Count Girls In

Empowering Girls to Combine Any
Interests with STEM to Open Up
a World of Opportunity

KAREN PANETTA, PHD, *and*
KATIANNE WILLIAMS

CHICAGO
REVIEW
PRESS

Published by Chicago Review Press Incorporated
814 North Franklin Street
Chicago, Illinois 60610
ISBN 978-1-61373-939-6

Library of Congress Cataloging-in-Publication Data
Names: Panetta, Karen, author. | Williams, Katianne.
Title: Count girls in : empowering girls to combine any interests with STEM
  to open up a world of opportunity / Karen Panetta and Katianne Williams.
Description: First edition. | Chicago, Illinois : Chicago Review Press, 2018.
  | Includes bibliographical references and index. |
Identifiers: LCCN 2017052811 (print) | LCCN 2018006454 (ebook) | ISBN
  9781613739402 (adobe pdf) | ISBN 9781613739419 (epub) | ISBN 9781613739426
  (kindle) | ISBN 9781613739396 (paperback)
Subjects: LCSH: Girls—Education—United States. | Women in science—United
  States | Science—Vocational guidance. | Science—Study and
  teaching—United States. | Technology—Study and teaching—United States.
  | Engineering—Study and teaching—United States. | Mathematics—Study and
  teaching—United States. | BISAC: FAMILY & RELATIONSHIPS / Parenting /
  General. | FAMILY & RELATIONSHIPS / Education.
Classification: LCC LC1752 (ebook) | LCC LC1752 .P36 2018 (print) | DDC
  507.1/073—dc23
LC record available at https://lccn.loc.gov/2017052811

Cover design: Mumtaz Mustafa
Cover image: Flashpop/Stone/Getty Images
Interior design: Sarah Olson

Printed in the United States of America
5 4 3 2 1

To my unwavering sources of sustainable, renewable energy, and loves of my life, my husband, Jamie Allan Heller, and my son, Benjamin Jayden Heller

—Karen

To Brian, Lucas, and Lily

—Katianne

CONTENTS

|||||||||||||||||||||||||||||||||||||||||||||||||||||||||||||||

AUTHORS' NOTE

A s a professor at Tufts University back in 2000, Karen noticed that her female students were struggling with an identity crisis of sorts. They were limiting themselves. Instead of being comfortable and confident in who they were as female engineers, they were trying to blend into a predominantly male culture. Karen formed the nonprofit Nerd Girls Foundation to encourage college women in STEM to celebrate their authentic selves.

As a journalist, Katianne has spent years having conversations with women working in all areas of STEM. These smart, capable women have found success by using STEM to help them pursue their passions. STEM has become the tool that allows these women to work on issues that are extremely important to them personally. An electrical engineer joins the ground crew that sent a solar airplane around the world; a clinical molecular geneticist works with an interdisciplinary team to develop organs-on-chips that will advance the ways in which we study diseases; and a computer scientist warns individuals that our social media imprints tell others way more than we think they do. It is impossible to hear their stories, as well as the enthusiasm in their voices, and not be inspired.

We are both parents. Karen has a son, and Katianne has a son and a daughter. When we set out to collaborate on a book, we knew we wanted to reach other parents. Parents hold the key to raising children who celebrate individuality, appreciate peers for their perspectives and differences, have the confidence to pursue their own interests, and believe that all children, regardless of gender identity, can work and play together in all activities. In addition, a parent's attitude toward STEM and toward diversity in STEM fields informs a child's beliefs, and positive experiences at home will counter exposure to negative stereotypes outside the home.

While today's kids have greater access to STEM activities than ever, there is still an opportunity gap. Those children who live in affluent school districts or attend private schools, who can afford to attend expensive courses and summer camps, who are at the top of their class, and who have parents who are already engaged in STEM have access to opportunities that other children may not. Sometimes, hearing about these activities that may not be available to one's own kids can make parents feel that the STEM door is already closed to their children. We hope that this book shows parents that this is not true. We believe that all parents can take steps at home to keep that door wide open, and that building a positive STEM attitude is the number-one way to achieve this.

Finally, we didn't write this book to tell parents how to maximize test scores or get their children into elite universities. We want to help parents raise authentic young women who have the confidence to put STEM to work in a way that best serves them and their passions. We believe in educating the whole child. We can all work together to raise children who appreciate science, believe in themselves, applaud the contributions of others, reach for the stars, and maybe change the world in the process.

PART I

|||||||||||||||||||||||||||||||||||||||||

What We Want for Our Girls

Once we believe in ourselves, we can risk curiosity, wonder, spontaneous delight, or any experience that reveals the human spirit. —E. E. Cummings

Maintain the Awesomeness

Little girls start out so full of spirit, joyously and chaotically marching to their own drums. They dance, they sing, they dress themselves in whatever smorgasbord of clothing makes them happy. Each day when they rise, they are ready to take the world by storm. They are interested in what everything is and how everything works. Their favorite question is why. They can be loud, they know what they want, and they are going to be presidents, astronauts, doctors, scientists, or butterflies. These girls are chock-full of awesomeness.

And yet, as the years pass, many girls lose their natural inquisitiveness, their enthusiasm, and even their confidence. Sometimes they lose their authenticity and put aside their passions in order to fit in. In the classroom, teachers see many girls begin to drift away from STEM subjects—science, technology, engineering, and math.

The reasons girls turn away from STEM are as varied and complex as girls themselves. Obstacles crop up in elementary school, middle school, high school, and even in college and beyond.

Some girls don't feel smart enough. Maybe they missed a key math concept in elementary school and were never able to catch up. Or they failed a test in middle school and their confidence plummeted. Or they were told by a teacher, parent, or peer that they weren't capable. It's not unusual for a girl to truly excel in math and science, to be one of the smartest in her class, and yet still doubt her ability.

Some girls look at the world and see confirmation that boys are made for math and science while girls aren't. They may think they see proof of this in the behaviors of their own parents, grandparents, or teachers. A girl may have heard her own mother say she's bad at math or had female teachers who show math anxiety or heard a trusted adult claim a girl should behave a certain way. Some girls, particularly at the high school or college level, encounter biased teachers. In fact, some girls have been led to believe that their math and science ability is innate and unchangeable—so what's the point of trying to be better?

Many girls aren't provided enough opportunities to engage in STEM, and the experiences they do engage in may be oriented toward learning styles that don't suit them. Teachers may not be properly trained, and the students might be left to fend for themselves. Girls can leave these extracurricular courses feeling frustrated if there isn't enough direction or disinterested if the subject matter doesn't appeal to them. Some girls who show no interest in building a car for a race may be more interested in project-based assignments like designing an animatronic puppet for a show, and yet they aren't always given that chance.

Some girls are interested in many subjects and feel that STEM is too single-minded and limiting. As they begin to look to the future they envision a job that involves communication and collaboration and that makes the world a better place. Because they don't know enough about STEM jobs, they assume the work must be dull and lonely. They picture themselves sitting at a computer in a cubicle all day or fitting together metal parts in a dirty machine shop.

As girls become teenagers, many want to fly under the radar. Instead of standing out, they want to blend into a culture that still expects girls to look pretty, not appear too smart, and be demure and deferential. They care greatly about what their friends think of them, and those girls

MEDIA THAT INSPIRES

TV shows such as *NCIS* and *Bones* have inspired a generation of women to pursue forensic science. Most applicants to forensics programs today are female. If only other forms of media were bolder—they too could have a positive impact on advancing women in STEM fields.

interested in boys will begin to form ideas about what might make a boy like them. Most will tell you that aptitude in math and science is not what boys find attractive.

Girls may think that they have to check their authentic feminine selves at the door to be an engineer or a scientist. They think they must fit into a male world and play by male rules. They assume in a STEM career they will have to downplay their own femininity. They begin to sense that there is something "boyish" about STEM: girls interested in STEM must have boyish interests and boyish brains.

As girls progress from kindergarten through college, they have to push through some pretty heavy obstacles. Luckily, parents and educators can remove many of these obstacles just by modifying their own behaviors and attitudes. Then, for those obstacles that remain, who better to help girls smash through them than parents and teachers?

Through Nerd Girls and our work with the Institute of Electrical and Electronics Engineers, we spend a good amount of time talking with woman scientists, engineers, and other STEM professionals, many of whom are excited to share their experiences and to act as mentors to young women. When we talk we are always interested in hearing how they ended up in STEM.

Most credit a parent. Many others credit a teacher.

The recurring theme isn't that these women had parents who worked in STEM fields themselves but that they had parents who encouraged their daughters, who played games with their kids at the coffee table, and who valued education even when they themselves did not hold a college degree. In other words, it doesn't matter what your background is. If you are a primary caregiver, you are in the number-one position to influence your daughter through everyday words and actions.

In addition, the women we talk to mention teachers or counselors at every stage who believed in them. They remember teachers who made math and science particularly engaging, who brought in real-world examples, who made a particular effort to talk about potential careers, or who took them aside to provide extra encouragement.

These can be the briefest of encounters. Think about how much good you could do in a short time by providing even small words of affirmation.

Unfortunately, even today, young women have stories about teachers who made them feel that they were lesser than. There are still high school guidance counselors who dissuade girls from applying to engineering schools and teachers who subject girls to gender bias in the classroom. Often, women who remember these stories relay them as the foremost reason they became determined to succeed in the field. They wanted to prove their detractors wrong. Such motivation is commendable, but we can't forget all the young women who have dropped out because of such comments.

This book will show you how to raise girls who will remain curious and inquisitive. You will learn how to avoid the obstacles—the myths, the stereotypes, the peer pressure, and the lack of information—that girls face from kindergarten through college that can cut confidence, derail aspirations, and turn girls away from potential careers. You will discover how to empower the young women in your life to develop their talents, dream big, and follow those dreams all the way to a fulfilling career.

You don't want them to miss out. Today's girls will be entering the workforce at a unique and exciting time. Technology is literally embedded everywhere, changing the minutest areas of our lives, and you can be sure that while it has already left its mark on the career landscape, some of the biggest shifts are yet to come. There will be not only amazing opportunities in STEM but also very few careers that aren't leveraging its components in some way.

And then there's the salary. While money isn't the sole reason to encourage a girl in STEM, people with STEM degrees earn more. On average, they bring home a salary 26 percent higher than their non-STEM counterparts. Those with STEM degrees who then enter non-STEM occupations still outearn those with non-STEM degrees. STEM fields are projected to grow at a rate of 13 percent from 2012 and 2022.

Parents want to prepare girls to be successful. We want them to lead lives of happiness and financial security. We also want them to stay true to their authentic selves. In this regard, we can do two things for them: encourage their natural talents and make sure that all doors remain open to them so that they have choices.

Parents don't know where their girls' interests will lead them, whether they will be doctors, engineers, marketers, artists, or any one of a million occupations, many of which are just coming into being. One college counselor routinely tells parents that no one can know what future careers will look like—job titles don't even exist yet for much of the work that today's children will be doing.

This doesn't mean parents should throw up their hands and wait to see what transpires. These jobs aren't going to fall from the sky. Our generation is already changing the landscape, and our children are going to take what our current workforce hands them and continue to innovate. They will apply these new technologies to education, health, manufacturing, business, transportation, and anything else they can think of. They will change the world by working in areas such as personalized medicine, the environment, and renewable energy.

Take, for example, the emergence of the internet of things (IoT). The idea of the IoT is basically that everyday objects are connected to each other and therefore able to send and receive data. The IoT gained ground humming along in our cell phones, watches, and the switches that let us turn on our porch lights while we are out at dinner. Now, all sorts of companies are scrambling to incorporate voice-based platforms like Amazon's Alexa into their products so that everything from cars to washing machines will literally do what we say. But things are just getting started, and this is small potatoes compared to the potential that technologists see for the future. Apply IoT principles to the creation of smart cities and imagine the benefits—but also the risks—of smart high-rises and office buildings, smart transportation systems, and smart power grids. Imagine the people this industry will employ.

Jeanne Beliveau-Dunn is CEO of the Internet of Things Talent Consortium, a group that includes power players from institutions such as MIT, Cisco Systems, GE, the New York Academy of Sciences, Pearson, and Rockwell. In a webinar for Meeting of the Minds, Beliveau-Dunn, who was named in the National Diversity Council's "2015 Top 50 Most Powerful Women in Technology," displays a slide titled "New IoT Job Roles" that lists some of the new types of talent that society needs as we digitize our cities and as city populations grow.

What are some of the jobs she sees for the future? Professional tribers, described as marketing folk who bring people together through digital platforms. Data scientists who mine and put to use all the data from all the things that will be connected in the future. Digital anthropologists. Virtual reality designers. 3-D printing technicians.

These and the many jobs that will grow in importance along with them will be fast paced and exciting. They will demand twenty-first-century skills like technological literacy, creativity, design, innovation, communication, and collaboration that will be as crucial as traditional core subjects. These jobs have no gender.

Girls and young women today are poised to be at the forefront of this remarkable change and opportunity. But in order for girls to reach that point, parents may need to put the past behind them and adjust how they talk to girls about science and technology. It is up to the people in the trenches to understand how attitudes toward STEM may be informing young girls.

Success depends on adults increasing their own STEM literacy and perceptions. What is your personal starting point? How do you feel about girls in STEM? Do you believe STEM fields are primarily for boys and a certain set of mathematically gifted tomboys? Are glitter-laden girls who love to dance and dress their stuffed animals excluded from loving science and technology? While everyone encourages preschool-age boys and girls to practice math and science, do you feel a subtle shift in your attitude once those same students reach fourth, fifth, or tenth grade?

Think honestly about your answers. If you're going to raise bright, creative, confident, and empowered girls who continue to believe in their awesomeness all the way through to the finish line—through college and beyond—you need to believe that girls are as capable and interested in twenty-first-century STEM as boys.

IIIIIIIIIIIIIIIIIIIIIIIIIIIIIIIIIIIIIIIIIIIIIIIIIIIIIIIIIIIIIIIIIIIIIIIIIIIIIIIIIIIIIIIIIIIIIIIIIIIIIIIIIIIIIIIIIIIIIIIIIIIIIIIIIIIIIIIIIIIIIIIIIIIIIIIIII

Putting It into Practice

- Ultimately, pursuing a career in STEM is a decision your daughter will make for herself. Encourage your daughter's natural talents and make sure that all doors remain open to her so that she has choices.

- Stay involved. Girls lose interest in STEM at different ages and for different reasons—but if you understand the many challenges girls face, you will be able to provide your daughter with the help, support, and encouragement she needs when she needs it.

- Don't underestimate your own influence. So many women in STEM credit a parent who believed in them, encouraged them, and placed a high value on education. While some of these parents are in STEM fields themselves, many are not. No STEM experience is necessary.

⚛ Not so sure about STEM? Take some time to reflect on how your own attitude may be limiting your daughter.

⚛ Look to the future. STEM, especially technological literacy, will be even more interwoven into everything we do. This means that no matter what career your daughter chooses, there's a good chance STEM know-how and confidence will help her do her job better and more efficiently.

‖‖

Whose Brain Is Really Better?

In 2002 researchers Victor Lavy and Edith Sand, economists from the University of Warwick and Tel Aviv University, set out to study both the long- and short-term effects of teachers' gender bias on primary school students. In other words, could teacher bias early in a girl's academic career actually have a negative effect on the courses she signs up to take in high school, the career she chooses, and, finally, the salary she brings home later in life? These researchers believe that the answer is yes.

Lavy and Sand examined the test scores of three sets of Israeli sixth graders between 2002 and 2004. When they compared the results of teacher-graded classroom tests to national exams with similar content, they found that while females outperformed males on the national exam, the males scored higher on the classroom tests. This happened only in a single subject—math. As the researchers followed the students through middle school and high school, that early gender bias continued to influence the affected students. Boys who had been "over-assessed" saw their scores on national exams improve and were more apt to sign up for higher-level math and science courses in high school. Girls who had been "under-assessed," on the other hand, saw their performance decline on national exams, and they shied away from higher-level math and science courses. Without these advanced-level courses under their belts, they are unlikely to choose a STEM field in college.

Oftentimes, gender bias is unconscious, manifesting in small ways. Well-intentioned parents and educators can simply slip up. Even parents who love their daughters and want the best for them sometimes, without realizing it, treat them differently. A little girl once wanted to get into the Nerd Girl's solar car, but her mother told her it was for boys. "Let your brother get in," the mother said.

Henry Houh and Rebecca Rapoport, cofounders of Einstein's Workshop in Burlington, Massachusetts, have seen this unconscious bias at play. They were working their booth at a maker fair one day when a mother approached with her two children. Both children enjoyed playing with the Zometool building toys that had been set out, but the mother talked about the math behind the toy with her son and talked about how pretty the toy was with her daughter. A second mother approached with her daughters, but while the girls were absorbed in play she inquired about opportunities for her absent son. These are not only missed opportunities but also send the subtle yet damaging message to girls that "this is not for you."

Why do we still subconsciously believe that boys are better suited for math and science to the extent that we let it influence how we grade our students and what opportunities we provide our children?

Scientists and psychologists have long studied the cognitive development of children and adolescents. Their results are generally confirmed by the legions of teachers whose classrooms act as minilaboratories. Overall, scientists reveal that young girls' brains have stronger neural connectors to enable faster processing of information. The cortical areas associated with verbal-emotive functioning are also more highly developed than in boys' brains, leading to stronger memory and listening powers. This also aids with the complexities of reading and writing. The corpus callosum, the bridge between the brain's hemispheres, is often larger and denser in girls than in boys, making girls stronger at multitasking and connecting words with feelings. Girls have higher levels of serotonin and oxytocin, which means that they may more carefully consider the consequences of their actions than boys.

On the other hand, the average boy has much more cortical area devoted to spatial-mechanical activity and less to verbal-emotive. He is quick with symbols, abstractions, and pictures. With less serotonin and oxytocin, he is more likely to be a risk-taker. At the very least, he really doesn't want to sit and listen to you talk. He wants to be moving something, anything. Everything is a projectile. Every wheel must be spun.

DIVERSE BUILDERS = DIVERSE PRODUCTS

As Karen's team of undergraduates worked on their solar car design, the boys weren't concerned with usability and safety—they focused on speed. The girls wanted to make the car safe and reliable. Speed was secondary. Diversity at the design table matters!

Everything must be touched and tinkered with. The boy brain is more apt to compartmentalize than to multitask.

Whether these differences are a product of nature or nurture has been often debated. The question is studied frequently, and there is quite a tug-of-war over the results. There are biological, neurological, and hormonal differences between the sexes—of course there are—and at the same time, there are societal norms telling us how to raise girls and how to raise boys. Scientists research this topic with the hope of answering some key questions: Are there things that girls are naturally better at? Are there things boys are naturally better at? And, last, are we perpetuating gender stereotypes that have zero biological basis?

A few years back, research seemed to indicate that some answers had finally arrived, and many declared that our brains are hardwired toward specific gendered aptitudes. Nature, not nurture, most determined how we act and think. But quick on the heels of this research came counterarguments decrying the research as flawed and inconclusive. British neuroscientist Gina Rippon from Aston University in Birmingham told the *Telegraph* that you cannot pick up a brain (literally) and declaratively differentiate it as either male or female. Any differences, she said, are due to the "drip, drip, drip of the gendered environment."

Perhaps the biggest takeaway from this is that many adults have preconceived notions that boys, good at analytics and reasoning, are good at math, which somehow has morphed into the idea that girls naturally are not.

Do boys have an easier time with math? Does it come more naturally to them, overall? Researchers have turned to student math assessments in hopes of arriving at an answer. There are many studies seeking to determine whether boys and girls fare the same on different math assessments, but the results vary. And, within test data that shows boys outperforming girls, the *why* is still elusive. Take, for example, the SAT.

Boys have consistently scored higher than girls on the math portion of the SAT. But why? Do boys have an overall edge when it comes to math? Is the test biased against girls? Are boys better at competitive and timed test taking? Do girls experience stereotype threat during testing, thus performing as they believe girls are expected to perform? Has gender discrimination in education left girls underconfident and underprepared?

Researchers have tried to tackle the gender question by looking at other assessments, such as the landmark Project Talent study. This longitudinal study was launched in 1960 and included over seventy-five thousand fifteen-year-old students given a battery of tests that measured, among other things, math aptitude. The test showed that girls had a slight edge in verbal abilities and boys had a slight edge in math abilities.

In the decades since then, researchers have conducted many other studies, using the initial Project Talent study as a baseline, and have argued their cases about whether there is a gender gap and, if so, whether it has been closing over time. Results are generally interpreted one of two ways. If you look at the average math test scores of boys and girls, you will see that any differences are statistically insignificant. On the other hand, if you look at what researchers call the "upper tail" or the "right tail" of test results (the top 5 percent), boys tend to be overrepresented in math and science. In other words, despite essentially equal average scores for boys and girls, more boys score in the highest echelon.

Some believe that this "right tail" is unchangeable. In 2005 Harvard president Larry Summers woke up one morning to find himself in the news, and not in a good way. He had hypothesized in a speech at an economics conference the day before that women were underrepresented as scientists at elite universities because they are not as innately highly gifted in math and science as men. Since then, we've heard the question "Why are there not as many women in STEM?" even referred to as the Larry Summers question. But that is not quite accurate, as Summers was hypothesizing about a different, much more specific question: Why are there more male scientists and mathematicians at the extreme top—namely, occupying the faculty positions at top universities such as Harvard?

Summers said in the same speech that he hopes to be proved wrong, and some researchers have been working at doing so. In 2009 Janet

Hyde and Janet Mertz reported that the gender gap in math, even along the right tail, has been closing over time. According to their work, the gap is smallest in countries like the United States that have greater gender equality both at home and in the classroom. While their research found that more males did indeed score in the 95th percentile grouping as well as the 99th percentile grouping (what we call the extreme right tail) of mathematical performance, they also found that this is a result of "changeable sociocultural factors, not immutable, innate biological differences between the sexes" and that the gaps have been closing over time. In another study from 2010 Jonathan Wai and his team from the Talent Identification Program at Duke University found that in the twenty year period that they studied the seventh-grade SAT scores of high-achieving students, gender differences disappeared in all but the extreme right tail, where they have been holding steady.

The answer, then, to "Which gender is better at math?" depends on how you interpret the data. Girls are performing well in math, but a higher proportion of the very top performers is currently male. But take note: The 2014 Fields Medal, a prize awarded since 1936 to mathematicians under age forty and often regarded as the most prestigious award a mathematician can receive, went to Maryam Mirzakhani, an Iranian math professor at Stanford, making her the first woman to be awarded the prize.

There is no empirical evidence to support the idea that girls should be directed away from STEM majors and careers on the basis of intellect. Outside of the gap seen at the extreme right tail—and even that may close in time—there is no proof that boys are any better than girls at the math skills necessary for STEM success.

Here's one last thing to think about. Take a boy with a test score that you might call average. When he says that he wants to be a scientist or an engineer or a video game designer, adults encourage him. Can the same be said for a girl with that same average test score? If she doesn't know what a civil or electrical engineer does, do parents and teachers take the time to tell her?

Too often we demand brilliance from our daughters before encouraging them in the STEM direction. We want them to be the top 5 percent or even the top 1 percent from the time they are young. If girls do not display an almost instinctual aptitude for math and science, we often assume STEM is not for them. That's not true, especially today.

There are many reasons for the loss of young women along the STEM pipeline—but assumptions about their innate ability should not be one of them. Our daughters have all the potential in the world, and we should be doing all that we can to make sure they have the confidence to go along with it.

Putting It into Practice

- Watch yourself! If you spent decades thinking of STEM as a "male" field, you can easily slip back into that way of thinking and let it affect the opportunities you provide and the feedback you give. Many parents and educators are guilty of gender bias—unfortunately, the message this sends to girls has a lasting effect.

- Put an end to the "Whose brain is better?" argument, even if it exists only in the dark recesses of your mind. For decades, researchers have studied the brain. Over the years, they have come to assorted conclusions about how male and female brains differ. The general consensus? Boys and girls may learn things in different ways—but girls are just as capable as boys. In fact, in a twenty-first-century world where creativity, communication, and collaboration are key, girls are well positioned for STEM success.

- Avoid perpetuating the idea that math skill is innate. Math will come easier to some, as all things do, but reinforce the idea that hard work does pay off.

- Align your expectations. We tend to want STEM girls to be the science fair winners and Math Olympiad champions, as if they must earn the right to want to be an engineer or scientist—yet we don't demand that of boys.

Meet Them
Where They Are

B ut wait, you say. I've got a girly girl! She's bright, sure, but she's a girl who loves to bake and sew and paint flowers on her nails. I've got a girl who is compassionate and kind. I've got a social butterfly.

Well, welcome to the twenty-first century, you parents of lucky girls. Here, girls are not required to "think like boys" in order to be successful. They can happily continue being themselves. In fact, here's how *not* to raise a STEM-loving child: Cram STEM down her throat. Insist on competition-style robotics programs when they are not her thing. Take away her dolls. Sit her at the table and load her up with math worksheets.

On the contrary, parents and educators should embrace a girl's particular interests. Girls do not need to change who they are to excel at STEM. They can love sports, ponies, BMX biking, lip gloss, and high heels. They can love to twirl, build, draw pictures of rainbows, hammer nails, collect stuffed animals, and paint rocks. It's all good.

In other words, adults should meet them where they are. In doing so, girls will flourish. They will develop the skills, confidence, and passions that will make them unique, authentic individuals, and that may just lead them to a career in STEM.

This doesn't just benefit daughters. It benefits everyone. It shows brothers and male peers that girls are on a level playing field and that everyone has something to contribute—even if they don't think and act the same. This generation can change the conversation. Society needs lots of scientists and engineers, but those who do the hiring aren't turning to women simply because they increase the worker pool. They need young women in particular to engage in STEM. They need their talents, experiences, and passions. They need the collaboration and creativity and life experiences that girls bring to the table.

Here's why: With a homogeneous group of collaborators, entire segments of populations are often disregarded or overlooked. The great, inspired ideas that come from the engagement of different backgrounds may never be realized.

Health care is a good example. After decades of being ignored, female heart disease is finally getting much-needed attention. Females diagnosed with autism spectrum disorders are so far in the minority that there is little research specific to their gender, and young girls with ADHD may go undiagnosed when their symptoms don't include hyperactivity. More women researching health fields could lead to more advancement in woman-specific health issues such as endometriosis, fibromyalgia, pregnancy and childbirth, female cancers, menopause, and birth control.

Katty Kay and Claire Shipman write in the *Atlantic* that "half a dozen global studies, conducted by the likes of Goldman Sachs and Columbia University, have found that companies employing women in large numbers outperform their competitors on every measure of profitability."

This is because women shake things up. They bring fresh perspective. Companies need and want women. Many, such as GM, Shell, and Verizon, are investing heavily in education programs that will help grow the pool of women and minorities in STEM fields, with the hopes that those people will one day work for them.

And yet, when girls do not exhibit the traditional, stereotypical inclinations of scientists and engineers, all too often no one encourages them or attempts to meet them where they are. This is understandable to an extent. When you have a little girl who spends her hours crafting, rollerblading, and playing dolls, it's easy to roll along with the traditional. But doing so only pigeonholes your daughter and limits her future. It is time to do away with the twentieth-century stereotype that painted STEM careers as best for those with "male" traits and interests.

Take, for example, siblings Ethan, twelve, and Elizabeth, eight. From a young age, Ethan showed an interest in mechanical things. As he began to draw, it was clear that he was very skilled at spatial ability. At age four, he sat gazing at the car pattern on his sheets and was able to articulate that he could estimate how many cars were on the sheet by counting one row across and adding that number as many times as there were rows, demonstrating that although he didn't yet know how to multiply he had a conceptual understanding of what multiplication was. He loved Lego sets and put together complex models quickly and with very little help. As he grew, his main interests were programming, robotics, and Lego bricks, and he took many classes in these areas. He was your stereotypical engineer-in-training.

Elizabeth, his younger sister, was social, athletic, and had a bubbly personality that both strangers and friends remarked on. From a young age, she told her parents that her goal was to be funny. She loved to laugh and make others laugh. She enjoyed ice-skating, basketball, American Girl dolls, Beanie Boos, crafts, coloring, writing stories, elaborate make-believe, and making cards and notes for friends and family. She had a room full of Lego Friends, and she enjoyed working on projects. She was a good student who liked to read and did well in all her subjects. She was so chatty in class that her first-grade teacher remarked that she hadn't yet been able to find a neighbor Elizabeth wouldn't talk to.

If you asked them what they'd like to be when they grew up, Ethan always said he wanted to be an engineer. He never wanted to be anything else. This is no surprise considering that he was aware of this career since he was a toddler. He'd flip his stroller upside down to play with the wheels and people would say to him, "You'd make a good engineer!" Elizabeth sometimes wanted to be a teacher and sometimes a nurse. She knew these professions and saw them modeled frequently by women she loved and admired at school.

Elizabeth would make a great teacher or nurse. She is personable, warm, and caring. Her interest in these careers will continue because she receives encouragement about what a compassionate teacher or nurse she would make. But Elizabeth should also know about the many other opportunities out there. If parents want to show a child like Elizabeth how her talents, interests, and personality align with a variety of STEM fields, how do they meet her where she's at?

First, embrace her interests and let her normal, everyday play naturally foster STEM skills. These interests could be sewing, art, music, stuffed animals, dolls, or sports. Creative play activities like sewing, art, and music not only develop the brain but also turn a child into a problem finder and solver. Autonomous play also helps define a girl's individuality and builds her self-esteem. If a young girl is in her bedroom happily dressing her dolls, don't pull her away and ask her to work on something less frivolous and more educational. Saying that only gears and building sets are "math and science" when her interest happens to be dolls sends the message that she must not be a "math and science" kid. Instead, provide her with materials to make her own clothes for her dolls—felt and masking tape, or fabric and a small sewing kit. Let her pick something from any clothes you are discarding and upcycle the fabric into something new. Give her a cardboard box to turn into a doll's bed, or a set of shoeboxes to become a multistory condo dollhouse. Use those gears to make an elevator. Help her see herself as a designer and maker.

Second, adults can widen her horizons and teach her about STEM by telling stories. While some girls will be thrilled when you dump a box of rods and gears in front of them, many more will be drawn in by a backstory. They like things to have a purpose and they like to rally around a problem that needs solving, especially a problem with a solution that will help humanity. Katianne has taught middle school students how to build simple circuits with LEDs. An important part of this activity is talking to the children about how LEDs are transforming the developing world. She tells the kids how three scientists won the 2014 Nobel Prize in Physics for their invention of the blue LED. This makes them laugh. What, they want to know, is so great about a blue LED?

The blue LED is so important because it was the missing piece of the puzzle in being able to make LED lamps. Today, LEDs are inexpensive, efficient, and last for a very long time. They work great with solar panels because you don't need a large photovoltaic cell. When the Nerd Girls set out to replace the lighthouse beacon on Thacher Island in Rockport, Massachusetts, the use of LEDs meant they only needed a lawn mower battery and a small solar panel. Before the LED, they would have needed a coffin-sized battery and a giant solar array. This is what makes LEDs a transformative technology in areas of the world where there is no access to electricity. They are cheaper and much safer than kerosene. They allow humanitarians to do what they were unable to do with compact fluorescents and incandescents—provide sustainable light to many.

This gives the girls context. Now, when they look down at the conductive tape, the coin-sized 3V battery, and the two-legged LEDs, they have a reason to get involved. They are now invested.

The more stories girls hear about STEM at work in the world around them, the better. Consider the STEM paths following. All four of these young women are personable, witty, eloquent, smart, creative, and caring. In their jobs they serve humanity, solve problems, collaborate, write, have adventures, travel, collect and analyze data, give presentations, and meet people from many walks of life. Last and most important, these women love what they do.

Medical Physicist Sheri Weintraub: Cancer treatment relies on physics—tomography machines like CT and PET use radiation to detect and pinpoint tumors, and then radiation is used again to shrink tumors. As a medical physicist, Sheri understands how radiation affects different organs, and she uses this knowledge as she works with oncologists and dosimetrists to develop safe and effective treatment plans for each patient. She oversees this plan, verifying the setup, accuracy, and safety of each piece of equipment before treatment begins. She also makes sure that the clinic is providing the best cancer-fighting care by commissioning new technologies and ensuring that they are safely integrated into clinical use.

Environmental Engineer Daniele Lantagne: Daniele has traveled to more than fifty countries to evaluate water treatment programs. She wants to know more than how water treatment tools like water filters work in the laboratory—she wants to know how these tools work once they are put into people's hands. Sometimes Daniele travels from village to village administering surveys: Are people shown how to use the treatment? Do they have the correct supplies? Do they have cultural or language barriers to using the tool? Without this input, aid can be ineffective. For example, after the 2004 Indonesian earthquake, many of the chlorine tablets distributed by charities and NGOs went unused because many Indonesians who received the tablets considered chlorine to be a poison.

Power Engineer Jessica Bian: Jessica keeps an eye on the North American power grid to make sure it stays up and running. In other words, no news is good news for the millions of people who take for granted that when they wake up in the morning their lights will turn on. Jessica has developed metrics to help identify potential issues in the system. "My job is like a doctor," Jessica says. "In a health checkup, a doctor measures body temperature, pulse rate, heart rate, stress level, BMI. That's what I do, find out the vital signs for the grid to see if it's close to collapse or black out." Jessica finds her job so interesting and critical because the power industry is in a major transition. As society works toward developing sustainable, efficient energy sources, strong communicators and collaborators are in demand. There are many opportunities for women to have a say in shaping this future.

Artist Heather Dewey-Hagborg: Heather is an artist and a scientist. She likes to explore our contemporary world and bring to the forefront through art those things that others might not spend much time thinking about, like privacy in a digital age. Heather, who was not a "math person" in high school, had the luck to take a computer science class in college with a great and motivating professor. She loved programming in Python, and she began to use it in her art. Her *Stranger Visions* project uses biotechnology to examine what biowaste humans might leave behind every time they drop a piece of gum, lose a strand of hair, or throw away a cigarette butt. From those pieces, Heather wondered, could she extract DNA in a way that would allow her to reconstruct through 3-D-printed sculpture what that person may have looked like?

When eight-year-old Elizabeth heard the above stories, she was particularly fascinated by DNA, each person's individual blueprint. This led to further talk about what exactly can be gleaned from this blueprint, as well as many questions about humans and other animals. She mentioned that being able to paint a picture of someone from the DNA they left behind would be helpful for catching thieves, which led to a discussion of whether that would be a good idea or not. From there, Elizabeth saw pictures of Heather and her work online. She noticed that at some point, Heather had her long blonde hair in a pixie cut, which Elizabeth liked. She was fascinated by the art installations, the rows of 3-D-printed faces mounted on a black background.

As your daughter becomes interested in new topics, you can continue to provide her with the tools to grow these interests in the same way that you provide her with sewing kits or craft materials to foster her existing hobbies. For a child like Elizabeth, a parent may take a children's book on DNA out of the library or find a video to watch online or set her up with gumdrops, licorice, and toothpicks to make a twisted staircase model of a DNA double helix strand. A girl will find such experiences, which all evolve organically from a story, useful whether she becomes a teacher, a nurse, an artist, or a biotechnology engineer.

In her studies of high school girls, Jacquelynne Eccles found that two forces push girls away from mathematical subjects: "how much they believe in the ultimate utility of mathematics, and how much they value working with and for people."

If we let girls develop their STEM abilities alongside their own interests and talents, they will be able to envision themselves in future careers and will understand the "utility of mathematics." By hearing stories from STEM fields, they will grow up knowing that the STEM careers of the twenty-first century very much involve "working with and for people."

Putting It into Practice

- Meet your daughter where she's at by marrying her hobbies with STEM. She may not be drawn to stereotypical STEM toys and activities, but this doesn't mean she isn't a "math and science kid."

- Tell stories about women in STEM. When girls imagine what they want to be when they grow up, they look to the women in their lives. If girls don't have the opportunity to spend much time with women in STEM fields, it is up to us to make sure they have access to their stories.

- Pique her interest. More girls show engagement in STEM projects when the project ties into a real-life problem, especially one with a humanitarian component.

- Make STEM part of the everyday language in your home. Talking about the role of Twitter after a natural disaster or the latest wearable tech will help older girls understand that math coursework is relevant and that STEM careers involve working with and for people.

 Be curious about the world around you, and share that curiosity with your daughter.

PART II

||||||||||||||||||||||||||||||||||||||||

Build a Strong Foundation

The whole art of teaching is only the art of awakening the natural curiosity of young minds for the purpose of satisfying it afterwards. —Anatole France

The Power of
Following Her Interests

I f we're going to meet girls where they are, we need to look a little closer at how to do that. If you have a daughter naturally drawn to building toys and construction sets, you may already think that she has the ability to one day be an engineer. This pathway, and your role as parent in encouraging those interests, is clear. But if your daughter is not drawn to those kinds of activities, you may find you need to change your mindset. You may already be aware of the mathematical benefits of playing a musical instrument, for example, but go beyond that to see your piano-playing daughter through a new lens. When you look at a child painting or sewing, you should see the world of STEM opening up to her in the same way that you would if she were sitting before you building a skyscraper. Instead of closing the door, look for ways to draw connections and widen opportunities.

Traditionally "non-STEM" interests are not as non-STEM as you may think. In today's interdisciplinary world, many people find career success by marrying STEM with a non-STEM passion or interest. This unique blend of experiences often drives creativity and innovation. There's inspiration everywhere. Take origami. Researchers are incorporating origami into robotics in amazing ways. MIT has an ingestible origami robot that, after being swallowed in a dissolvable capsule, can unfurl itself inside a child's stomach to retrieve a button battery before it can do harm. NASA hopes the Pop-Up Flat Folding Explorer Robot

(PUFFER) can one day make it to Mars, where its ability to fold flat will allow it to tuck into small spaces.

Innovators use their creativity to combine their unique experiences in new, never-considered ways. Resist the idea that only the young girl who focuses on one solitary pursuit will become an expert in that particular field. She's a kid, after all. Let her develop a broad range of interests. Let one pursuit lead to another. That's where "childlike wonder" comes from, and raising lifelong learners is what keeps it alive.

Childhood is a time for young children to explore, have adventures, experiment, and be fascinated by the world around them, all while building the strong foundation upon which more specialized skills may one day sit. If your daughter's play develops the habits of mind and the broad skills that will be useful across many disciplines, she will be set up for success in STEM and in life.

Build a Strong Foundation with These Habits of Mind

Many different types of play help young children develop the habits of mind that they need to be successful in a STEM field. When we look at the whole child, habits of mind like self-esteem, creativity, perseverance, and a sense of self are much more important than niche academic achievements. No matter your daughter's interests, incorporate the following into her play-filled days to help her develop a strong foundation:

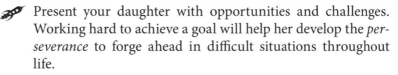 Provide the supportive environment that will allow your daughter to develop a healthy sense of *self-esteem* that gives her strength as she encounters both academic and social challenges.

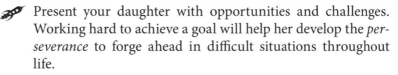 Present your daughter with opportunities and challenges. Working hard to achieve a goal will help her develop the *perseverance* to forge ahead in difficult situations throughout life.

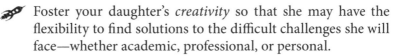 Foster your daughter's *creativity* so that she may have the flexibility to find solutions to the difficult challenges she will face—whether academic, professional, or personal.

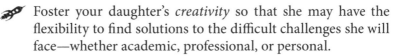 Give your daughter time, permission, and tools to develop her unique talents and interests regardless of social norms

and your own desires so that she may discover and embrace her authentic *sense of self.*

Focus on Broad Skills, Not Specialized Skills

Many different types of play naturally teach the broad skills that are critical to STEM success, including computational thinking, spatial ability, media literacy, and digital literacy. Almost any hands-on activity is teaching one of these foundational skills:

- **Computational thinking:** Computational thinking describes the way we logically define and approach a problem. It's the method used by computer scientists to write code, and it involves defining the steps that make up the problem, breaking large tasks into smaller chunks, and recognizing patterns and repetition. Teaching programming is of course one way to instill these skills, but computational thinking is not just the domain of the computer scientist. These thinking skills are actually used across many disciplines—including health care, international relations, economics, law, and engineering—to tackle and solve large-scale issues. In addition, computer science itself permeates all disciplines—programming is a tool that allows everyone to automate tasks, solve complex problems, and analyze data.

- **Spatial ability:** Spatial ability is the ability to envision an object in its 3-D location. Children develop spatial skills through playing with manipulatives and through use of spatial language such as *above, below,* and *under.* Spatial ability is used in all fields that incorporate physical design, but it is also used to help us do a better job of packing the trunk for a beach vacation. Interestingly, spatial ability can also affect the way we approach math and logic problems that don't have anything to do with physical space. While studies show that boys have a biological advantage in this area, studies also show that these skills are easily learned.

- **Media literacy:** Media literacy is the ability to engage with different forms of media, both high- and low-tech—books, newspapers, social media platforms, music, video games, commercials, and the like. A media-literate person is able to assess, analyze, and evaluate what one sees and hears. Understanding how content is created, as well as the special interests behind the messages, is empowering. A person can use this understanding to make informed decisions, a skill that is vitally important for both personal and academic success.

Digital literacy: Digital and media literacy overlap; both skills enable a person to consume and interact with digital media such as websites and social media platforms. Digital literacy, though, focuses on a person's ability to live in a digital world. For early learners, digital literacy might encompass learning to type, to use different programs, and to navigate the internet. It teaches a person how to *find* information online, as well as how to then evaluate it, and it teaches how to create with technology. A large part of digital literacy training is imparting good digital citizenship, which includes teaching your daughter not just how she can use technology in positive and responsible ways but how she can stay safe.

DANCING ROBOTS?

You never know what opportunities might arise if you follow your interests while keeping your mind open to STEM. Margo Apostolos turned her love of dance into a career that has included working with robotics at NASA's Jet Propulsion Laboratory. It all began when she audited a mechanical engineering course and, upon viewing the stilted way robots were working along a car-manufacturing assembly line, asked the question no other student was asking: *Can't they move more gracefully?* Margo was invited to work alongside engineers to bring her understanding of human movement to robots. Over the years, Margo has worked with the Mars rover team, studied how robots could be used to remove rivets from airplane wings, and researched how humans could use robots to repair satellites in space.

So go forth and encourage your girl to develop her passions, whatever they may be. And if she is missing a skill—if she's an excellent logical thinker but struggles to put a 3-D puzzle together, for example—don't despair. STEM is a wide and varied assortment of fields, made up of a wide and varied assortment of skills.

The following sections discuss just a few of the many interests that you may currently consider non-STEM. You'll learn not only how these interests naturally inform a child's STEM knowledge but also how to integrate additional STEM skills if desired. These aren't lesson plans, and you aren't expected to tackle all these ideas with your daughter. Let these serve as examples that shift the way you view your child's own interests—whether listed here or not—and that prepare you to support her as she develops her unique talents.

Art

Why It Matters

Artists and scientists (not the mad scientists in movies or on television and certainly not Rick Moranis in *Honey, I Shrunk the Kids*) are very nearly opposites, aren't they? They'd make poor friends and awkward bedfellows. Science is exact, we decided at some point. Art is messy and creative. Artists and scientists do not coexist well.

In fact, Shirley Malcom of the American Association for the Advancement of Science calls this phenomenon of separating art from science an "artificial bifurcation." John Maeda, president of the Rhode Island School of Design who holds both a degree in electrical engineering and computer science from MIT and a PhD in classical design from Tsukuba University in Japan, says that scientists and artists are much more alike than prevailing stereotypes would have us believe: "We know that the scientist's laboratory and the artist's studio are two of the last places reserved for open-ended inquiry, for failure to be a welcome part of the process, for learning to occur by a continuous feedback loop between thinking and doing."

The benefits of art are varied:

 An artist has the freedom of self-expression and creative growth without the fear of being right or wrong.

 The artist is challenged to decide what to create and with what medium.

Other times, the artist must decide how to create something with personal meaning even when given constraints.

 Art brings us together. It is a way to understand each other. An appreciation of art brings with it an appreciation of other viewpoints.

 As technology becomes integrated into every aspect of our daily lives, we need engineers to design products that are beautiful and stylish.

 Through art, we can visualize and better understand the beauty of mathematics such as classical or fractal geometry.

 Through art, we develop spatial ability. We project 3-D images onto a 2-D canvas through perspective. We further play with perspective through styles such as cubism.

 As adults, an ability to express ourselves visually allows us to create prototypes, sketch designs, and give presentations to educate others or market our ideas.

 Artists may become comfortable with a variety of simple and complex tools such as wire cutters, soldering irons, pottery wheels, and handsaws.

How to Develop Interest

 Provide the highest-quality materials you can and teach your daughter to care for them. Specialized materials give a young girl the idea that she is being taken seriously. A nice tin of colored pencils and a sketchbook make an excellent gift.

 Instead of prepackaged craft kits that don't encourage creativity (like foam stickers kits), create an artist box stocked with an assortment of creative supplies. Depending on your child's age, you might include some of the following:

+ Construction paper or card stock
+ Newspaper or recycled plastic tablecloths for drop cloths
+ Felt
+ Glue, glue sticks, and glue guns for older children
+ Tape—duct tape, masking tape, cellophane tape

+ Popsicle sticks
+ Rubber bands of varying sizes
+ Scissors
+ Markers
+ Colored Pencils
+ Paints, brushes, and cups
+ Brads

Make recycled goods part of your home art center:

+ Egg cartons
+ Cardboard rolls and sheets
+ Orange juice containers
+ Milk containers
+ Plastic bottles
+ Packaging materials like Styrofoam and bubble wrap
+ Old sheets, curtains, and pillowcases
+ Old clothes like button-up shirts
+ Wire coat hangers

Art is messy, and adults don't always have time to supervise an activity and its clean-up. Set aside a specific time and place each week for art messiness. Teach your daughter how to clean up after herself—to shake the drop cloth out, fold it, wipe down surfaces, and return everything neatly to its place.

Give your daughter autonomy. Don't say no to her ideas. Be positive. If something sounds outlandish, ask her how she thinks she will do it. Help her brainstorm, encourage her to make a plan, and then let her try. Let her succeed or fail on her own terms.

Sit on your hands. Your daughter's sense of pride comes from doing the work herself—even if her lines are crooked or she uses too much glue.

You can play too. Sit and work on your own project, no matter what your skill level, and have fun doing it. Model perseverance by learning and practicing new skills and being proud of first efforts. Model self-esteem and the enjoyment of creating by finding joy in your art.

How to Further STEM-Art Connections

STEM doesn't have to be high-tech. There as so many ways that STEM can inform art:

 Origami reinforces spatial awareness and geometry skills.

 String art involves angles, measurements, patterns, and fractals, as well as the engineering principles of design, and is good for all ages and skill levels. For young children, you only need card stock or cardboard and yarn. Older artists often work with plywood, small brad nails, and thread or embroidery floss.

 Attaching rubber bands, balloons, parachutes, or propellers to projects encourages young artists to create art with movement.

 Cardboard sculptures or structures like dollhouses and doll beds can be made without the use of tape or glue by cutting slits in the cardboard.

If you are ready to bring some tech to your daughter's art, small DC motors and LED lights are fun additions to an artist box. Small motors can bring art projects to life. A DC motor is about the size of a spool of thread and costs only a few dollars; the packaging should tell you what size battery or solar cell to use with it. Use motors to create spinning art and sculptures, or to add a spinning component to a piece of 2-D artwork. With LED lights, conductive tape, and coin cell batteries, girls can incorporate lights into greeting cards, paintings, and more. With felt and Velcro, they can make light-up jewelry.

You can stock up on LEDs and motors at an electronics store. If you find this overwhelming, you can ease the learning curve by purchasing a bare-bones kit with electronics components that are useful for learning and then reusing. Add one of these to your daughter's art box and she'll be able to add motors and lights to her creations. For example, the Electricity Science Wiz kit created by Penny Norman (recommended ages five to ten) contains a motor, buzzer, LED light, and easy-clip wires. The Investigating Electricity Kit (ages twelve and up) sold online at Home Science Tools includes a small motor, battery holders and batteries, alligator clips, lights, a switch, and wire, among other items.

In addition, there are many opportunities to merge technology and art through computer software and apps. Some artists draw digitally using drawing programs, special styluses, and drawing boards like those made by Wacom. CAD programs are great for modeling 3-D designs, and even for 3-D printing. There are stop-motion animation programs for all skill levels. You'll find more about these computer programs and apps in chapter 5.

Cooking

Why It Matters

It's hard to find a more everyday STEM task to enjoy with your kids than cooking or baking. The applied math and science are already there, and the learning doesn't need to be front and center—it can be a sliver of the activity itself. Measuring ingredients, for example, is a small part of the baking process, and yet talking fractions or ratios allows us to incorporate the language of STEM into our everyday lives, helping girls become comfortable and confident native STEM speakers.

There are many benefits to cooking:

 Reading and following a recipe requires young chefs to practice active reading.

 Recipes are algorithms—follow the steps and you should arrive at the promised product. Discussing variations along the way ("I wonder what would happen if we did this in the wrong order?" or "I want to make this recipe in a mini-muffin pan—what do you think we need to do?") helps develop computational thinking skills.

Cooking presents the perfect hands-on approach to fractions, proportions, ratios, time, and many other mathematical concepts.

Cooking is chemistry, the science of many different chemical reactions and physical reactions such as changes of state.

Children build creativity when they are given some free rein in the kitchen to modify or create their own recipes.

How to Develop Interest

- Children have so much fun cooking and baking with adults—so abandon your expectations, get in the kitchen, and have some fun.

- Encourage your daughter to pick out recipes and plan meals.

- When there's time, let your young daughter get distracted from the recipe or encourage her to deviate and invent. Maybe the recipe calls for three-quarters of a cup of flour, but first she wants to see how much of the three-quarters of a cup will fit in the one-third cup, or she wants to sprinkle flour on the counter and write her name. Remember her age and let her play.

- Encourage curiosity by taking the time to both ask and answer questions. Asking "What happens when we . . ." allows children to become active experimenters. The goal isn't as much the final product—it's the experience.

- Be cognizant of how often you answer questions with "I don't know" because you are busy or distracted. Show your child how to look up (research) answers to questions. Write down the question for later if now is not a good time.

- By age eight or nine, girls are ready for some autonomy in the kitchen. A girl this age is capable of following an easy recipe for cakes or muffins on her own. Help her gather the ingredients, be there for helping with the oven and electric mixer, but stay out of her way as she pours and stirs, and watch her mistakes happen. (In the words of two nine-year-olds, "Remember that time we forgot to put the *blueberries* in the blueberry muffins?")

- Sometimes there are failures. But there's always next time, and as with any innovation process girls can try to figure out what went wrong and talk about the modifications they will make next time. They can take time to reflect.

How to Further STEM-Cooking Connections

As children get older, understanding the chemistry that makes the magic happen helps them become better chefs—they are able to predict outcomes, which means they can create new recipes or adjust existing ones for improvement or for a different flavor. In fact, hands-on science classes that teach cooking have become popular on college campuses, particularly with nonscience majors looking to fulfill a science requirement.

If your daughter is interested in cooking, continue to encourage her. The science kits at toy stores might make nice gifts, but the easiest and most effective way to teach her is to get into the kitchen and use the real thing. Here are some activities that don't require special kits:

- **Ice cream:** You don't need an ice cream maker to make ice cream at home. You need salt (any coarseness), cream, sugar, ice cubes, a few sealable plastic bags, and a whole lot of shaking. What's going on here? Salt lowers the temperature at which water freezes. This is why if you sprinkle salt on ice in wintertime, the ice melts—the salt has actually lowered the melting point of the ice, so whereas normal water might freeze, the salt and water solution will not. This brine actually gets colder than the freezing point of water itself—and that's what we're after. For the ice cream ingredients to freeze, the temperature needs to be lower than water's freezing point of 32 degrees Fahrenheit, so salt gets us there.

- **Bread:** Use a simple recipe to try your hand at making bread at home. Yeast are hungry little sugar-loving single-celled organisms. When you feed them sugar, they will ferment— which means that they convert the sugar to alcohol and carbon dioxide. The carbon dioxide gets caught in the bread dough, which is what causes the dough to rise. When the dough is baked, the alcohol evaporates and the yeast die off, leaving behind nice air pockets. (Through its use of organisms to make breads, cheeses, and yogurt, fermentation is one of the earliest forms of biotechnology!)

- **Apples and lemon juice:** Sliced apples turn brown because of a process called oxidation—when the cells of the cut apple are exposed to the air, the air enters these cells and a chemical reaction occurs that creates brown chemical by-products called melanins. Lemon juice contains ascorbic acid (better known as vitamin C). If the apple slices are squirted with lemon juice or dunked in a lemon-water bath, the oxygen is instead attracted to the ascorbic acid, saving the apple—at least for a while. Try different juices with different amounts of ascorbic acid, or see how long it takes those lemony apple slices to succumb to oxidation.

Use the language of science and mathematics as you cook, but don't turn the activity into a big lesson. You're there to have fun and these words are just part of your vocabulary:

Hypothesis: A best guess as to what will happen based on what one already knows.

Chemical reaction: The ingredients have combined to make something new—and they can no longer be separated. Baking a cake contains a few chemical reactions—like the baking powder that produces gas bubbles to make the cake fluffy instead of dense.

Physical reaction: The substance may appear different, but it is still the same substance. Ice, for example, is still water. Frosting piped into rosettes is still frosting.

Ratio: How much of one item exists in relation to another. Michael Ruhlman wrote a cookbook titled *Ratio* (he calls it an "anti-recipe book") built on the idea that you can create anything in the kitchen as long as you have memorized certain fundamental ratios. The ratio for a basic cookie mix, for example, is one part sugar, two parts fat, and three parts flour.

Proportional: When two ratios are equal. One half of a twelve-inch pizza is proportional to two quarters of a twelve-inch pizza. Six inches is proportional to half a foot.

Middle school and high school girls may express an interest in where their food comes from. Encourage their interest in sustainability, pesticides, organic food, farm-to-table dining, or gardening.

In addition, teach girls about the large role chemical engineers play in food science. They help perfect that secret sauce, create the processes for making the smoothest chocolate bars that still have that nice crisp snap, and create new technologies for food packaging, better flavor, and improved texture. They find ways to safely increase the shelf-life of products and eliminate food-borne pathogens. There are many human beings on the planet to feed, and not all of them have easy access to fresh local food.

A girl with a burgeoning interest in chemical engineering will soon find out that it's not just about food. Chemical engineers are responsible for the absorbent pellets in diapers and the fire retardant in parking garages. Their expertise is needed across many industries, including health care, pharmaceuticals, biotechnology, environmental safety, and even aerospace.

Cooking, Crafts, and STEM

Cooking inspires curiosity for our physical world as well as for its many people and cultures. Through the kitchen and garden, we can broaden children's horizons, deepen their imaginations, and foster their appreciation for the Earth and its inhabitants—all of which will help grow empathetic young scientists and innovators. Meredith Outwater, founder of Gourmet Globetrotters, shows us how families can prepare snacks from around the globe while complementing them with coordinating crafts, games, books, art, and movement.

Travel to India and prepare naan with a mint chutney. Naan incorporates yogurt into the yeast-based recipe and requires kneading, which is fun for little hands. There are many types of chutneys, or sauces, to try. A simple tomato and mint chutney brings many different colors and aromas to explore. Pair that culinary adventure with a look at Diwali, the Hindu festival of lights, which ushers in their new year. Read *Lighting a Lamp: A Diwali Story* by Jonny Zucker to younger children, color mandalas, use colored flour to create rangoli designs, and craft diya-inspired lights with glass baby food jars, tissue paper, and glue. Or explore yoga poses by printing or purchasing yoga cards. Talk about breathing,

continued on next page . . .

. . . continued from previous page

balance, flexibility, and strength. Older children may do sun salutations and younger children may enjoy playing "Yogini Says," which is played like Simon Says but using yoga poses.

Or venture to Egypt and whip up pita and hummus. Pita is a pocketed flat bread that may have originated in Mesopotamia, and hummus seems to have come from the same area. Both tend to be friendly to less developed taste buds. Egypt offers many paths of exploration. Talk about mummies and let children wrap each other in toilet paper or white streamers for a giggle, create sarcophagi out of flat egg carton tops and markers, or offer children toothpicks and mini marshmallows and ask them to build pyramid-inspired structures. The Sahara lends itself to many discussion topics, as does the Nile River. You may focus on how camels survive in these conditions—from their extra eyelid to their large eyebrows to their humps that store fat (not water) to their hooves. Fill a shallow pan with sand and have children push a small flat object (e.g., a penny) into the sand and then have them use the same force to push a cardboard cutout of a hoof. It won't sink; discuss why!

Roll sushi in Japan and try folding origami; make pot stickers in China and build creative dragons out of shoe boxes and craft supplies lying around the house; puree a borscht in Russia and make matryoshka dolls from paper; mix up tzatziki in Greece and make an Olympics-based obstacle course; whip up cheese puffs in Brazil and create the Amazon rainforest in a glass jar; prepare crepes in France and try your hand at impressionist art. There are so many corners of the world to explore!

Sewing

Why It Matters

Sewing requires creating, planning, measuring, and constructing. In fact, it uses so much of the same methodology used in the engineering world that some recommend teaching sewing to undergraduate engineers.

Erin Winick, an undergraduate at the University of Florida, happens to be both a sewer and a mechanical engineer. Her grandmother and her mother introduced her to sewing when she was younger, and she kept it up alongside other hands-on activities like building sculptures out of Lego bricks and making Rube Goldberg machines with objects she found around the house.

It wasn't until she was in college that she realized how much her sewing had helped her. She explains sewing's relationship to mechanical engineering like this: "I realized that I had gotten a lot of training from sewing that really put me on a path to engineering. Much of what I had learned in making patterns and building these complex designs was actually turning something that was 2-D from a pattern into something that was 3-D for someone to wear, which is something that people don't often appreciate. There's a lot of engineering in that. In college, I took 3-D modeling classes where I had to use spatial awareness to be able to craft engineering-related parts. Some girls have trouble with that because they don't have a lot of opportunities to build their spatial awareness skills. I never did because sewing helped to fill that gap."

On top of that, a sewing machine is a machine, and a fairly complex one at that. Knowing her way around a sewing machine helped Erin as she learned to use lathes and mills, to weld, and to manipulate sheet metal.

Erin has successfully used STEM to enhance her own interests and skills. In her senior year she combined her interests in fashion design, 3-D printing, and STEM outreach to create a company called Sci Chic that shows the creativity and fashion present in STEM. She creates 3-D-printed jewelry and accessories inspired by science and engineering concepts. In her free time, she experiments with 3-D printing on fabrics, a connection she never would have made without her experience in sewing.

How to Develop Interest

- Punch holes around a paper plate and provide small children with a large dull plastic needle and yarn.

- Draw simple patterns (circles, stars, hearts) on paper and show your young daughter how to pin them to fabric. Cut two matching pieces, turn inside out, sew, and stuff to make a pillow.

- As your daughter advances, give her a small sewing kit filled with embroidery thread, kid-sized needles and sewing scissors, cotton for stuffing, a measuring tape, and felt so she can make projects of her own design.

- Teach older girls how to use a sewing machine and follow patterns. Let girls plan, measure, cut, and experiment. If you don't sew, is there someone in your family or neighborhood who does?

- Many other activities introduce sewing concepts, such as knitting and crocheting. Many girls enjoy making bracelets, rings, and necklaces with gimp, Paracord, embroidery thread, or elastics. Duct tape is fun for no-sew wallets and purses.

How to Further STEM-Sewing Connections

Introduce your daughter to smart garments—or e-textiles. If you could incorporate electronics into clothing, what would you do? In the future, how might the medical community use e-textiles embedded with sensors to monitor your health? Envision a bandage that tracks the status of a wound: researchers at the University of Bath have collaborated with a team of clinical researchers at a pediatric burn center to help young burn victims by developing a dressing that turns fluorescent green when it senses infection.

A daughter interested in e-textiles can create pillows, puppets, quilt squares, and more that light up, make sounds, or vibrate. SparkFun Electronics is an online retailer that aims to make such electronics projects more accessible. They not only sell the components but also offer easy-to-follow tutorials. They sell the LilyTwinkle, one of the easiest LilyPad

Arduino boards. It has a small microcontroller, smaller than a quarter, that requires no coding and is designed specifically for use in e-textiles. (A microcontroller is a computer embedded into a system in order to make the system do something.) Your daughter can connect up to four LEDs to the LilyTwinkle, which runs off a 3V coin cell battery, for a soft firefly light, or connect four LEDs to another LilyPad Arduino board called the LilyTiny and each light will behave differently. She can add the lights to felt masks, Halloween costumes, or anything she desires. She will need the board, a pack of LilyPad LEDs, a LilyPad coin cell battery holder, a coin cell battery, a LilyPad switch to turn the lights off and on, and a bobbin of conductive thread that acts as the wiring.

Music

Why It Matters

Playing an instrument can actually change your brain. As little as fifteen months of musical training may increase the volume of white and gray matter, and may make other changes that grow both auditory and motor skills as well as improve cross-talk between the right and left hemispheres. Music can strengthen verbal fluency, information processing speed, and other cognitive functions that will stay with you throughout your life, even if you put your instrument down.

In fact, the greatest benefits of studying a musical instrument may be long term: recent studies demonstrate that the brain changes that result from music training in childhood can protect the brain from memory loss and cognitive decline as we age. So join your daughter! And singers rejoice: while this research was specific to instruments, other research has shown that singing also shows signs of improving left- and right-brain cross talk.

More immediately, in playing the piano or another instrument, your daughter may not be thinking about numbers, but she is working with beat, rhythm, melody—all based on mathematical concepts, especially fractions. Learning fractions is such a major benefit of playing music that incorporating music into math class can help students learn. Susan Joan Courey, assistant professor of special education at San Francisco State University, worked with a team to develop a music-based educational program called Academic Music that took the Kodaly method of musical education and integrated it with the learning of fractions. The Kodaly method, based on the teaching style of Hungarian composer and educator Zoltan Kodaly, has a heavy emphasis on folk songs and, especially at the beginning, emphasizes body movements such as clapping and drumming while de-emphasizing language, thus removing language as a barrier. For six weeks, half the third graders in the study were given Academic Music instruction, and half were not. After six weeks, the children in the music program scored 50 percent higher on their math tests than the other group.

Let's not forget that music is also a great outlet for creative expression; it reduces stress, provides opportunities for companionship and collaboration, and is a hobby that can be carried into adulthood.

How to Develop Interest

If your daughter is interested in an instrument, invest in her hobby by buying an instrument and signing her up for instruction. Unfortunately, music can be an expensive pursuit, and the high price is prohibitive for many families. Look into renting or buying second-hand instruments, or consider a keyboard as a more economical way to bring an instrument into the home. Many older kids will pick up instruments such as guitars with their own money and teach themselves. Advocate for band, orchestra, jazz band, and choir in the schools, and donate unused instruments to programs that will gift them to children who cannot afford them.

Many sophisticated music apps give children access to music. Garage-Band provides a collection of instruments at your fingertips; ImproVox is used for recording and sharing vocals. JoyTunes' Piano Maestro teaches piano by actually listening to what you are playing on your keyboard or piano and letting you know if you did it right.

NOT PITCH PERFECT? SO WHAT!

Too much pressure is put on kids to sing in tune. When they don't sing in tune, hearing "you can't sing" discourages them. The best singers say it is when they "sing like they don't give a damn" that they find their best voice. Anyone can and should sing. Find your own inner music!

How to Further STEM-Music Connections

 Learn how to make instruments. Steel drums, shakers, xylophones, tambourines, bells, maracas, drums—these are all fairly easy to make with inexpensive recyclable materials.

 Build a speaker with paper plates, magnets, copper wire, card stock, tape, scissors, and glue.

Digitally mix music, create content, and produce online.

A Place for the Arts

Today you are likely to hear educators talk about STEAM. What is STEAM, and how is it different from STEM? The *A* stands for the arts, but the reasoning behind this insertion can be a little difficult to follow.

STEM made its entrance into the K–12 vernacular in the 1990s. At that time, there were few courses actually *called* STEM in K–12 schools, and a "STEM course" referred to a typical math or science class. Calculus was STEM. Biology was STEM. STEM courses gained a reputation as any pencil-and-paper-pushing math and science classes for left-brained intellectuals. Throughout the tech boom of the '90s, these courses rose greatly in importance, and if a school, crunched for both time and money, had to choose between STEM and anything else, STEM usually won. There wasn't much engineering or technology in schools at that point—the driving factor behind the rise in STEM was increasing student achievement in math and science. In fact, the acronym first bandied around was SMET, but that was wisely discarded.

Today, the STEM class that your daughter might take is much more focused on engineering and technology. It is often a project-based course that encourages open-ended inquiry and design to solve problems. Ideally, students would find that it is a fun and interesting class that encourages creativity and is not just for those who excel in math and are book-smart in science.

Rebranding these newer STEM courses as STEAM courses is a move meant to draw focus to the art and design inherent in STEM. For many working in the field, whether these courses are called STEM or STEAM doesn't change anything. Either way, these are the classes that might plant the seeds for such innovations as the origami robots mentioned earlier. These are hands-on classes that might emphasize function—strength of a bridge, a working 3-D puzzle—as well as design, and particularly a blend of the two. Not only that, but the projects introduced in a successful class are attractive to children who aren't focusing on careers—they just want exciting ways to experience music, technology, art, and other interests. To parents, on the other hand, the name change can make a big difference in perception—STEAM can sound more inclusive, more accessible, and more interesting.

Everywhere in the STEM world, though (even without the *A*), design does matter. Elegant code sits behind beautiful and intuitive apps. There's no unlinking the fields. Today, everything in technology is about human-technology or human-computer interaction. The moment you include the word *human*, you are introducing the necessity for understanding people, psychology, sociology, anthropology, history, and culture to create technology that truly benefits humanity.

At NASA art is often used to communicate technology and big data. A light sculpture at NASA's Jet Propulsion Laboratory depicts the commands sent from Earth to satellites and the data sent back to Earth in return. It's beautiful and informative. Karen's course Animation for Communications is an example of using art to communicate. Animation is effective for educating populations who can't read or write and is highly effective for educating children with autism.

The focus on STEAM in education will hopefully bring renewed focus to the importance of the arts. Unfortunately, fine arts are the first to suffer during any economic downturn, and schools are often forced to suspend programs such as art, music, theater, and dance. And sometimes those programs don't come back for years—which means students entering school during a bad economic cycle may miss out on the benefits entirely.

Former US education secretary Arne Duncan found that a 2009–2010 arts education survey painted a "good news-bad news story"—with the bad news confined mostly to low-income areas. The recession had little impact on arts programs in many school districts, but low-income areas suffered a wide opportunity gap. Four million elementary school students do not receive visual arts instruction at their schools, and music instruction in high-poverty high schools has dropped from 100 percent to 80 percent in the last decade. Why is this important? Duncan reported that "low-income students who had arts rich experiences in high schools were more than three times as likely to earn a B.A. as low-income students without those experiences."

The award-winning Harmony Project gives us a glimpse into how the arts can be life-changing. The Harmony Project is an L.A.-based youth program with the motto "Give Music, Change Lives" that serves youth from low-income areas. Students receive an instrument and professional instruction five times a week. Nina Kraus's team at the Auditory Neuroscience Lab at Northwestern found that kids studying music through the Harmony Project became better listeners. When students' listening improves, their ability to follow directions, read, and focus all improve as well. The team believes that cultivating these abilities may be one way to close the achievement gap for low-income children. As Harmony's website states, "Learning to play an instrument takes patience, persistence, and focus—the same qualities students need to excel in school and in their future career." Every one of the fifty-two graduating seniors in the program in 2015 was accepted to college.

Advocate for the arts. Help make sure that these crucial programs don't get cut. The arts help students and communities, and are important to our future. Science and the arts are interwoven and symbiotic. STEM fields need people with art backgrounds. John Maeda doesn't see technology flourishing without art by its side. "Art and design are essential to humanizing technology," he writes. "You need both in order to create balance and fuel true innovation."

It's Better to Create
than to Consume

Legend has it that when the printing press was popularized, Swiss biologist Conrad Gessner requested regulations on the book trade because of a concern with information overload. Since the sixteenth century, we've continued to climb this media ladder—comfortable with the media that we're standing on, genuinely scared about the dangerous implications of anything above. Radio threatened books, television threatened books *and* radio, and the personal computer and the invention of email threatened society as we know it. ("E-Mails 'Hurt IQ More than Pot'" read a 2005 CNN headline; the article referred to studies showing, among other things, that IQs of those who divided time between work tasks and email dropped an average of ten points, as compared to the four-point drop seen after marijuana usage.)

Teens today have their choice between many competing social media sites. Facebook, Instagram, Snapchat, Twitter, and Tumblr all serve specific purposes and audiences. A typical teen sends and receives thirty texts a day either through SMS or through services like Kik and WhatsApp. As they become teens, girls prefer social media sites and are drawn to visual sites such as Instagram, Snapchat, Pinterest, and Tumblr. While teen and tween girls spend the majority of their time on social media sites, boys tend to favor video games.

It makes perfect sense that teens are embracing the internet as a place to build community, share images, and play, but the difficulty is that they are experimenting in a nonprivate global space with no forebears. Open the doors to technological change, and all sorts of things come along with it. Depending on how we use it, technology can improve us, informing and educating us on worldviews in a way that hopefully leads to tolerance and respect for other cultures, ethnicities, and genders—or it can do the exact opposite.

Instead of taking a protectionist approach, grow your daughter's digital citizenship skills by staying involved and informed, and by enforcing age-appropriate usage. Simply tracking screen time doesn't allow for differentiation between the many ways our children use technology. Help children go beyond texting, watching shows, and playing games by teaching them to recognize whether they are creating, connecting, consuming, or some combination thereof.

Watching television, as well as playing many video games, falls into the consume category, as does anything that turns us into couch potatoes or tablet zombies. There is little brain power involved; we are not progressing toward a learning milestone, and we are not learning a new usable skill.

The majority of your child's screen time should be spent creating. In creating, she is using technology as a tool and likely developing both computational thinking and digital literacy skills. No matter what your daughter is interested in, you can find opportunities online for her. In some cases, she is not only creating but also getting used to software programs that might be similar to those professionals use.

Take a word processor, for example. Children can use word processors to write stories and poems, create signs for lemonade stands, design birthday cards, compose letters to newspapers, and illustrate books. Other applications like 3-D CAD programs have a much more specific use. Here we walk you through a number of different creative endeavors girls can undertake with the aid of technology.

Live-Action Movies

Filmmaking can act as an entry point into the creative arts for children, and it teaches skills that transfer across many applications—to complete a project, students must take something from their imagination and attempt to bring it out into the world. They must plan the project, lay out storyboards, write a script, devise settings and costumes, and find the materials, spaces, and actors to make their vision a reality. Finally, they must edit—cutting out excess and revising their original plan—to create the strongest possible product.

Making movies is empowering. Some movies are collaborative efforts where children must argue for their artistic vision but also be willing to compromise, while other movies are solo projects that allow an artist to have complete control over creative expression. In fact, making movies gives those children who might normally be overshadowed by their peers the chance to control the narrative. It allows them to tell their story their way, grows their creativity, and gives them a platform. Making movies is a way for teens to effect change and connect students to their communities and the world; the end result brings students a much-deserved sense of accomplishment.

Student moviemakers need little more than a phone or tablet to create movies that give them a voice. Also, the learning curve is small—most teens today are already familiar with making and editing videos. Thanks in part to this accessibility, certain nonprofits are finding great success in bringing moviemaking to teens, especially in underserved areas.

Getting Started

🚀 Apple offers iMovie for free on most of its devices. Windows Movie Maker is free for your PC. Adobe Premiere Elements, Animoto, and PowerDirector are highly rated video editing software packages.

🚀 Encourage your children to try these at home:

+ Create movie trailers for imaginary movies
+ Film a video message to a future self
+ Combine video clips and photographs from throughout the year to make a birthday memory for a friend or family member
+ Create a parody of a music video, movie scene, or television show
+ Film a comedic interview

🚀 Learn more about digital rights at the website Teaching Copyright (www.teachingcopyright.org), a project by the Electronic Frontier Foundation that includes lesson plans for teaching students. YouTube also has pages that discuss

VIDEO ACTIVISM

The MyBlock Education Program based in New York City (www.myblockedu.org) helps students become active citizens through the use of video. The program works with schools to develop a personalized curriculum that works within time and budget constraints. The program loans schools video equipment and provides education materials and a teaching artist who visits the school to run workshops on both video literacy and active citizenship. In this way, teens become involved with their communities through filming short movies about their neighborhoods. Videos are then uploaded to a virtual video map of New York City.

copyright and fair use (see www.youtube.com/yt/copyright and www.youtube.com/yt/copyright/fair-use.html).

 Don't just create—become part of the community. Share films by hosting a film festival for amateurs, even if it's in your backyard. Visit film festivals and independent art houses to expose children to ideas outside of the mainstream.

Animation

Technology has brought amazing advances in animation. In fact, in the traveling Pixar exhibit, the public had the chance to see the enormous computing power behind the intricate filmmaking steps of modeling, rigging, surfaces, sets and cameras, animation, simulation, lighting, and rendering. Take Merida's hair in *Brave*. It was critical to her feisty character that Merida have that long curly red hair—but at the time, no one knew how to animate hair like hers, with all those curls moving in different directions at all times. It took six months to determine if it could even be done, and then it took two years of work involving many STEM professionals to build the computer simulation. From there, they put the curly-hair simulator to work.

Above all else, animation is an art broken wide open by technology, and it is interesting today to see the way different techniques are blended together to create beautiful effects. *The Little Prince* (2015), for example, combined computer-generated animation, paper cutouts, and stop-motion. With the technology in our homes, kids too can create all sorts of amazing animations.

2-D Animation

If your girl loves to draw, she may be interested in animation. It can be a little tricky to draw on the computer with a mouse, although this method is perfectly good for beginners. Serious artists may want to invest in a pen tablet that they can connect to their computer for creating digital artwork.

Animation-ish by FableVision Learning is a nice entry-level package. This software was designed by Peter H. Reynolds, the award-winning author and illustrator of *Ish*, *The Dot*, *Someday*, and *I Am Yoga*. In Animation-ish users progress through three different skill levels as they learn how to create their own motion cartoons. (The simplest level requires only three frames.) Like traditional animation, this program works by layering drawings with small movement in between, and then playing those at a certain speed.

Stop-Motion Animation

Stop-motion animation creates the illusion of movement by taking successive photographs of objects. It's easy to do at home. All kids need is a computer and a webcam, or a mobile device, and an editing program. Today, as tablet and phone camera quality continues to improve, apps have made stop-motion videos even easier to make.

Many kids make stop motion movies with Lego bricks, but you can use anything from dolls to friends to cereal boxes to clay figurines. The frame-by-frame format lets kids create humorous physics-defying scenes—they can show themselves being dragged around the room by a toy car, for example.

This is really for kids of all ages—kids as young as first grade can make their own rewarding animations, and this interest might even lead to a career someday; successful movies like *The Boxtrolls* and *Fantastic Mr. Fox* used stop-motion animation.

A good place to start is the HUE Animation Studio. This brightly colored book comes with lessons, ideas, a small piece of clay, and a free download of their award-winning animation software for your computer. You will also need a webcam.

Programming

The Scratch programming language is a great tool for beginning animators. Developed by the Lifelong Kindergarten Group at MIT Media Lab, it provides a different experience than either of the previous examples because the creator can add code to enhance the animation. Take a simple animation of a car driving from the left side of the screen to the right. In a program like Animation-ish, animators might use cut and paste to create fifty frames that show the car, where in each frame the car is relocated a small distance to the right. Play the animation and it looks like the car is moving.

In Scratch users can draw a car, drag it to the left-hand side of the screen, then add a line of code to the car that basically says move two spaces along the x-axis, pause for a fraction of a second, and repeat this process fifty times. The effect is similar—press play and the car moves across the screen.

Animating through Scratch allows the maker to create an interactive experience. One can program the car so that when a user clicks on it, it beeps, changes direction, or comes to a stop. When a user clicks on the Up Arrow, the car can move along the x-axis by larger and larger jumps—first by twos, then fives, then tens, generating the illusion of acceleration.

Webpages

Web design has certainly come a long way. Today, kids can create a beautiful and striking webpage very quickly. Webpage design strikes high on the rate of return and low on the frustration level.

Sites like Weebly and Wix offer free hosting and unlimited pages. The templates are drag and drop. Young entrepreneurs can set up websites to advertise or sell items. Artists can display work. Photographers can create slide shows. Writers can produce online literary magazines or zines. Parents may password-protect pages in order to maintain control over who is looking at their children's online content.

3-D Printing

3-D printing may sound complicated, but it's not that hard to get started. Online or downloadable programs allow users to drag, drop, and connect simple shapes onto a 3-D axis.

Then, once your child has some experience, she can use math and programming concepts to create more complicated designs. Working with an x-y-z coordinate system while creating 3-D objects will certainly make learning those concepts in math class a little bit more relevant.

If a student doesn't have access to a 3-D printer at home or at school, don't let that stand in the way:

- Local community makerspaces such as those found in public libraries will often be able to help with 3-D printing. Many of these makerspaces offer classes for kids as young as eight. Beginners of that age usually start out on easy-to-use programs like the free cloud-based BlocksCAD, a 3-D CAD program (www.blockscad3d.com) developed by Einstein's Workshop specifically for young children. If your daughter doesn't want to take a class, she can often use the onsite computers or bring her own design in the form of an STL file from home and rent the 3-D printers, usually at a per-minute charge.

- SolidWorks, a maker of 3-D CAD software, has developed Apps for Kids (appsforkids.solidworks.com) to introduce young children to the 3-D printing world. Apps for Kids either provides kids with a blank canvas or allows them to upload an image that the program then transforms into a 3-D model. A real-life object—a favorite toy, perhaps—can be turned into a 3-D model that can then be stretched to make it longer, wider, bigger, or smaller. It can be colored, painted, or adorned with stickers. And then it can be printed and delivered to home.

- Tinkercad (Tinkercad.com) is a free web-based 3-D CAD program. It stores the user's models as STL files, which she can use to print on her own printer or send to one of Tinkercad's third-party printing services that will print the product and send it to her. There are lots of user-created files to borrow and tinker with—cars, soccer stadiums, airplanes, and cups abound in the Tinkercad gallery. Many artists use Tinkercad to make sculptures, jewelry, or household objects like vases and pencil holders.

Laser Cutting

Laser cutting is similar to 3-D printing in that artists use a computer application to visualize and create a design that is then stored in a particular format and sent to a machine. So, what can a girl do with a laser cutter?

Laser cutting involves using a laser to make high precision cuts into a material. The laser cutter has traditionally been found in industrial manufacturing applications, and so it is a great machine for aspiring engineers.

Instead of painting pottery for handmade gifts, girls can create beautiful cards or wall displays of images that are cut into wood, acrylic, plastic, textiles, cardboard, foam, and more—all depending on the laser cutter. Girls can create multiple layers of laser cuts that can be cut, stacked, and glued together to form a sculpture.

As students become more advanced, the possibilities are endless. Laser cutters may be 2-D, but they are often used for rapid prototyping in industrial applications. This means that during the design process of, say, an ergonomic chair, the many parts can be cut on a laser cutter out of wood, metal, or plastic and then assembled. Designers can even add electronics to their prototype for a quick and dirty look at their vision before spending time on an actual product that will likely need some pricey tweaks.

In this way, laser cutters have tons of applications. Take dollhouse and doll furniture construction. Can your daughter design the pieces of a doll chair, table, or bed? What about the walls of the house itself? When her laser-cut pieces arrive like a package from IKEA, she can assemble them with glue, screws, nails, or even tabs she has built into the cuts. Pinterest is an excellent place to get some visuals of the possibilities of laser cutting, although there are a lot of intricate projects! Start simple and let your daughter build up skills. After some 2-D work to familiarize herself with laser cutting, such as creating simple shapes or initials, move on to projects that can be assembled easily. Three simple laser-cut wood pieces can be combined like a 3-D puzzle to make cats or dogs; a single piece of leather can be laser cut with stitch holes to form the parts of a wallet. Laser cut four animals and add holes at the tops to make a mobile.

You can find laser cutters in many of the same places you'd find 3-D printing. Makerspaces near you may have laser cutters. If so, they may offer courses for children as young as early elementary school, and you can likely rent the laser cutter as well. Some makerspaces charge for materials, while use of the laser cutter is free.

Create Worlds

A nine-year-old girl is giving Katianne a *Minecraft* tour: "I like that you can make a whole bunch of different stuff, like mansions. They have a whole bunch of different characters. They have squids, fish, salmon, pufferfish. . . . You can even make your own character. . . . Sometimes you learn natural resources that come with a world. Like I found a cave. It has coal and gold and diamonds that I have to mine. In Survival Mode, there are chickens and cows, rabbits, sheep, pigs . . . you find ovens to cook them. So it's like really living a life. You have to hunt and everything. It's the same exact thing as being outside except everything's in blocks and you can fly. . . . I love rabbits. When you feed them they can get together and make a baby. . . . This is a craft table where I can make stuff. I'm making lots of stone pickaxes because when you use them they die out."

This is the world of *Minecraft*—this never-ending pile of virtual bricks and, if you're in the mood, monsters. It's a sandbox—hop on in, play, and explore. If there's one thing that can bond a bunch of kids of different ages and abilities, it seems to be *Minecraft*. Siblings who normally might be fighting are sitting together. Maybe they're destroying each other's virtual mansions, or maybe they're sharing knowledge on what to do when you've created more pigs than you know what to do with. Our friend says this about her older brother: "He's helped me learn how to make certain things . . . like we have a lot of battles with each other and he helps me make cannons and machine guns first."

While video games may have a bad rap for promoting antisocial tendencies, *Minecraft* is very much a collaborative game. Stuart Duncan, a Canadian web developer and father of a child with autism, created the Autcraft *Minecraft* server because he wanted to create a safe space for his son to play. He didn't expect a huge turnout, but *Minecraft* is very popular among children with autism, likely because there's a certain structure and predictability to the game. There are more than seven thousand members on Autcraft today. As the children play, researchers are discovering that children with autism bring what they learn about communication and social interactions back to the real world. In fact, researcher Kate Ringland journeyed into the Autcraft virtual world to study how people with autism learn from *Minecraft*.

If your daughter loves *Minecraft*, encourage her to build. Embrace *Minecraft* and open-ended games like it. These games may be in a different format than we are used to, but kids are learning collaboration and problem solving while also building spatial ability and computational thinking skills.

If your daughter discovers a technology that she has a knack for, challenge her to take her interests to the next level—one in which she creates instead of consumes. Those who enjoy building in *Minecraft* might take a class in which they learn to program their own mods in Java. A moviemaker might one day be one of the many engineers who work on-site in the film industry—from software engineers for computer-aided film, to mechanical engineers for props and sets, to light and sound engineers. A young woman who gets into Scratch because she likes to draw may discover that she enjoys designing video games, which could then lead to a career developing simulation tools for NASA. The path is rarely straight—we never know where an interest will take us.

STUDYING TECH

Studying how people use technologies—like this study of how children with autism develop social skills and build friendships through *Minecraft*—is in itself a STEM career called human factors.

Adults, Check
Your Attitude

Girls enter grade school passionate and gung ho about science. Who doesn't love learning about caterpillars and the moon? But something happens as they make their way to upper grade school. If we parents and educators still maintain a broad influence over children at this age, could we be part of the issue? This chapter looks at how adults' own complicated relationships with math, science, and gender stereotypes can give girls a disadvantage right from the starting block.

The goal is to create a sustainable, hospitable environment, a place where a girl is assured that she has the same worth as a boy and that she will be taken as seriously as a boy. It is important that a girl learn—despite the way girls and women may be portrayed in popular media—that she and her friends are smart and capable with bright futures and have the same right to educational and career opportunities as boys.

Everyone plays an important role here. Girls look to the women in their lives for cues on how they should think and behave, so it is critical that girls see their mothers, aunts, teachers, and so on engaging with STEM in positive ways. A father who expresses his enjoyment and appreciation for math and science will also have a profound influence on his daughter, and if he shares that enjoyment with her, even better.

It's important that the home be at least one place that is free from gender bias and STEM stereotyping. With this strong foundation, a girl who encounters bias and stereotypes in her life will be much better equipped to handle them.

Our Relationship with Math: It's Complicated

Unfortunately, it's not uncommon to hear mothers say they hate math or that they're not good at it, preferring to leave the job of helping with math homework to dad. Such remarks can have a negative impact. They confirm for a child, whether son or daughter, that women as a gender must not be good at math or science. From then on, daughters have the added burden of stereotype threat—every time they dip a toe into those math or science subjects, they risk confirming this negative stereotype. This is an added challenge for a young woman every time she submits an assignment or takes a test—a bad score that may be shrugged off as an off day for the boy sitting next to her may, in a girl's eyes, represent proof that girls as a gender are not good at math and science. Instead of digging her heels in and studying harder next time, she may feel it is better to quit.

Even when girls are simply made *aware* of the stereotype, they may psych themselves out of performing as well as they would have otherwise. In 2003 a group of students sat down to take a math test. Some were told beforehand that female testers have historically performed worse on this test than males. The girls in this group scored lower than a control group that had not been informed of any gender differences in scoring.

When girls get the message that they're not smart enough, even if the implication is subtle, and even if it comes unwittingly from their own parents, it makes it more difficult for them to succeed. These remarks can be a simple sentence. They can be serious, unintentional, or meant to be funny. But they still can undercut her drive and confidence.

That is why parents and educators need to examine their own attitudes, and that can take work and self-reflection. Diana, a speech therapist and mother of two, has a clear memory of her high school math teacher returning a graded test to a friend and telling the friend that she had *done well for a girl*. "From that moment on," Diana says, "I knew that no one had any expectations for me to succeed, and so I stopped trying." As a mother, Diana began to wonder if her negative attitude toward math was keeping her from encouraging her own children to pursue more math and science opportunities. Stories like this one illustrate why changes to this mindset are often slow and generational, but taking steps to overcome our own issues with math will help crank the wheel of change a little faster.

Julie, also a mother of two, recalls that when she was young, her mother stayed home with her during the day, working part-time a few nights a week at a department store. When an older cousin needed help with math coursework for nursing school, she asked Julie's mother to help her. This may not seem like a big deal, but it was for Julie. It changed the way Julie perceived her mother. Suddenly, her mother was someone that people came to for help with math. Never having thought of her mother in this way, she was surprised, and also very proud. Julie's understanding of her mother and father was based on common stereotypes, yet just like that her malleable mind took in this new information. She came to know that her mother, who had stayed home with the children, kept house, packed lunches, and cooked dinners as everyone else went about their very important activities, was actually smart.

As Jean Piaget explained more than half a century ago in *The Construction of Reality in the Child*, children take in new information and acquire knowledge rapidly, from multiple sources and without much discernment. This knowledge becomes their view of the world, and so adults must take care not to subject young minds to gender stereotypes. Parents, caregivers, and educators must always be aware of what they are modeling and keep lines of communication open for frank and honest discussions to counteract the gender biases that both girls and boys are apt to encounter on a daily basis.

Putting It into Practice

- Reflect on your own STEM history. Everyone's story is different. If you dislike these subjects, when did that begin? What happened? What was difficult for you, and what are some of the possible reasons?

- Share your own negative experiences, but frame them as learning experiences. Reinforce that your negative experience doesn't translate to your daughter: "I wish I hadn't listened to that teacher because he/she was wrong about me."

- Stop yourself from talking negatively about STEM in front of your children. If you struggle with math, that's not the same as hating math.

- You use math all the time. Make that math part of your household language so your children develop mathematical fluency. One big issue kids have with word problems is that they take math and mix it with language from an adult world they don't yet understand. Talking up math in the home will help them with the word problems they will encounter by middle school involving sales tax, tips, commissions, measurements, coupons, sale prices, bank interest, and the like.

- It's important that daughters see the female role models in their life participating in STEM, so don't shy away from helping with math homework.

- If you don't know how to do something, that's OK. One of the most effective ways of learning is to teach someone else, so go that route: "I don't remember much about direct proportions. Why don't you walk me through your notes and the examples in your book and see if you can help me remember?"

- Bring your own style and flair to homework help. Make up songs to help memorize facts, or make up silly word problems.

- Brush up on math through websites like Khan Academy. This models for children that you are a lifelong learner, that you don't give up, and that not understanding is part of the learning process.

- When you are frustrated, stop yourself from destructive language like "Why will you ever need to know this?" or "This new way of doing math is ridiculous."

- A "bad score" to a girl may be a B! Make sure she knows that there is nothing wrong with a B. Even if the score is a D or an F, reassure her that everyone gets a bad grade once in a while. Do you hit every baseball pitched to you?

It's Not Just Parents—Early Educators May Have Their Own Math Anxiety

In their search for role models, early elementary school children often look to adults of the same gender. Since over 90 percent of elementary school teachers are female, our young daughters find potential role models right in their classrooms. What happens, though, when one of these teachers has math anxiety?

Elementary teachers are inspired to teach for many reasons, and some have the same math anxieties as other adults. In college surveys, elementary education majors report the highest levels of math anxiety of any major; unfortunately, as these teachers-to-be work toward their degrees, there are often not enough math requirements to help them overcome this anxiety.

Researchers at the University of Chicago set out to study whether this anxiety transferred to the teachers' first- and second-grade students. At the beginning of the school year, researchers told children two stories— one about a student who was good at math and another about a student who was good at reading. The children then drew these students, and the researchers recorded whether the children chose to draw girls or boys. At the end of the school year, they found that the only students who saw their math performance decline over the course of the year were girls who prescribed to gender stereotypes (good at math = boy, good at reading = girl) *and* were taught by a math-anxious female teacher. Boys

"After my daughter's parent-teacher conference, I mentioned to her that her teacher had said she (my daughter) really liked math. Her teacher had actually said she was doing really well in math, but for some reason I inadvertently used the word 'like.' My daughter thought this was a big joke and brought it up for weeks. But something happened. She continued to do well in math, but now she also had this confidence I hadn't seen before. She started to get this math swagger. I don't know— did the fact that her teacher thought she 'liked' math validate that she was good at it, that she was a 'math person'?" —Heidi, mother of an eight-year-old

and those girls with no such gender stereotypes showed no decline in performance.

In other words, those young female students who came into the class-room with the idea already in mind that girls were no good at math found this confirmed by their teachers. These students took on their teachers' math anxieties as their own, and their performance showed it.

||||||||||||||||||||||||||||||||||||||||||||||||||||||||||||||||||||||||||||||||||||||||||||||||||||||||||||||||||||||||||||||||||||||||||

Putting It into Practice

- You put a lot of effort into helping your daughter do well in school, but it's just as important that you spend time setting the foundation for success by noticing and combating any gender stereotypes she encounters. Make sure all children know that all genders excel at math so that an adult's math anxiety doesn't leave its mark.

- Mothers, grandmothers, aunts—volunteer in the classroom for a math-related activity so that your daughter and her classmates see one more example of a woman who enjoys math.

- Break down problems and laugh at your own mistakes. Have lots of examples that allow you to say things like, "I thought this was tricky at first, but practicing and asking myself lots of questions helped me narrow it down to smaller steps," or, "Shoot. That doesn't look right. Let's see if we can find a mistake."

- Remind children that math is a puzzle that can be challenging at times. Sometimes kids need to look at a problem from another angle, or put it aside to let their brains rest. Reinforce that different students learn in different ways and at different speeds.

- Create a climate where mistakes are celebrated—no mathematician ever solved a vexing theorem without a good deal of scribbling and erasing.

- Remind children that some people work best alone, with no eyes upon them. For some, having to work at the whiteboard compounds mistakes. This even happens to parents and teachers, and that's OK. If students see adults recover and even laugh at their mistakes, they will model this behavior.

 Math anxiety makes those who experience it underperform—stress and concern prevent them from reaching their true potential. It's critical that interested adults help their children build math confidence.

Keep Math in Perspective

Mathematician Bertrand Russell said, "The true spirit of delight, the exaltation, the sense of being more than Man, which is the touchstone of the highest excellence, is to be found in mathematics as surely as poetry."

Unfortunately, there aren't many students today who would agree. They're stressed about school in general, but math seems to be at the top of the list. Of course some kids learn math easily, but for many others it becomes a scary, stressful thing and they feel like they're always trying to catch up.

Math is important, but telling young students that the only path to a STEM career is through a rigorous set of math classes—classes that they may be invited into based on academic performance on a single test—can backfire. A child begins to feel like the path to a STEM career is set very early in life, and if she is not chosen, if she misses the boat, she'll be left behind. Not being accepted to an honors math course in middle school or even elementary school should not be a barrier to entering STEM fields later. Some kids are late bloomers, and while a few of those late bloomers won't let their late arrival at the game stop them, others will.

In 2013 biologist E. O. Wilson, at that time an octogenarian, wrote an essay in which he challenged the necessity of math in the sciences. While teaching biology at Harvard, he witnessed many students forgo a career in science because they didn't feel they had the necessary skills to even pass the math courses required for the degree. "This mistaken assumption has deprived science of an immeasurable amount of sorely needed talent," he wrote.

This essay produced a number of dissenting opinions. Writers took issue with Wilson's belief that "many of the most successful scientists in the world today are mathematically no more than semi-literate," and argued that if this were true at one point, it is certainly no longer true today.

There's no question that math is important—but as Andrew Hacker observes in his book *The Math Myth and Other STEM Delusions*, math pedagogy, as well as the way in which it is decided who needs what math and at what time in their lives, is imperfect, and there is little doubt that students abandon math because of these systemic faults.

To be sure, STEM fields today require proficiency in math. It would be surprising to see another E. O. Wilson, who grew up attending "relatively poor" schools and didn't take calculus until he was thirty-two and already a tenured professor at Harvard. But there is truth in what Wilson says: students assume STEM majors require rigorous math *and* they assume they are not smart enough. What Wilson seems to be saying isn't to fear math—it's to forge ahead. Learn the math you need to learn. Don't be afraid of the unknown that might lurk around the corner. "For every scientist, there exists a discipline for which his or her level of mathematical competence is enough to achieve excellence," Wilson says.

Nicole Sallak Anderson is CTO of SapientX. She's also a futurist, a blogger, and has written the fiction books *eHuman Dawn* and *eHuman Deception*. When she was a senior in high school, she decided to pursue computer science in college. At the same time, she "had a bad case of senioritis," dropped precalculus, and didn't take any math her senior year. "I loved software but didn't like math," she writes. "You see how my narrative is already different?"

The narrative is different, but not for the reasons one may think. It's not uncommon for someone to love the logic and math in computer science while disliking precalculus or calculus—but so few take the necessary steps into programming to figure that out. Computer science and higher-level math are very different, and while there are likely computer scientists out there who use such math, such as those who work in economics or physics, the majority of programming jobs don't require it.

What makes Anderson's narrative different is that she didn't let this decision hold her back. She went on to Purdue University, where she owed a small debt for her earlier senioritis, but by then she was ready for it: "Fast forward to the next fall and I failed the entrance exam for Calculus I. Failed it. I had to take a remedial math class for computer science majors, which was basically the precalc class I should have taken in high school. Worse, because I wasn't in Calculus I, I couldn't take the first computer science course in the sequence, CS 180, and instead had to take a FORTRAN class with the IT students. Better yet, *neither* of these classes counted toward my computer science degree. Basically, I was already a semester behind and I hadn't even started college.

"Yet never once did I think I should quit or change majors. Why in the world would I give up a career in software just because I wasn't a genius at calculus? The thought never occurred to me. Instead, I took the remedial semester and entered Calculus I, as well as CS 180, in the spring and aced them. The remediation set me up for success. It enabled me to become a stronger student. Four years later, I graduated on time and headed out to work for Motorola."

> *"Why in the world would I give up a career in software just because I wasn't a genius at calculus? The thought never occurred to me." —Nicole Sallak Anderson, CTO at SapientX*

Unfortunately, girls are held to a higher standard on the math-success scale. A fourth-grade girl declaring that she wants to be an electrical engineer seems to be a cute anomaly, and many adults may automatically assume she must be "good at math." The same assumptions aren't applied to boys, though. All sorts of boys want to be engineers, scientists, and video game designers. Maybe they like math as nine-year-olds; maybe they're even good at it. Maybe not. Chances are, even if their grades aren't as good as their female counterparts, they still plan to become engineers or scientists. They are interested in something—say, for example, robotics or programming—and math is one of the hurdles they must clear along the way. With an eye on the distant prize, they head through the different challenges, and even if they squeak through a high school or college math course with a D, well, they made it through, didn't they? That's success. For those without that key interest, though, math can become the primary deciding factor, the gatekeeper—if you are good at math, continue in this direction; otherwise, here's the exit.

If your daughter measures success by the number of As on her report card, reinforce that grades are short-term goals. Tell the stories that will help her set long-term goals to push her through difficult coursework and survive less-than-perfect grades. Show her that math class is not the gatekeeper to a STEM career. As E. O. Wilson wrote in his essay, what makes a great pioneer in science isn't necessarily the same quality that makes a great mathematician, but the two can always collaborate.

|||||||||||||||||||||||||||||||||||||||||||||||||||||||||||||||||||||||||||||||||||||||||||||||||||||||||||||||||||||||||||||||||||||

Putting It into Practice

- Reinforce that some STEM careers are more math heavy than others.
- Math classes can be difficult. Make sure she knows she doesn't need to be perfect. Math is only a part of the story.
- Reinforce that math ability comes with practice.
- Don't discount your daughter's STEM interest even if she struggles in math.
- Spend time discussing different STEM careers so that your daughter can develop interests and career aspirations.
- The math courses that your daughter may need to complete in order to obtain a degree do not necessarily correspond to the math that she will use daily in her future career. Can it be a challenge to pass those courses? Absolutely. But that does not mean she won't enjoy or thrive in her career.

|||||||||||||||||||||||||||||||||||||||||||||||||||||||||||||||||||||||||||||||||||||||||||||||||||||||||||||||||||||||||||||||||||||

Failure Is Not an Option—It's a Necessity

Little in learning is as important as failure. It's an intrinsic part of the learning process. Unfortunately, girls often expect perfection and may give up if they don't feel they are great at something.

Compared to boys, girls are often better behaved in the classroom and take fewer risks—sometimes, it has been argued, to boys' detriment. In *Raising Cain*, Dan Kindlon and Michael Thompson advocate for a more gender-balanced elementary classroom, one that allows for and takes into account boys' problems keeping still and greater difficulty multitasking or focusing on reading. The grade school classroom can be a girls' world—female teachers teaching in ways that best fit young girls. If this environment is not good for boys, it's probably great for girls, right?

Not always. Social psychologist Heidi Grant Halvorson explains that the feedback girls receive during these years—as compared to the feedback boys receive—reinforces the idea that they are either innately good at something or they are not. "Bright girls believe that their abilities are innate and unchangeable, while bright boys believe that they can develop ability through effort and practice," she writes. For this reason, the brightest girls can be the quickest to lose confidence and to give up when they face a challenging problem. Bright boys, on the other hand, often feel challenged by the difficulty of the material. They want to scale the mountain. Frequently, girls want to find a mountain that better suits them and what they believe are their innate abilities.

How does this happen? According to Halvorson, researchers believe that the praise girls often receive in elementary schools for their traits—they are able to sit still, they are able to focus, they are "good girls"—as well as the more generic feedback they may receive, such as how smart they are and what good students they are, implies that their success, their "goodness," is something innate and unchangeable. They were lucky to have been born that way.

Boys, on the other hand, often pinball through elementary school with their fair share of admonishments to be still, finish their work, and keep their hands to themselves. They constantly receive coaching on how to be successful through comments that might sound something like "If you would just sit still" or "If you would just focus." The result, then, is that boys learn that through hard work and adaptation, through sitting still and focusing, through trying harder or using different strategies, they are able to succeed. In other words, they develop a flexible mindset, as opposed to a fixed mindset.

Eileen Arnold, an engineer who majored in violin in college, says that one of the greatest things she learned from studying the violin was that practice does in fact make you better. She had seen it firsthand, and she knew it could be done, whether in music or math. So another benefit of music—or of any pursuit, sports or art or music—is this flexible mindset, this understanding that hard work does pay off.

You may have read Malcolm Gladwell's *The Tipping Point*, which claims that ten thousand hours of mindful practice should make anyone pretty good at something. Sometimes, between the fear of failure *and* the fear of reinforcing stereotypes, it's hard to convince a girl who has failed a math test that she can work harder, try a different approach, and find success. She might feel it is much easier to just give up.

Unfortunately for many young girls, a bad experience may eliminate the entire subject as a career option. Most students encountering any failure in math, science, engineering, or technology get frightened, think it is too hard, and quit. Adults have to get the message through to students that making mistakes and understanding how and why they failed at something are how people learn. In outreach visits with students, Nerd Girls representatives always ask, "If you play on a sports team and you lose the game, do you quit the sport?" Of course not! You train harder and try not to make the same mistakes. It's the same for any STEM discipline.

As schools move toward teaching twenty-first-century skills and more classrooms become areas of open-ended investigation, experimentation, and collaboration, girls will grow more comfortable with the idea of failure. Hopefully, both boys and girls will become immersed from a young age in a scientific methodology that encourages them to hypothesize, experiment, examine erroneous results, revise, and begin all over again. Look at the innovation process. It involves, through failure, honing in on a solution to a problem, be it a computer program's functionality, a scientific experiment in a chemistry lab, or a piece of writing or artwork or music.

There is one other important thing to note about failure today, which has less to do with academic achievement and more to do with building a student's sense of pride and responsibility, and this is allowing your children to make and own their mistakes. You can't fix everything for them, and, in fact, the stakes get higher as they get older. When the day's homework sheet is left at middle school, for example, put the onus on the student to solve the problem. Can a friend take a picture of the worksheet and send it? Teach your children to solve their own problems and to accept responsibility when they cannot. Teach them also that your time is valuable.

When a parent or educator steps in and solves the problem for them, the student may be on the right track, but they know that their decisions are not what got them there. They have not had that burst of confidence from figuring something out for themselves.

Girls have enough trouble with perfection as it is. Help them understand that the world did not fall down around them when they had to deal with a situation on their own, when they broke something and had to own up to it, when they were less than perfect. Doing so makes them stronger and more capable.

Telling kids they are always smart also sets them up for a rude awakening, especially when they get to college. Effort does equal results, but that doesn't necessarily mean perfection.

Putting It into Practice

- Treat your own failures as part of the learning process.

- Use praise such as "You worked really hard on that! I'm not surprised you got a good grade," as opposed to "Of course you did well! You've always been so smart."

- Greet your children's failures with an "Oh well! That happens to all of us! Let's talk about what you might try next time," "Let's see if we can figure this out together," or "Why don't you take a little break, and then let's try it again."

- Monitor homework and test grades, but don't micromanage. Give your daughter the opportunity to correct course on her own, as she will need to in the real world. One way to do this is to give her the opportunity to come to you. Instead of saying, "I see you got a 60 on your science quiz," ask her how her science quiz went, and then help her to reflect and formulate a remediation plan.

- If you do see a trend of poor performance, teach your daughter how to be proactive: work together to determine a course of action, and make sure she's involved. For example, instead of speaking to a teacher yourself, prepare your daughter so that she can initiate that conversation. If this will be difficult for her, get in touch with the teacher: "Joy is supposed to come talk to you about her recent test grades, but she's nervous. Could you help her get the conversation started?"

- Find a way to help your child catch up. Set up a system for increased feedback from the teacher, and if necessary, investigate tutoring or a remedial class.

- Use examples of perseverance that are close to home, not just those of celebrities and sports superstars. This means your own failures.

- Don't jump in. When your daughter is about to do something wrong, don't correct her right away. Give her a moment to realize her mistake herself.

- Teach your child to use technology as a learning tool. Suggest that she take a picture of important assignments when done. That way, if she forgets the paper, she has a backup. Meanwhile, if the teacher doesn't return a paper in time, the student has her own copy to study from.

Home Life

Gender roles at home is one area where we have seen big changes in the last few decades. In 1983 Michael Keaton made us laugh portraying a dad unable to effectively parent his three kids in *Mr. Mom*. Today, for a majority of families, that premise might not even make sense. Dads are more involved than ever. Stay-at-home dads are still less common than stay-at-home moms but are not unheard of and are widely accepted. Single dads run households and complete many of the tasks that traditionally fell to mothers, including braiding hair and packing lunches.

In March 2015 researchers from the University of British Columbia published a paper in *Psychological Science* titled "The Second Shift Reflected in the Second Generation: Do Parents' Roles at Home Predict Children's Aspirations?"

The answer was yes. This study looked at not just the parents' beliefs (e.g., dad may call himself a feminist) but also how both parents acted out those beliefs in their busy homes. It turns out that a father's actions carry a lot of weight. Fathers who believed in an equal division of household tasks and who walked the walk by doing their share of the work had daughters who expressed a greater desire to work outside the home and who had a broader view of potential careers.

Alyssa Croft writes that this study is important "because it suggests that achieving gender equality at home may be one way to inspire young women to set their sights on careers from which they have traditionally been excluded."

So, sharing the laundry and the cooking is one way to do it, but it's not the only way—maybe you live in a more traditional household where the chores happen to fall along gender lines, or where the mother stays home. Even in more traditional homes, parents can set the right tone by respecting each other's contributions, by reinforcing that the division of labor makes sense for reasons beyond gender (one parent is home and has time to do the laundry, for example), and by making sure everyone pitches in for dinner preparation or cleanup.

Sheryl Sandberg wasn't raised in a gender-neutral home—her father worked outside the home, her mother worked in the home, and chores were divided along gender lines—but she was raised to think that she could do anything. "My father always took me seriously," she says. This is something we hear often from women who have achieved success in STEM fields. Electrical engineer Alice Parker recalls how her father helped her and her brother build a boat in the basement just because they asked if they could. The boat never even fit through the door.

Katianne recently spent an afternoon with a group of middle schoolers who were working on a project in their STEM class. A group of young girls had been working on a model home that was the envy of all their male classmates. Their home was structurally sound, perfectly painted, and had also been modeled precisely in 3-D CAD software. As an extra touch, the girls had added a set of lights around the front door and had used an Arduino LilyPad to program the lights to display in different colors and patterns. When Katianne asked who had done the work, the girls shrugged and looked surprised. "My father did it," one of the girls said. "Did he show you how?" She shook her head, looking again as if this were an absurd question. This father had truly missed out on a wonderful learning opportunity with his teenage daughter.

|||||||||||||||||||||||||||||||||||||||||||||||||||||||||||||||||||||||||||||||||||||||||||||||||||||||||||||||||||||||||||||||||||||||||||

Putting It into Practice

- Parents who take their children and their endeavors seriously are more likely to raise innovators.

- Let your daughter's voice be heard. Do not define "good" as quiet and submissive.

Kids can both learn and spend quality time with older family members by helping out with all sorts of household projects. Give children opportunities to learn how to use hammers, screwdrivers, levels, tape measures, and other tools around the house. Employ their assistance when . . .

+ hanging a shelf,
+ sawing a board,
+ building a pinewood derby car, or
+ taking the batteries out of toys or holiday decorations.

Are both sons and daughters helping with the cooking, cleaning, and laundry? Are siblings working together to complete chores—folding towels, picking weeds, or raking leaves? Showing that the family is a team and everyone pitches in on everything makes a difference.

The Power of Role Models

In 1983 David Wade Chambers devised a test called the Draw-a-Scientist Test (DAST). The idea was to determine at what age scientist stereotypes first appeared. At what age, for example, do we decide that scientists are the sort of people who wear glasses and lab coats? The DAST has been performed many times over the years in many countries, and while it measures many different stereotypes, it has come to be known primarily as an indicator of gender bias—the majority of children draw male scientists.

By exposing boys and girls to more diverse role models, adults can help them see scientists and engineers in a nongendered light. This means more than sitting in on the occasional talk with a female scientist or engineer. You will have the most impact if you broaden your idea of who makes a good role model and your idea of what kids respond to in their role models.

Who Makes a Good Role Model?

Where are the female STEM role models? Where are all these people who will inspire girls to greatness—who will show them that if they cherish education, believe in themselves and each other, and stand strong in the face of opposition even when going against traditional feminine norms, then they will write their own rich life story? Who of the following do you think would make a good STEM role model for your girl?

A mother who has always struggled at math returns to school to get her nursing degree, pushing through and getting the help she needs to pass her math courses

 A father who respects women and continuously encourages and engages his daughter in the same way that he does his son

A stay-at-home mother who takes the time to notice patterns in nature when out with her children

A mother who works long hours to support her family, makes wise financial decisions, and brushes herself off after failure and bad news

Astronauts Sally Ride, Ellen Ochoa, and Judith Resnick

 An elementary school teacher who encourages girls and boys alike to have a love of numbers and patterns

A civil engineer who comes to your child's school to talk about her career

You get the idea. They all would. Don't equate "STEM role model for girls" only with female STEM professionals who visit schools and speak to science classes. You can draw your daughter's attention to the role models all around her once you reframe your thinking.

If you don't work in a STEM field yourself, then what exactly are you modeling? You are modeling perseverance and attitude. You are responsible for saying, "You can do this," for helping your daughter to feel encouraged, supported, and believed in so that she feels strong and confident and sees the world as a place full of possibility where failure is at best a learning experience and at worst a momentary setback.

Primary caregivers are a child's first and most influential role models. What are the gifts that you would most like to impart? Strength in the face of adversity? Assertiveness? A love of learning? Whoever you are, whatever your position in this world, you have gifts to share. Do not undervalue yourself.

In the 1980s when Noramay Cadena was just a year old, her parents packed up the family and left Mexico for California. Her father had a high school diploma. Her mother had left school after the second grade. Both parents found jobs as factory workers in San Fernando Valley. The summer Noramay was thirteen, she was awoken early every morning to head off to her job as an unpaid intern at the bungee cord factory where her mother worked. This was all her mother's idea, and Noramay was not happy about it. Five days a week she sat next to her mother at a long table assembling bungee cords. They clocked in and clocked out. A bell rang when it was time for lunch, and another rang when it was time to go back to work. This is the gift her mother gave her.

"I hated the experience at the time. I realize now that it was her way of very clearly and tangibly demonstrating what my life would be like if I didn't pursue a college degree," Noramay says.

Noramay was accepted to MIT, and when she left for the East Coast, she wasn't alone. She had a baby when she was a senior in high school, and her young daughter traveled across the country with her. Noramay went on to earn three degrees from MIT and is a strong role model for her daughter as well as the many other young women she encounters in the community and in her work. Today, Noramay is an award-winning engineer, cofounder of the nonprofit Latinas in STEM, and cofounder and managing director of the hardware accelerator Make in LA. Her daughter, now a sophomore in college, is a business and marketing major.

Underrepresented Role Models in STEM

Girls have to see people like them in STEM careers to envision themselves in such an environment, but studies show that girls don't respond to role models who are too attractive, too feminine, too geeky, too accomplished, too old, or even too masculine.

Hmm. We've rejected a lot of potential women. Who's left?

Girls need a variety of role models. Inspiration is not one-size-fits-all. In sports, role models are abundant. A fantastic coach leaves a strong impression on a child just starting out, inspiring a love of a new sport. A child sees an older neighbor always outside shooting baskets or welcoming kids of all ages and abilities into a pickup game. Young players admire older players on their team. You might take kids to see a high school, semipro, or professional game—where all the players carry the responsibility of being role models to young fans.

Kids need STEM role models in the same way—plentiful and diverse. A narrow view of what makes an acceptable STEM role model for girls robs them of opportunities. The assumption is that young women are better able to envision themselves in a STEM field when they are introduced to role models whom they identify with. (The logic runs, "I'm like this person, and they can do this, so therefore I too can do this.") Well, who do girls identify with?

A young woman raised in a culture where girls are discouraged from STEM careers needs to see women from that same culture blazing the trail. Debbie Berebichez is a physicist, STEM advocate, and cohost of the Discovery Channel's *Outrageous Acts of Science*. She was raised in a conservative community in Mexico where girls were discouraged from pursuing careers in STEM. "In high school, I was told that if I were too smart, I would never be liked and it would be challenging for me to find a husband," she says. She defied teachers, parents, and even friends, though, when she won a full merit-based scholarship to study physics in the United States. She became the first Mexican woman to graduate with a PhD in physics from Stanford University. For young women growing up in similar environments, it is important, Debbie says, that we "make these women aware of others who have traveled the same path and succeeded."

Other times, it is not as necessary that the role model be a woman. Young women can identify with role models not because they see them as identical but because the role models, too, are different than expected. Research from the University of Washington found that girls overall respond to role models who "do not embody the STEM stereotype" of being male, Caucasian or Asian, and a bit nerdy. A girl thinks, *I don't fit the normal stereotype, and neither does this person. If they can do it, I can do it.* This leaves us a much larger pool of men and women from a variety of ethnic, racial, and socioeconomic backgrounds as potential role models.

Are We Supposed to Be Feminine or Not?

On the heels of that study came another that concluded that feminine role models actually demotivate girls because girls feel that these two different ideals are simultaneously unattainable. In other words, they buy into the old "I can't be both pretty *and* smart!" myth.

If you look at this study, though, you see that researchers collected their data in a very particular way. The middle school girls participating in the study didn't interact with these feminine role models—they only read about them. They may have read a magazine article about a woman who had a record of achievements in STEM but also expressed an interest in fashion magazines, for example, before they completed a survey that tended to show that their interest in STEM either hadn't changed or had actually decreased.

This, of course, strikes a chord with Karen—she formed Nerd Girls to battle the very perception that a woman can't be both feminine and talented in STEM. Perhaps it is true that reading articles about women who are pretty and smart demotivates girls. Perhaps it depends on how these particular articles are written—if they, for example, are informational articles stressing a woman's individual achievements as opposed to persuasive pieces that bring the reader along for a ride that leaves them feeling inspired and included.

The idea that STEM role models should be discouraged from presenting any traditionally feminine norms is worrisome. It also doesn't align with what we have witnessed. Through Nerd Girl outreach, girls of all ages get to see the Nerd Girls in action—not just read about them. The personal connection is crucial. These women are confident, friendly, approachable, and smart. Moreover, they seem to genuinely like each other's company and work well together. They shine as they answer questions. They are proud of their knowledge, and they are excellent teachers. On top of that, young girls see the respect their male classmates have for the Nerd Girls.

Of course, there aren't enough Nerd Girls for them to be in-person role models for everyone. There is a sore need for more role models who can speak to young women directly, especially those in high school, college, or in their early careers. Someone once presented this conundrum: "So, the way to get more females interested in STEM is to have more females in STEM." Well, yes! Perhaps this is why so many STEM women are so passionate and so willing to spend their time mentoring younger women. They know that their active participation all the way though the pathway helps their younger peers feel supported and encouraged. Though women in certain STEM fields may still be underrepresented, fortunately they tend to be a highly mobilized group with a high percentage of involvement in working with younger women.

The Problem with Superstars

Sometimes, well-intentioned adults who talk about STEM with girls tell them only about the girl superstars, and in a way that emphasizes their very particular accomplishments. High achievers should be celebrated and receive recognition, and girls certainly should hear their stories. But many girls will ultimately see that level of success as unattainable.

Courtney Gras is a young electrical engineer from Ohio who started her own company and was given a spot on the Forbes 30 Under 30 in the field of energy. She also runs a consulting business that helps young entrepreneurs. As a role model, she has given much thought to her own journey. When Katianne interviewed Courtney for the Institute of Electrical and Electronics Engineers' *Women in Engineering Magazine* back in 2016, she asked Courtney, "You've accomplished so much—if I'm a young student I might be thinking, oh, I can't do that—I would never be a 30 under 30, etc., and so I would never be so successful. What would you say to someone like that?"

Courtney put it like this: to try to replicate anyone else's successes will do nothing but limit you. When you think about it, it's easy to see that it will also demotivate you—since it's impossible. The broader message needs to be that when we dedicate ourselves to a cause that we are interested in and that fits our natural abilities, over time we will find our own version of success.

A role model should talk about this. She should say something along the lines of: "You may be sitting there thinking that you could never do what I did. And no, of course you can't do exactly what I have done. I am not here to tell you how to be me. I'm here to tell you that if you wake up every morning and work hard at what interests you—you will, through a series of small steps, some so small they are barely noticeable except in hindsight, have your own version of success."

How to Bring Role Models into Your Daughter's Life

It's important to read about historical trailblazers, but kids need to hear about women who are making enormous advances in STEM today. Here are just a few examples:

Ellen Ochoa: Ochoa is the first Hispanic female astronaut and the first Hispanic director of the Johnson Space Center.

Mildred Dresselhaus: Known as the Queen of Carbon for her years of research into the electrical properties of carbon, Dresselhaus loved her work so much that she kept returning to her MIT office long after she had "officially retired."

Hadiyah-Nicole Green: One of fewer than one hundred black women physicists in the United States, Green received a $1 million grant to develop a cancer treatment that relies on a combination of nontoxic nanoparticles and harmless lasers.

On Facebook, follow groups like these and you will see stories of inspirational women daily in your feed:

Amy Poehler's Smart Girls

Girls Who Code

IEEE Women in Engineering

A Mighty Girl

NASA

National Girls Collaborative

Nerd Girls

Society of Women Engineers

TED Talks are short but inspiring! Search www.ted.com and you are sure to find a talk that matches any interest. Start by checking out the following:

McKenna Pope: Want to Be an Activist? Start with Your Toys

Kenneth Shinozuka: My Simple Invention, Designed to Keep My Grandfather Safe

Christopher Bell: Bring On the Female Superheroes!

Wanda Diaz Merced: How a Blind Astronomer Found a Way to Hear the Stars

Lidia Yuknavitch: The Beauty of Being a Misfit

Reshma Saujani: Teach Girls Bravery, Not Perfection

Tavi Gevinson: A Teen Just Trying to Figure It Out

Natalie Warne: Being Young and Making an Impact

Lauren Hodge, Shree Bose, Naomi Shah: Award-Winning Teenage Science in Action

Beau Lotto and Amy O'Toole: Science Is for Everyone, Kids Included

E. O. Wilson: Advice to a Young Scientist

In-person visits: Encourage schools to bring in a variety of STEM professionals to talk to the class. If this is you, make sure to present the story, not the résumé. Give students something to be interested in and something to relate to. Let them know that you make mistakes, that maybe you weren't the smartest in the bunch, but that you worked hard and persevered. Talk to the students about the diverse people you work with, and how important that mix of people is.

Age up: Find role models a few years older than your daughter so that she has achievable aspirations and can see herself at "the next rung on the ladder."

Groups:

FabFems.org is a searchable database of women role models from around the world who are available for local after school visits, field trips, job shadowing, or even online role modeling.

Girls Inc. serves over 140,000 girls across the United States and Canada. It is a home base for girls—a center available on average thirty hours a week that instills the message that girls are strong, smart, and bold. Most Girls Inc. centers are in low-income areas. One of the many programs they offer is Operation SMART—Science, Math, and Relevant Technology.

PART III

||||||||||||||||||||||||||

Help Her Down the Pathway

Let us choose for ourselves our path in life, and let us try to strew that path with flowers. —Émilie du Châtelet

Grade School:
The World of Possibilities

Who Ate Our Creativity?

It's a spring evening at the softball field. The girls are seven and eight, and they've got their hats on, batting gloves in back pockets, softball bags clipped in a row along the fence. They are having a blast. They are excited because they are finally considered old enough to play this organized sport, and yet the rules are somewhat confounding and perhaps a bit confining.

One girl lies on her stomach by the bench. In the field, others chase butterflies and do headstands. Parents yell to them to get in their "ready position"—they dutifully crouch and Velcro their hands to their knees. A moment later their heads are down, maybe even swinging as they feel the end of their ponytails circle the ground. Or if they bend even farther, they discover they can see right through their legs into the outfield. Sometimes they twirl or draw names and hearts in the dirt.

Parent coaches shout to them to be ready, to pay attention—the adults want the girls to learn the rules of the game and, more important, don't want them to get beaned. But it's a slow game, especially at this age, and the kids' attention spans are short.

Sports are vitally important—they keep girls physically active, help them develop motor skills, teach them teamwork, introduce them to competition and sportsmanship, build confidence and self-esteem, show them the benefits of hard work and practice, and inure them to failure. These are sought-after skills in the workplace, and 75 percent of the women who've made it to the executive C-level know it—they report that when they see college-level athletics on a candidate's résumé, they're interested.

Still, it's important to balance organized competitive activities with time for free play. In team sports, there's a possibility that one will mess up and let others down. There are adults to listen to and rules to follow. There's a requirement to show up whether one feels like it or not. None of this is true of unstructured play. Organized activities have their benefits, but they are different from those that result from a girl giving her imagination free rein—tearing around the neighborhood on a bike she pretends is a motorcycle, stopping when she feels like it, diving into a pile of leaves she imagines is a deep pool, then heading home because she's hungry. The girls in position on the softball field are practicing discipline and focus—but they are not free to follow their whims. As much as they may want to talk to their friend behind them, wander away from their position, or chase after a butterfly—they're not supposed to.

Make sure there's time in the schedule for doing nothing. In other words, make room for boredom. Of course, even if parents buy into boredom as an intellectual ideal, implementation can be painful. As any parent who's been snowed in with a few kids knows, that transition period when children first realize they have nothing to do can be rough. But children need to be bored at times. If adults fill up every moment for them, and then use screen time to fill the gaps, children never experience boredom as the incubator of creativity.

Psychoanalyst Adam Phillips writes, "It is one of the most oppressive demands of adults that the child should be interested, rather than take time to find what interests him. Boredom is integral to the process of taking one's time." Through true lying-on-the-floor-staring-at-the-wall boredom, children can begin to realize their own desires; they can embark on wonderful journeys, whether in their minds or in the physical world. Give them this gift, and your children will draw on these youthful adventures well into adulthood.

As a child, Japanese video game designer Shigeru Miyamoto liked to explore the countryside alone. One day he came upon a cave, and so he sat and enjoyed the peacefulness and the play of shadows on the cave walls. He came back to the site many times, eventually even venturing there at night with a lantern. Miyamoto went on to become the creator of *Donkey Kong* and *Super Mario Bros.*; he drew on this formative time at the cave when imagining the underground realms for *The Legend of Zelda*.

Other children invent and then revisit the same imagined world again and again, sometimes giving it a history, a language, and a geography. World-play to this degree is generally seen as a sign of creative giftedness, and many of those young children have gone on to successful careers (a high number of MacArthur "genius award" winners created worlds in childhood). Some of these childhood worlds belong to literary masters—like J. R. R. Tolkien's Middle-earth and the Brontës' Gondal.

These are stories of remarkably gifted individuals, and this detailed and vivid world-play seems to be a way to recognize and even measure marked intelligence in young children. It sounds like creativity is an innate skill, a sign of a natural intelligence. So, this brings us back to the question of nature versus nurture: Are we born creative? A few minutes on Pinterest and very few of us feel creative, at least comparatively. Who hasn't said at one time another, "I'm not that creative," putting creativity comfortably in the wheelhouse of arts and crafts, mistakenly marrying it with artistic talent?

We can define creativity broadly: a creative thinker exercises both divergent and convergent thinking. Divergent thinking is expansive— when we think divergently we generate a number of different ideas. It's what many of us recognize as brainstorming—casting a wide net. We then follow this up with convergent thinking, which means we sift through our ideas, maybe looking for patterns, combine a few ideas together, and look for connections—all to sculpt the best possible results from this initial basket. These ways of thinking combine to make creativity.

If you begin to think of creativity in this way, it spreads far beyond the art room. An engineer must be creative, as must a scientist, a policy maker, a teacher, a lawyer, and a mathematician. Creativity means that when we find ourselves in a situation, we are able to find our way out of it; creativity is first and foremost a life skill.

When looked at from this angle, it's easier to see how creativity can be cultivated—although we may never reach the genius level, the extreme right-tail of creativity, where dwell the Brontës, Tolkiens, and Miyamotos. Creativity can be enhanced by being open to experiences, by being interested in the world, by spending time in a state of boredom, by expressing emotion through the arts, and by being aware of divergent

Jump-starting Creativity

Teach your child how to brainstorm an idea for a project or a writing assignment by using one of the following methods:

1. Brainstorming as two-step process. When your daughter tries to determine a topic to write about, encourage her to first cast a wide net—write down any idea she thinks of, no matter how absurd. Then look back at that list and pick the ideas that most interest her. For each of those, drill down—write down all the thoughts she has related to that idea alone, no matter how absurd.

2. Freewriting. It's not uncommon for children to feel some anxiety over a writing assignment. The open-endedness of writing a paragraph about a favorite holiday or maybe a poem about a time they felt happy can be overwhelming and time consuming as they fret over whether they are "doing it right." Help your daughter by teaching her a freewriting exercise—write the topic at the top of a piece of paper, and then spend one minute writing anything that comes to mind. She must keep writing. If she writes "taco hamburger fish," that's OK—the process is meant to relax the brain and get it in creative mode.

and convergent thinking. It is no wonder the youngest among us—those askers of why, those puddle jumpers and bug watchers—usually score sky-high on creativity scales. It's also easier to see why it is so important and worthwhile to spend time growing your child's creativity. You may not be raising the next Picasso, but you might be raising a child who will one day be able to amuse a group of conference attendees when a projector breaks down or who can reroute a trip through trains or ferries when airline reservations fall through.

THE IMPORTANCE OF CREATIVITY

Creativity means that when we encounter a problem, we are able to recognize options; creativity is first and foremost a life skill. If we find ourselves unable to pay our rent, or if we are laid off, creativity allows us to move forward in a productive way instead of becoming paralyzed.

In the United States IQs have continued to rise roughly ten points per generation. In 1966 Ellis Paul Torrance and his colleagues developed a creativity index called the Torrance Tests of Creative Thinking that, similar to the IQ test, determines a subject's CQ, or creativity quotient, with the aim of predicting future creative achievement. Today this test is widely used worldwide.

In 2011 Kyung Hee Kim took a look at roughly three hundred thousand CQ scores in the United States and found that scores had been steadily rising since the mid-1970s, but that in the 1990s they began a tumble that still shows no sign of stopping. Results indicate that across all ages, Americans are becoming less motivated to be creative—a decline that is seen as "steady and persistent"; surprisingly, this was particularly true for children in kindergarten through third grade. This decline may indicate, he says, that our youngest children—our unencumbered wanderers—have actually become "less likely to see things from a different angle . . . less capable of the critical thinking skills processes of synthesis and organization and less capable of capturing the essence of problems."

What is depressing creativity? Certainly, we can think about pointing a finger at the changes in education, where emphasis has moved away from creativity in the classroom and toward standardization. In K–12 education in America, we have watched as creativity has been peeled away from the classroom in favor of testing prep. Creativity became the province of the arts—it existed in the art room, surely, but where else? On top of that, art classes were pushed aside for more classroom learning time.

In 2010 Jonathan Plucker, then a professor at Indiana University, toured schools in Shanghai and Beijing. A scholar in education policy and talent development, he frequently collaborates with colleagues around the world. He told this particular gathering of faculty that American schools were shifting toward standardizing curriculum, rote memorization, and national testing. Then, Plucker says, "After my answer was translated, they just started laughing out loud. They said, 'You're racing toward our old model. But we're racing to your model as fast as we can.'"

Some schools are now turning to more project-based teaching methods, possibly due to Common Core standards for mathematics and reading as well as Next Generation Science Standards that incorporate twenty-first-century skills. This may be surprising, as Common Core is often associated with testing, but the Common Core standards themselves emphasize creativity, collaboration, communication, and critical thinking through cross-disciplinary learning. You might see, for example, a middle school class reading Gary Paulsen's *Hatchet* and then constructing a raft like the one described in the book.

American schools and the teachers within them, though, are still judged by student test scores, and many schools have no choice but to devote serious classroom time to pencil-and-paper work. Teachers want to spend time on creativity, but many still feel so stifled and overwhelmed by paperwork and standards that they have little time to work creativity into lesson plans. There is much work to do in this area, to be sure.

But the story starts much earlier than this. School can't be the sole problem with our little ones. There is a natural and developmentally inevitable decline of creativity that occurs throughout childhood—some call it the fourth-grade slump; others say it occurs more around sixth grade. It can continue through high school as adolescents juggle conformity and socialization with their own autonomy. But creativity should be very high in early childhood, so why the decrease from kindergarten to third grade? What is happening at home that is changing our creativity?

 Increased time is spent on technology as opposed to free play.

 The rise of sports and other organized activities takes time from free play.

 Helicopter parenting prevents children from making their own decisions and flexing their creative problem-solving muscles.

Parental involvement places great emphasis on the end product, on a "right way."

 Busy lives take time away from having meaningful conversations, reading stories, and general interactive play with our children.

Education policy changes slowly, but what happens in your home doesn't have to. As parents, we need to be informed about trends in learning and advocate for continued changes to our public schools—all of them—that will prepare our children for the twenty-first-century workplace with its emphasis on creativity and collaboration. At the same time, families can encourage creativity at home. Scott Barry Kaufman and Carolyn Gregoire write in *Wired to Create* that "pretend play is more common for children whose parents talk to them often, read bedtime stories, and explain things about nature and social issues." With that in mind, try the following at home to build creative muscle:

 Fill your house with books and toys.

 Grow your own creativity.

 Work together on projects at home—project-based learning does not need to be confined to the classroom.

Make time for boredom by turning off devices.

Spend time with your children at home when you all have nothing to do. Follow their lead. What sounds fun? Poke around the yard; pretend the living room is an ocean and the couch a pirate ship.

 Make school projects a time to create instead of buy.

 Set aside time in the weekly schedule for uninterrupted free play.

Provide opportunities for kids to work on endeavors that have no right and wrong outcomes, and sometimes hold back from correcting them. Listen to them. Validate their marvelous ideas.

Fun with Chalk

What's better than chalk? Chalk is an interactive canvas. It's inexpensive—you can find it at the dollar store. Drawing with chalk encourages great creativity. Here are a few activities to inspire your young one.

1. Have her draw herself (and friends) in a scene: outer space, underwater, soaring over the city like a super-hero—and take pictures from above.

2. Help her turn the sidewalk or driveway into a road-way for scooters and bikes: draw lane lines, street signs, and toll booths.

3. Encourage her to use chalk to draw the backdrop for stop-motion animation with dolls, stuffed animals, or people.

Can I Put My Name on Your School Project?

It's easy to get caught up in school projects. Whether grade schoolers need to dress up as Susan B. Anthony, make a diorama of animals in winter, or build a Styrofoam model of an animal cell, projects that blend crafting and glue and multiple trips to the craft store quickly become family affairs. Step back and let your daughter work on her own, and although she may not have the prettiest poster in the class, you will have helped grow both her creativity and her self-esteem.

A child who works very hard on a project will be proud of the accomplishment. A child who sits by while a parent takes over will learn that one's own work is not good enough, and only when stronger, better, smarter reinforcements are called in does the project look "how it is supposed to look." Think of your role as providing direction and input by being a consultant, not a manager:

> Teach artistic methods. Consider saying something like, "If you'd like I could show you how to put layers of torn green

construction paper in your diorama so it looks like grass." If, after that, she tells you she'd rather use green glitter glue, so be it.

- Young children need your guidance for breaking a project down into manageable chunks. Sit with your daughter, bring in a calendar, and model how you do this. If the teacher has sent home a schedule, review it with your girl to see how it fits into her upcoming activities.

- Children's imaginations are huge and what they envision may be unattainable. When you need to, step in and teach your daughter how to evaluate an idea: "I know you'd like to build this six-foot Eiffel Tower out of toothpicks by next week. How do you think you'd get it to school? How many toothpicks do you think you'd need? How long do you think it will take? You have a birthday party, church, and soccer practice this weekend. Let's sit down and talk about your ideas. Then, if you decide you can't do it, I can help you think of a really great alternative."

- As your child gets older, transfer more of the scheduling responsibility to her. By third, fourth, or fifth grade, she should begin to shoulder this by making a schedule and sharing it with you. Periodically check in with her on her progress and show her how to creatively carve out time to work. If she is overwhelmed, ask how you can help or what can be removed from a busy schedule. Emphasize the importance of school.

- Don't buy expensive props, and ask classroom teachers to set spending limits if they haven't already done so. Encourage creativity by using what you have or by buying craft supplies similar to what is in your art box. Most costumes can be created with felt sheets, a glue gun, and a collection of old clothes.

- Children cannot create in a vacuum. Girls with only their own experiences to draw upon may end up frustrated when they need to take the reins and pull something creative out of the hat. If your family takes trips to museums, reads together, looks through art books, and appreciates nature, when it comes to create, your daughter will be able to draw upon these experiences. Going to the theater, whether it be local school productions or professional, is a great opportunity to file away ideas on how set designers and costume artists create basic sets and costumes that require the audience to use their imagination. You can nudge your child along when she is stuck by reminding her of past experiences, taking her to the library, or helping her find resources on the internet.

🚀 Destination Imagination and FIRST Lego League are two after-school activities that encourage creativity through teambuilding and competition. Destination Imagination starts as early as first grade, and FIRST Lego League starts in fourth grade.

The Makerspace—and Why It's Great

It's half past seven in the morning at the Summer Street School in Lynnfield, Massachusetts. The opening bell is an hour away, and the halls are still quiet—but the media center is bustling. Children huddle on the floor negotiating the path of a marble run. Two boys wander through the stacks using an iPad to direct a small spherical robot. Twin girls pile plastic cups into an impressive castle, and when a boy in a red sweatshirt lifts his head from his Makey Makey kit and calls out "Can someone help me with this?" a pony-tailed girl puts down her scissors and comes to his side. Amid all this, elementary school media center specialist Alex Caram stands back and surveys the scene.

This is the Summer Street School makerspace. Caram (with lots of help from the PTO, parent donations, and the support of the school staff and the town superintendent) has created a fairly low-budget space for students to experience STEAM and the creative joy of making. On this particular morning, Caram is running a special before-school makerspace class. The roster is full and there's a wait list. During school hours, many teachers block off time every two weeks to bring their students to the makerspace. And then, perhaps best of all, through the course of the school day, the makerspace is open to any child who wants to use it.

Caram gave up her small office ("I never used it anyhow," she says) and turned it into a room full of nicely organized bins and buckets full of craft supplies and recyclables as well as a few foldout work tables. In the media center itself, there is a Lego wall, and shelves hold squishy circuits and conductive tape for electronic projects. Tablets and Chromebooks mean lots of opportunities to code in Scratch or to make stop-motion animation movies.

With creativity on the decline, makerspaces like this are a way to get creativity back in schools. "When I was a kid, we did a lot of project-based learning. Because of curriculum changes, we got away from that. So this isn't new," Caram says, sweeping an arm around her space. "Because of testing, you have to sort of have a way to market it. Because the curriculum has to be so structured now, there's just not enough classroom time—and a makerspace fills that gap."

An important tenet of the makerspace is that children lead the way. While the impulse may be to put more structure around it—to tie projects to curriculum—too much of that would rob students of the key benefits. Caram prefers to teach them skills in small lessons (if they want—otherwise, they are free to keep doing what they're doing), although she is open to giving teachers access to the space for wide-open projects. When the second graders were studying bridges, for example, they came to the library to build. The children weren't constrained in what sort of bridge they could create, and at the end of the day every bridge looked different.

The benefits of the makerspace to the school have extended well beyond growing creativity: it has become a place to celebrate different types of learners, a favorite hangout on a stressful day, and a place to build community.

There are many different reasons kids find their way to the media center to spend time being makers. Maybe it's to help alleviate anxiety, to take a mental break, or because the child needs movement. The makerspace has proved to be a great resource to children who struggle in typical classroom settings. "These are the kids who really shine doing other things. The makerspace lets us celebrate them," Caram says.

In these younger grades, there's not too much difference in the ways boys and girls use the makerspace. The girls really enjoy the robotics. All the kids particularly like Sphero, an easy-to-use white ball that rolls around the room based on input on a tablet. Caram might offer a coding lesson in the makerspace here and there. "The girls who come away from coding and really like it—I'm surprised," she says. "You have to expose them all to it. I couldn't have guessed who would be really into coding, but you sit some kids in front of the computer, and you see them get to the point of 'Oh! I'm good at this!'"

The makerspace has worked out so well that other towns in Massachusetts are sending representatives to tour the media center and meet with Caram to see how they can incorporate makerspaces into their own schools. If your child's school doesn't have a makerspace, consider leading the way.

Here are some tips for starting your own school makerspace:

- Start by getting buy-in from the principal, the superintendent, and the PTO.

- It doesn't need to be a room. It can be whatever you have—a makerspace can exist on a cart.

- It will get a little crazy. And messy. And that's OK.

- It doesn't need to be high-tech. Start small. Set expectations.

- The art teacher is your friend. Coordinate with him or her. The art teacher will know all sorts of great information—from what level projects are appropriate undertakings for what ages, to how to keep glue dispersal neat, to tutorials on how to hold materials together without tape or glue.

Why Can't We Teach Math the Old Way?

At the start of the century, a group of educators; businesspeople from such places as Apple, Microsoft, and Cisco; and policy makers like those from the US Department of Education came together to form a group called P21—the Partnership for 21st Century Learning. They developed a framework that included over eighteen different skills. A number of states committed to include the skills in their educational standards, assessments, and professional development, but the National Education Association says that "over the years it became clear that the framework was too long and complicated." P21 interviewed leaders and boiled the framework down to these four necessary C skills—critical thinking, communication, collaboration, and creativity.

These skills aren't new, but the need for them is great, and so parents should be concerned with how they are taught. In fact, when Andrew J. Rotherham and Daniel Willingham reported on "21st Century Skills" back in 2009, they surmised that since these skills have not historically been regulated or assessed, the chance to learn these skills has always required a bit of luck for the average child. For schools coming on board, implementing these skills requires a large change: in order to succeed, teachers need strong support in the form of smaller class sizes, more time for teacher collaboration, money for technology, and staff to help with maintaining these technologies. Rotherham and Willingham also cautioned against assuming that teachers would intuitively know how to teach the four Cs. They reasoned that while most teachers believe a project-based classroom is a good idea, they still need extensive training in how to manage this sort of student-centered environment, as well as how to teach and assess these skills.

Skip Fennell, project director of the Elementary Mathematics Specialists and Teachers Leaders Project at McDaniel College, has worked for math reform in the United States for decades. Fennell was one of the writers of the Principles and Standards for School Mathematics in 2000. At that time, several of the writers, including Fennell, wrote about "the need for elementary-based math specialists to deliver the curriculum because of the mathematical and instructional challenges inherent in the Standards." In fact, Fennell says he's been "knocking around with the notion and need for elementary math specialists" since the late seventies. His feelings hadn't changed when it came time to help with the writing, review, and implementation of the Common Core State Standards for Mathematics (CCSS-M).

Launched in 2009, the CCSS-M represent a sea change in the way math is taught in the United States, and the four Cs are an integral component. Just as Rotherham and Willingham cautioned about the four Cs, Fennell knows that in order for the new math standards to work, teachers need support and training. Elementary teachers are generalists, Fennell says, expected to be "equally proficient and passionate about all of the subjects they're responsible for," and, consequently, short-term professional development in implementing a rigorous math program just isn't enough.

Without the investment in teacher training, everyone involved has a reason to be frustrated. We know that a child who is asked to do something unfamiliar without a clear explanation will become turned off to math. That resistance to mathematics is hard to undo. The math problems that frustrated parents post on social media sometimes seem to demonstrate how hard it is for teachers to assess a student's higher-order thinking skills with just pencil and paper. Other times they seem to show that parents are misinformed, quick to judge, or resistant to change. "Why can't we teach math the old way?" some ask.

Before going back to the old way, there are other options—an increased focus on math specialists, for one. In an ideal world, every grade school and middle school would have one. Unlike a reading specialist, who may take small groups out of the classroom to work on skills, math specialists spend the majority of their time with teachers. Because they are experts in mathematical pedagogy, the largest chunk of their time might be spent working directly to train the trainer either in large settings, in smaller grade-level groups, or by visiting other district schools. They spend much of their time coaching teachers—preplanning, coteaching, and observing teachers in an informal environment that has nothing to do with licensure and everything to do with helping teachers improve their teaching of mathematics.

Fennell's Elementary Mathematics Specialists and Teacher Leaders Project engages with math specialists in Maryland and partners with them to take that work out nationally, but there are roadblocks. "In any state in this country you can get certified and receive accreditation as a reading specialist. Only 20 states offer math certification. So while there is interest, the interest is not at the level of reading," he reports.

Then there's the money. Who would say no to the idea of a math specialist? Everyone loves the idea, but finding room in the budget is another story. And if a district does hire a math specialist, that position can get diluted very quickly as administrators see the importance of expanding the program to other schools but don't have the budget to hire more specialists. The specialists end up strained, spending one day a week in each of the schools they cover, and so they have less impact and aren't able to do the job they were hired to do. "If I'm a fourth-grade teacher, I can't wait until next Monday to see you. I need to see you right now because I need help on this concept," Fennell says. He has seen math specialists be told they need to pick up reading as well. "You have this really great idea, but to save money or to claim you're reaching all of these needs, you're going to spread that person so thin, and then the job is not what he or she was doing," he says.

Going back to the old way is not the answer. Schools need a more rigorous curriculum that emphasizes critical thinking, communication, collaboration, and creativity, but one that is implemented so as to give teachers and children the chance to succeed. Math specialists are a way to help.

|||||||||||||||||||||||||||||||||||||||||||||||||||||||||||||||||||||||||||||||||||||||||||||||||||||||||||||||||

Putting It into Practice

- 🔬 Don't advocate for the old mathematics—advocate for stronger teaching of more rigorous mathematics in a way that also introduces the fun and beauty inherent in the subject.

- 🔬 Does your school system employ math specialists? If not, request one.

- 🔬 Discuss frustration with assignments in appropriate ways so that your child doesn't emerge feeling pitted against mathematics and her teachers. "This problem doesn't make sense to me, either," and "The way this problem is written makes it very difficult to understand what you need to do" are both constructive. "The Common Core is awful" and "When are you ever going to need to know this?" are not.

- 🔬 Encourage your child to voice concerns with math problems in a positive, proactive way, and encourage teachers to break down resistances to mathematics by being open to discussions about the difficulties students had interpreting problems. Validating the students who misunderstand a problem lets students know that they are not trying to decipher a secret code—they are part of the conversation.

- 🔬 Fennell discusses the need for discussion with "student stakeholders." Parents and teachers can learn a lot about math attitudes by listening to students of all ages reflect on their classroom experiences.

|||||||||||||||||||||||||||||||||||||||||||||||||||||||||||||||||||||||||||||||||||||||||||||||||||||||||||||||||

Elementary Math

While many students are prone to argue "What's the point?" about algebra, trigonometry, even geometry, the basic skills of elementary school math are necessary for many jobs and set the foundation for the advanced math that follows.

In 2006 Johns Hopkins researcher W. Stephen Wilson published a paper titled "Elementary School Mathematics Priorities" in which he lays out five building blocks. These are the skills your child needs to master in elementary school. Breaking early math into five digestible blocks is a useful way to give parents access into their child's math world. These building blocks are probably not surprising:

1. Numbers
2. Place value system
3. Whole number operations
4. Fractions and decimals
5. Problem-solving

Your daughter will loop back and forth between these skills throughout elementary school, reinforcing concepts and gradually adding greater complexity. As she progresses, she will see that these skills, while introduced separately, are interconnected. You cannot add 436 to 782 without understanding place value.

Your daughter will likely find some of these concepts difficult. Unfortunately, the last few decades haven't demonstrated a great increase in student understanding of fractions. In 1978 thousands of eighth graders were given a multiple-choice question that asked them to estimate $12/13$ + $7/8$. Only 24 percent chose the correct answer of 2. In 2014 researchers studying the difficulties of learning decimals and fractions re-created this test—albeit with a much smaller sample size of forty-eight eighth graders at a single affluent suburban school system. Only 27 percent answered correctly. What is the significance of these low percentages? Understanding fractions tends to be a bellwether for future performance. Understanding fractions in the fifth grade has been shown to correlate with math achievement in tenth grade.

How to Bring Grade School Math into the Home

1. **Make good use of car time.** Students need to know their facts cold. They must be fluent in the basics—addition, subtraction, multiplication, and division—in order to progress confidently in math. Very often, an elementary school homework schedule will ask students to spend fifteen minutes on math facts in addition to reading for twenty minutes, but in the business

of everyday life, this doesn't always happen. It's hard to work fifteen minutes of math into the day in addition to everything else. It helps to assign the practice a space. Every time you're in the car, practice math facts. This means that on the way to soccer practice, or piano, you can ask ten questions to keep skills sharp. Giving your child fact fluency is one of the best things that you can do for her future success in math.

2. **Purchase power.** When your child asks you to buy something for her, practice mental math and estimating by making her do the work. "About how much will three of those cost?" or "You can pick out the favors for your birthday party. You have twenty dollars to spend."

3. **Don't feel you need to reinvent the wheel.** Many excellent videos and interactive games online can beef up your child's understanding of concepts like fractions and decimals while also teaching her effective learning habits. Make sure to watch with her so that you can answer questions. Check out the websites for Math Antics or Khan Academy to get started.

4. **At-home activities are child's play.** Learning activities should be fun, interactive, hands-on, and inexpensive. Your child will get the most out of at-home activities if they are more than one-shot deals. Find games that you can return to again and again to build on established skills.

5. **Speak the language of math.** Math is based on precision—and that applies to the language of math as well. When helping your child with math, make sure you are speaking the same language. Define the terms. Don't dive immediately into a problem as if pressed for time. Slow down. Ask questions. "What are we talking about? How did your teacher explain this in school? What are the words we need to know, and do we agree on what they mean?"

6. **Model problem-solving.** When you are working on a problem, model the process for your child by talking it through and then even writing out the equation, even if you can do it in your head.

Fraction Play

Around eight or nine years old, children begin studying fractions. Understanding fractions is key to many more advanced math concepts, so it is important that a child have a firm and confident grasp of basic fraction concepts (writing and comparing fractions, for example). Play this game with your second or third grader once a week—make it part of a routine while you are baking cookies on Sunday night or maybe during an after-school snack on a quiet weekday.

You will need a chunk of clay, dough, or sand-polymer mix. A malleable clay allows children to divide and combine easily—four small balls easily transform into one large whole, which is then easily broken into three balls. That's pretty much the gist of it—child's play. In addition, have scraps of paper and a pen handy, and on a few slips of paper write the words *Halves, Thirds, Fourths, Fifths, Sixths, Eighths,* and *Sixteenths.*

1. Talk the talk. Introduce the term *equal shares* by saying "I'd like to divide this dough into equal shares. How should we do that?" Explain that *equal* means the same and that a *share* is another word for piece, part, slice, or section. Explain that *divide* is to break something into pieces, so by "dividing something into equal shares" we are breaking something into a bunch of pieces that are the same size.

2. Have your daughter divide one of the balls into equal shares to make sure she understands the concept. ("How many pieces?" she might ask. Maybe you say two, or maybe you tell her it's up to her.) Make sure to name what she has created: "Oh, you divided the ball into halves," or "You've divided the ball into fourths."

3. Have her put the ball back together to make a whole. Explain what she has done by using the language:

"A *whole* is all the pieces back together in one piece. Now we have one ball." (You might perhaps segue here into the difference between *hole* and *whole*, even writing them out and explaining that they are homonyms like *two* and *to*, and that their meanings are completely different!)

4. Ask her to divide the ball into *Halves*, showing her the card so she can see the word and how it is spelled.

5. Using the cards, ask her to divide the ball into fourths. (Does she realize she can divide each of the halves again?) Continue this with eighths and sixteenths. As play progresses, keep talking about the steps you are taking.

Playing in this way may be enough for one day, and besides, by now your cookies may be ready. The next step, whether during this playtime or next week, is to strengthen the connection between words and numbers. You might say, "OK, now give me one half," which would mean to divide the whole into halves and give you one. Ask for one eighth, one sixteenth, and so on, for a while, and then ask for three eighths, or six sixteenths. This can continue multiple times in the kitchen as your daughter becomes familiar with the language and begins to assign mathematical meaning to the fractions she is creating.

Once she is comfortable with talking about fractions in this way, continue with the same game but write down what you are asking for as well as saying it: $\frac{1}{2}$ is one half, $\frac{1}{4}$ is one fourth, $\frac{2}{3}$ is two thirds, and so on, so that she can begin to combine the words with their mathematical notation. Examine the notation and discuss what it looks like.

Now that she has the mathematical representation in front of her for the first time, ask her if she can explain what the top and bottom numbers mean: the bottom is how many equal

continued on next page . . .

. . . *continued from previous page*

shares our dough is divided into, and the top is how many shares we are taking. Give each a name: numerator (top) and denominator (bottom). Soon, you can progress to only writing the fraction and not speaking at all.

From here, your child has a basic understanding of what a fraction is, and in future weeks you can begin to play in all sorts of ways. Eventually, you can begin to explore how different fractions relate to each other:

1. Ask questions like, "Which is larger, ½ or ¼?" Four is a bigger number, so a child who doesn't yet understand the concept of fractions will say one fourth, and explaining why this is not so can be very confusing. However, if you are playing with clay, it becomes much easier. Have your daughter create one half, and then have her create one fourth so she can see for herself which is larger. Emphasize language here—say, for comparison, "Which is bigger, six or four? Six whole cookies or four whole cookies? Six? OK. Now, which is bigger, one sixth of a cookie or one fourth? Do you hear the *th* on the end? I'm not saying 'six' but 'one sixth.' What does that mean?" Do this activity until your child seems to have achieved fluency in this area, progressively asking more complex questions.

2. Ask her to divide the whole into thirds. Then take one of those thirds and slice it in half, and pick up one of the halves. Can she tell you what quantity you are holding? If not, tell her to slice the other two balls in half as well. Does that help her see that you are holding ⅙? (One student exclaimed, "Oh! It's much easier to see once they're all the same size!")

3. Introduce the words *equivalent fractions*. Equivalent fractions may not look the same, but they have equal shares of the whole. (If you were to squish the ²/₄ pieces together, the ball would be the same size as the ½.) Note how important it is that your daughter is fluent in the mathematical terms of *equal*, *shares*, and *whole*—and what a big difference fluency makes in defining what an equivalent fraction is. Just as math concepts build on each other, so does the terminology, and if your daughter manages to miss the terminology in one area, defining and understanding will be that much more difficult in the future.

Don't Wait to Fill Gaps in Mathematical Knowledge

If your daughter is struggling in math, model perseverance even in the wake of her frustration. Evaluate the situation and take the necessary steps to get her back on track. Aim to build both her confidence and a strong mathematical foundation:

 Reinforce that everyone learns at different speeds and in different styles. What works for one student may not work for another—as active learners, kids need to be open to trying different approaches to see what works best.

 Keep the teacher informed. Let him or her know how much time your daughter spends on her homework, how much help you provide, and how much stress it may be causing your daughter.

 Request remedial math programs that can help students who are missing grade-level skills.

Maintain a flexible and positive mindset—spending extra time now will set her up for future success. Let her know that one bad grade does not define her.

✈ Consider a tutor. Look for one who "gets" your daughter and who has experience with grade schoolers. Clearly define your expectations—are you looking for your daughter to practice her multiplication through hands-on learning? Would you prefer that the tutor review concepts but not help with homework?

"In sixth grade I had a really bad math teacher. I learned nothing and I didn't do well on our state assessment. I got put into a Math Help elective in seventh grade where we relearned everything, and right after that I got moved into Advanced Math." —Meagan, a high school junior looking at engineering schools

---

It's Never Too Early for Media Literacy

As children look around them for clues and patterns as to how the world works, what they watch on television or see online plays a huge role. What a child sees and reads becomes the foundation upon which she builds her hypotheses about how she should look, how she should feel, how she should act, and what she should care about.

Unfortunately, media is still dominated by negative portrayals of girls and women. "Smart girls" and "popular girls" are often portrayed as mutually exclusively categories, with the two groups pitted against each other. The smart girls may be depicted as socially inept geeks, while the popular girls are shown as social butterflies primarily concerned with "getting the guy."

It's tempting to brush off such stereotypical portrayals as trivial, but exposure to these ideas can affect a girl's perception of a STEM career, a girl's perception of herself, and a boy's perception of the girls around him. According to a FEM Inc. white paper, these stereotypes may become embedded in a person's subconscious such that "people with no measurable explicit prejudice demonstrate implicit biases, not only towards other people but also towards themselves." Worse, the authors assert that "once these patterns are in place they can have significant effects on a person's behavior and achievement."

Even young children see shows, movies, cartoons, and commercials that have subtle stereotypes. When you can, sit with your daughter and talk about what you are watching. For young children, this might mean saying, "Did you notice that commercial showed all the girls caring only about how they looked? That's silly—all the girls I know care about lots of different things."

FEM Inc. notes that media also has the power to break stereotypes, and seeing positive role models (whether real or fictional) can counteract negative influences. This means drawing attention to media that sends empowering messages, even if it's through small comments like, "Did you see how that girl was so good with computers *and* she was a soccer player, too? I like that she has different interests, just like so many girls I know."

As your daughter matures, help her strengthen her media literacy skills by continuing the dialogue. Sarah Gretter, senior learning designer at Michigan State University Hub for Innovation in Learning and Technology, offers the following suggestions for teaching her that all media are constructions that arise from particular special interests. A strong media literacy foundation will empower girls, giving them agency to debate and disagree with content.

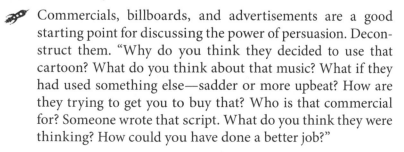

- Begin by discussing media literacy in traditional content such as picture books in early elementary school. You can slowly integrate more digital media as your daughter grows.

- Teach your child the term *active participant* and then teach her how to be one. An active participant in media becomes part of a conversation. She questions what she consumes: *Who made this? What makes them an expert? Do I believe what they are saying? Do I like what they are saying? How does it make me feel?*

- Commercials, billboards, and advertisements are a good starting point for discussing the power of persuasion. Deconstruct them. "Why do you think they decided to use that cartoon? What do you think about that music? What if they had used something else—sadder or more upbeat? How are they trying to get you to buy that? Who is that commercial for? Someone wrote that script. What do you think they were thinking? How could you have done a better job?"

As you contemplate when to give your child cell phone privileges or access to computers, consider what is appropriate given her stage of development. Online content is both professionally produced and user generated, and users are expected to be sophisticated enough to recognize the difference; oftentimes this sophistication is beyond a child's developmental abilities.

While you may consider a protectionist approach to certain content, remember that your child doesn't exist in a vacuum, and her friends will have access to media that you'd rather they didn't. Build open lines of communication so that your daughter feels comfortable telling you about what she sees or hears when she is not with you. Then, together, you can discuss what she saw and how it made her feel.

Permission to Speak Up

You can expect that well-meaning adults will occasionally say things to your child that may reinforce gender stereotypes. In the same way that parents are beginning to teach young children to be active participants in media, they can also model reactions and teach kids strategies for speaking up when someone, even an adult, has made assumptions about them that they feel are untrue and biased.

Your daughter may feel very unsure and shy, but girls can come to understand that they can be "good" while still speaking their minds politely and respectfully. As she grows she will continue to face difficult interactions, and experience from a young age will make it easier for her to stand her ground.

One way to address this is to teach her to ask frankly for clarification by saying, "What do you mean by that?" This gives the offender the opportunity to rephrase his or her expression.

FILM A COMMERCIAL

Parodying a commercial, infomercial, or movie trailer is a fun way to investigate and play with media as a construct.

Programming Time!

In late 2014 President Barack Obama became the first US president to write a program. His was very simple:

moveForward(100);

He wrote this line during a Code.org "Hour of Code" event at the White House. Over the last few years, Hour of Code events worldwide have helped to pull back the curtain and show all of us that an hour is all it takes to get started with programming. It's not that complicated after all.

Obama also started the CS for All initiative to bring computer science to K–12 students across the country and to balance inequities in opportunity. His program includes financial backing to train teachers, build regional partnerships, and provide equipment. In explaining the program, a White House blog noted the demand: nine out of ten parents surveyed want computer science taught at their children's schools. But it also mentioned the urgency. In 2015, 22 percent of students taking AP Computer Science were girls. Only 13 percent were African American or Latino.

Very likely, you would like your daughter to try her hand at coding, but you might not know where, or when, to start. Following are some tips.

Start Now—but Not Necessarily with a Computer

Coding is not about the specific programming language. It is about developing computational thinking skills and learning logical thinking mainly through the creation of algorithms. Coders need to be able to look at problems sequentially and identify all the different decisions they are able to make that result in different outcomes. You certainly don't need a computer to teach logic; in fact, when you're teaching a very young child, it may be best not to have one at all.

For instance, if you ask your child to come up with an algorithm to make a peanut butter and jelly sandwich, she may start by saying "Put peanut butter on the bread." Well, there are lots of steps that have to be taken to do just this! Open the jar, use a spreading device to put a specific amount of peanut butter on the spreader, but then what do you do with it? Oops—we forgot the bread. So, maybe we correct our algorithm to get the bread ready first. It may go something like this: Get the bread, open the bread package, remove two pieces of bread and place them side-by-side on a plate, and so on.

Somewhere along the way, you decide it's time to get the peanut butter, and so you add that to your algorithm. If you're designing with an eye for efficiency, though, you'll realize that you should have grabbed the peanut butter when you grabbed the bread.

Essentially, students are learning to be more thoughtful and detailed in their communications. They are learning to slow down and think about all the logical steps and sequencing that has to happen for an action or activity to occur. While beginning algorithms incorporate a linear set of steps, more complex algorithms will contain conditional branches ("If it's above 60 degrees wear shorts, else wear pants") and loops ("Take a card from the deck. Hand a card to the person on your left. Move to the next person. Repeat this until there are no more cards left.")

Defining algorithms teaches children to really focus on the details, something that can be hard to do in today's content-driven world. For example, if you want someone to draw a fox without telling that person explicitly to draw a fox, what differentiates a fox from a cat?

Identify the crucial details by speaking in terms of shapes, lengths, and position on a page: *Draw a bushy tail. Draw pointy ears.*

The website CS Unplugged contains a large library of activities for teaching computer science concepts—all without the use of technology. Children collaborate and move around the room (or the great outdoors) as they work on fun activities that actually help them understand what's going on inside their computers.

Interest ignites once you pry open the door and start asking questions. How *does* a computer store all those pictures that we take in such high quality? What's sitting inside that box? What does my picture look like in there? The activities are made for school or home, and they are easy for non–computer scientists to understand. They have also been translated into at least a dozen languages. Data compression (like that in HBO's *Silicon Valley*), binary numbers, sorting and searching algorithms, and much more—real-world analogies and games can give your daughter a basic understanding of what's going on behind the scenes, and this can make the computer seem much more accessible.

Itching to Write Code in the Classroom

Coding can be introduced in elementary school, but it is essential that teachers receive full support to learn effective ways to do this. Many teachers don't have experience coding themselves, so the process of adding a coding requirement must be well planned and well supported.

Understanding Algorithms

You don't need a computer to play these games that will help your kid develop her computational thinking skills:

1. Come up with algorithms for the following:

    + Getting dressed in the morning

    + Making grilled cheese

    + Wrapping a present

    + Finding a word in a word search

    + Building a paper airplane

    + Making a friendship bracelet

    + Guessing a number between one and twenty

2. Draw a design or picture, shield it from view, and then attempt to get others to replicate your drawing through your words alone.

Remember, bad experiences can alter the path of a child's career! Coding should be used as a fun and exciting way to complement and reinforce concepts already in the curriculum. Imagine seeing a math formula for fractals come to life in color to make art or making music from algorithms!

For coding, the programming language and the program's intent must resonate with kids. Robotics is very popular. With simple commands, students can watch their program control movements in real life. They can program a robot to use sensors to find objects, get through a maze, or play games.

Animation is another fun option for students. As with robotics, students quickly see the results of their work. Getting something out of programming motivates students and instills confidence to delve deeper into the field.

To start kids off, show them the final working product first. In robotics, this might mean you get them hooked by showing them the robot being controlled by a computer. Tweak a line of code to make the robot do something different—to move left instead of right, for example.

|||||||||||||||||||||||||||||||||||||||||||||||||||||||||||||||||||||||||||||||||||||||||||||||||||||

Putting It into Practice

- Never programmed? Be a fearless role model and try out an Hour of Code tutorial. There are different tutorials for different ages and interests. They're online and can be done at any time, although some may have machine requirements or require downloads.

- Start with a board game like Robot Turtles to teach logic and basic programming. Play games like Battleship, Blokus, chess, checkers, or Qwirkle, and draw attention to the algorithms governing decision-making. You can play many of these same games against a computer—how do you think those programs were written?

- Have a child who wants to learn at home or take an after-school class? Make it more fun and enhance learning by teaming up with a friend.

- Hour of Code not offered at your school? The Hour of Code website offers a sample email that you can send to your school principal: https://hourofcode.com/us/promote.

SIT UP STRAIGHT

As your child begins to spend time on tablets, smartphones, and computers, teach her proper posture. After extended time on computers and other devices, children—and adults—may experience long-term damage to hearing, posture, and eyesight, as well as repetitive strain injuries.

⚛ Looking for an easy-to-program robotics kit? Try Sparki (ArcBotics), Sphero (Sphero Edu), or Dash and Dot (Wonder Workshop). Looking for a more advanced robotics kit? Try Lego Mindstorms.

⚛ Try out Scratch at http://scratch.mit.edu. A key feature of Scratch is the ability to look inside other projects to see how they were made and even to appropriate the code for your own use. This means you can find a project you like and tweak it.

Spatial Ability and the Pink Aisle

Most of us have passable spatial ability, so what's the big deal? Unless your kid wants to be a mechanical engineer or an architect, why should she work to further develop these skills?

Interestingly, spatial ability skills help us model mathematics problems in a more visual way. Yi-Ling Cheng and Kelly Mix found that spatial ability training helps with mathematics, particularly algebraic missing-term problems such as $4 + x = 9$. In their study, they gave a baseline test to a group of children between the ages of six and eight. They then gave some students a lesson in mental rotation, while the other students worked on a crossword puzzle. (A mental rotation test might show you a drawing of a shape, often made out of blocks, from one angle. You are then asked to pick the picture that shows the same shape from a different position.) Those in the spatial training group saw their math improve significantly compared to the control group.

Spatial skills are easily learned. A 2010 Israeli study found that after 116 Israeli first graders participated in eight training sessions on mental rotation tasks such as reproducing images from memory and perceiving objects from different angles, gender differences in spatial skills disappeared. Similar tests have achieved the same results with young adults.

Construction toys help build these skills, and for a long time these construction toys were marketed mainly to boys via "the blue aisle." As more young women become engineers, more STEM toys that appeal to girls are hitting the market—many developed by young women engineers and entrepreneurs. This is evidence that as more women enter the

STEM workforce they are bringing divergent and fresh ideas. Today's girls benefit as these women build the toys they wished had been available when they were growing up. Creative building kits Roominate and GoldieBlox are examples of this new market. As established toy makers find that there is an audience here, they are working to fill this need, although not without some controversies.

In 2012 Lego came out with their new mostly pink, purple, and teal Lego Friends line. They had tried and failed a few times before to reach the massive yet elusive girl market, so they took no chances here. This time they went right to the target audience and spent four years talking to thirty-five hundred girls and their mothers. These weren't just any girls, though—these were the girls who did not play with Lego products. They found that these girls wanted to build just as much as boys—but they wanted to build different things and, yes, they expressed that they wanted to build in different colors.

Lego Group vice president Nanna Ulrich Gudum was responsible for the Lego Friends product line, and she explains what she saw, "The girls we talked to let us understand that they really wanted a LEGO offering that mirrors what the boys experience, but in a way that fulfills their unique desire for redesign and details and combined with realistic themes in community and friendship."

When the line first came out, it was met with a large petition. Parents didn't like that the friends were sitting around pools and salons in Heartlake City, didn't like the colors, didn't like that the traditional minifig had been replaced with the "mini doll," and, most important, didn't like that there was this decidedly girl-versus-boy segregation in the toy store to begin with. In other words, was Lego going the wrong way by making a girlish Lego Friends line instead of making all their products more gender neutral? One father commented that Lego Friends were nothing more than dolls disguised as Legos.

But more girls are building. Before Lego Friends, girls accounted for around 10 percent of Lego players. That percentage has gone up sharply since. Overall, according to the *Wall Street Journal*, one year after the launch of Lego Friends, three times as many girls were building with Lego sets.

The best solution would be for Lego commit to making sets that are interesting and relatable to a variety of children. There should be many more female minifigs in traditional sets so that both boys and girls benefit. Many girls were building planes, space shuttles, and cars with Lego bricks long before the Lego Friends line came along, so let's give more girl role models to this set of girls who constituted the Lego Group's core female audience before the advent of Lego Friends (and let's not forget the many boys, too, who see gender stereotypes at play in the overrepresentation of male minifigs). There has been some small movement here. In a contest to design new minifigs, a set of women scientists won; the minifigs were then sold in an overwhelmingly popular but limited set.

If your daughter likes Lego Friends, watch the message that you are sending. If you dislike Lego Friends because they are "really nothing more than dolls," then you are telling all those little girls who love pink and purple and dolls that to also love building they need to change—because serious builders aren't interested in "girly" things.

Putting It into Practice

 Teach preschool- and kindergarten-age children spatial concepts by using spatial words:

+ Location—behind, before, beside, below, above

+ Shape—straight, curvy, wavy, round

+ Shapes—triangle, square, octagon

 Read picture books that have spatial words like *Rosie's Walk* by Pat Hutchins.

Play hidden-object games: Is it under the bed? Is it on the bed?

Play chess or tangrams.

Build with tiles, blocks, and marble runs.

Do puzzles.

Learn origami.

Practice art—draw, paint, and sculpt.

All Camps Are Not Equal

Camps and after-school programs can be an excellent way to grow or maintain your daughter's interest in STEM. They are very popular today, and you can likely find a camp for anything from architecture to biotechnology to robotics.

It's not as simple as filling out an application and writing the check, though. There are a few things you and your daughter should investigate first. When it comes to extracurriculars at a young age, one bad experience is all it takes to turn a child off for good. Before signing up, consider the following:

The Ratio of Girls to Boys

A girl may love a subject but be disheartened to discover that no other girls appear to share her love. This may be especially true for older elementary girls—younger children mix easily, but around third grade gender differences become more noticeable, and it is not unusual for girls to suddenly shy away from joining a group of boys.

Ask the camp for the ratio of boys to girls. If the camp has a much higher number of boys than girls, check in with your daughter to see if this is OK with her. Even better, find other girls to join her. If no other girls are available, listen seriously to her reservations, should she have them, about being one of only a handful of girls—or the only girl—and decide together whether this is the right experience for her.

Diversity of Activities

Look for camps that offer a wide range of activities. Kids, like adults, have their own preferred way to spend a day. They may love, hate, or be indifferent to group work, crafts, skits, competitions, nature walks, art, sing-a-longs, being outside, being inside, bugs, animals, dirt and grime, chaos, or structure.

The enjoyment (or lack of enjoyment) of their day will influence your daughter's perception of the camp's focus, even if what she didn't like has nothing to do with it. A bad experience at architecture camp one year because she didn't like the food, didn't have a good buddy, or felt the afternoons were boring may signal the end to a budding interest in architecture. When looking for a camp or after-school program for a grade schooler, go for breadth over depth.

Equity of Interests

Call the camp and request a syllabus so that you can see how the program is structured. Look for evidence that the camp activities appeal to a wide range of interests and personalities. For example, designing a sneaker is an activity that will appeal to a broad range of children. Most children wear sneakers, and yet can bring their own individual wants and needs to their design—do they want a sneaker that changes color, lights up, dries quickly, or never smells? Better yet, look for out-of-the-box creativity in activities that ask kids to combine two different types of footwear into one innovative new product, like a dress shoe that is as comfortable as a sneaker—or converts to one! This forces kids to think about the pros and cons of, say, sneakers and high heels and then work to incorporate the best of both worlds. Look for activities that satisfy different entry points into STEM, such as the idea of helping others. Footwear is a problem for growing children in developing countries. How would you design footwear that can "grow" with a child?

Know Your Daughter

Sit down with your daughter and ask her a few questions to make sure you understand her motivations. What is she hoping to get out of camp? What is she concerned about? What does she imagine it will be like? Camps are a very positive experience, and they can help both to further nascent interests and introduce new ones.

Pay attention to what your child likes—not what you want her to like. You don't want your child to be you. Take everything you think she should know or be interested in—and put that aside so that her own interests can flow in. It is not about forcing her. What grabs her attention? You may find yourself shocked sometimes by what she likes. A six-year-old who gets hooked on learning Mandarin Chinese? An eight-year-old who loves bugs? Why not?

Animals as Inspiration

Many young girls have an affinity for animals, so animals are a wonderful way to talk about science and engineering. Introduce your daughter to all the ways in which engineers have been inspired by the animal kingdom.

KEEP QUIET

The largest mistake adults make when introducing STEM projects to young children is spending too much time up front explaining the lesson to be learned. With buckets and bins of exciting supplies sitting before them, kids can't focus. Get to it!

Humpback whales: If you take a look at the fins on a humpback whale, you see that they have interesting contours. Those knobby not-so-little bumps might seem like some sort of unwanted growth, but they actually reduce drag across the whale's fin, and if you can lower the amount of drag that's slowing you down, then you can increase your lift. The blades on fans and wind turbines are smooth—but what if engineers add humpback-whale-like ridges to the blades? Fans and wind turbines would be much more efficient. Now there's a cool idea for a school science fair project.

Frogs: How can surgeons get a tiny camera-carrying robot to make its way across the slippery internal abdominal wall of a patient without falling—and then get it to release its grip without harming the patient? Mechanical engineers at the University of Leeds are looking to tree frogs and the hexagonal-patterned channels on their feet for the answer!

Geckos: Geckos can walk—and run—without falling when scaling sides and bottoms of structures. How can they do this? They have millions of tiny hairs called setae on the pads of their toes. Mimicking this feature could lead to lots of applications: a 2.5-pound gecko can support 293 pounds and *still* run fast! Industry sees lots of applications for a superstrong adhesive that leaves no residue—the Ford Motor Company, for example, has partnered with Procter & Gamble to investigate how moving to a gecko-inspired adhesive in their car parts might make separating parts for recycling a possibility down the road. More

importantly, perhaps we could tape a television to the wall—
and take it down whenever we wanted to.

Sharkskin: Sharkskin is actually made up of tiny overlapping
scales called dermal denticles (so called because they resemble
teeth). These scales have even smaller grooves running through
them that help with aerodynamics so that sharks swim faster.
The rough shape also prevents parasitic algae and barnacles
from attaching. Researchers at the Fraunhofer Institute are
working on a textured paint that creates a layer like this dermal
denticle. One day, this paint could be added to wind turbines or
airplanes to make them more efficient. Other scientists at Shark-
let Technologies hope to develop a product based on sharkskin
that will help hospitals minimize the spread of germs.

Butterfly wings: Butterfly wings are covered by tiny scales that get
their color either from melanin (browns and blacks) or from the
particular way light scatters across the scales (iridescents). Take
the brilliant-blue morpho butterfly—we see this color because
some colors of light are canceled out while others are reflected.
Engineers working at mimicking the way the butterflies scatter
light to make color could change the ways in which we make
electronic displays on televisions, cell phones, and computers,
and even the way we make paints and fabrics.

Plant burrs: In 1948 Swiss electrical engineer George de Mestral
pondered whether there was any use for those annoying burrs
that he had to pick from his clothes (and his dog!) after walks
in the woods. It took him eight years of research and experimentation to come up with the product we know today as Velcro. Apparently, he was made fun of for his invention—but the
laughs surely stopped once NASA came calling.

BIO-WHAT?

Biomimetics (or biomimicry) is the process of looking to
nature for inspiration in engineering.

Harbor seals: Harbor seals have very sensitive whiskers that they use to navigate through the dark and to track food. They are able to sense the smallest disturbances in the water around them. Researchers are working at developing sensors that mimic the seal's whiskers in order to improve autonomous underwater vehicles and maybe even develop self-driving trucks.

When you and your child are walking through your neighborhood, hiking, or visiting the aquarium or the zoo, talk about the field of biomimetics. Discuss what is special about even the tiniest insects and tallest trees—and daydream about how we as humans might be able to use that same technology.

Let Her Know What's Out There

Charlotte is an articulate fourth-grade girl with an excellent handle on many things STEAM. She attends an after-school camp that includes STEAM in its activity rotation. In school, she attends a STEAM class once a week taught by a full-time STEAM teacher. It's her favorite class. She is able to not only explain what STEAM stands for but also give examples of what she has learned in each area. The one subject she isn't able to expound on, though, is engineering. What does an engineer do? She can only describe an engineer as "someone who makes things and fixes things, like cars," which, while accurate, does not sound particularly exciting and does not adequately show the expansiveness of the many careers that make up engineering.

In *One Nation Under Taught*, education leader and author Vince Bertram reveals that in a study of graduate students and professionals in the sciences, over 40 percent first became interested in their fields between kindergarten and fifth grade. The time is now. What is missing for many students today is simply exposure—and this is fortunate because that should be fairly easy to fix.

If parents and teachers do a better job of talking about STEM careers and of showing students the relationship between these careers and the toys they cherish, the products they use in their daily lives, the ideas they dream about, and the problems in the world that they want to solve, they may leave a lasting impact.

Elementary school children are ready for career stories like the following:

🚀 If you're a mountain goat, how do you walk up steep mountains? Can we engineer a winter hiking boot that mimics a goat's hooves? What other animals could we investigate to see how they stay warm or how they travel? (Materials engineer)

🚀 Mind-controlled minihelicopters and drones fly by picking up the electric signals sent as a person thinks about directional movements. How could this technology be used to help occupational therapists design tools for use by those with disabilities? (Mechanical engineer, human factors engineer, electrical engineer, computer engineer, computer scientist)

🚀 Smart houses and the internet of things—what items in your home would you like to be able to control with your smartphone? Or program for when you are not at home? (Mechanical engineer, electrical engineer, computer engineer, computer scientist)

🚀 What would you do with a robot? How would you design a robot to do your chores? To play with you? To keep you and your family safe? What challenges might you face? (Mechanical engineer, electrical engineer, computer engineer, computer scientist)

🚀 We can make tiny RFID tags—so little we can attach them on the backs of bees! These tags let us track items. Any time these tags pass by a receiver, we can see which tag went by, as well as what time and other information that we can then store on a computer. Some people want to use them to track honeybees so we can come up with ways to save the dwindling honeybee population. RFIDs also are attached to articles of clothing at a store—they beep if you try to leave the store with the RFID still attached. What would you use RFID tags for? (Electrical engineer, computer engineer, computer scientist)

In 2013 the Next Generation Science Standards were first published after an effort led by individual states and many other critical partners. These standards looked to model countries such as Japan, Singapore, and Finland and aim to blend life, physical, and earth sciences with engineering and technology.

The following chart shows some of the Next Generation Science Standards concepts by grade and matches them to the related careers that you and your daughter can read about at the end of this book (see page 206). Kids love real-world examples. They love hearing their teachers and their parents tell stories, so talk up the following careers and show your daughter the connections between these careers and the science she is learning about every day:

Grade	Scientific Concept
K	Forces and Interactions: Pushes and Pulls
K	Interdependent Relationships in Ecosystems: Animals, Plants, and Their Environment
K	Weather and Climate
1	Waves: Light and Sound
1	Structure, Function, and Information Processing
1	Space Systems, Patterns, and Cycles
2	Structure and Properties of Matter
2	Interdependent Relationships in Ecosystems
2	Earth's Systems: Processes that Shape the Earth
K–2	Engineering Design
3	Forces and Interactions
3	Inheritance and Variation of Traits: Life Cycles and Traits
3	Interdependent Relationships in Ecosystems: Environmental Impact on Organisms

We Have Your Back

As your daughter becomes one of the big kids in grade school, you start to see that she is standing on the precipice of a strange new world that seems to have new rules. You weren't expecting this until middle school, or at least fourth grade, but there are girls out there who can be quick to tell your daughter that she isn't doing something the right way,

Related Career Examples
Mechanical Engineer, Civil Engineer
Park Naturalist, Zoologist, Wildlife Biologist, Materials Engineer, Civil Engineer
Meteorologist, Atmospheric Scientist, Architect, Civil Engineer
Electrical Engineer, Astronomer, Physicist
Chemical Engineer, Materials Engineer
Atmospheric Scientist
Materials Engineer, Chemical Engineer
Civil Engineer
Civil Engineer, Petroleum Engineer, Mining Engineer, Geologist, Geophysicist
Human Factors Engineer
Mechanical Engineer, Civil Engineer
Geneticist, Microbiologist
Environmental Engineer, Civil Engineer

continued on next page . . .

Grade	Scientific Concept
3	Weather and Climate
4	Energy
4	Waves
4	Structure, Function, and Information Processing
4	Earth's Systems: Processes that Shape the Earth
5	Structures and Properties of Matter
5	Matter and Energy in Organisms and Ecosystems
5	Space Systems: Stars and the Solar System
5	Earth's Systems
K–5	Elementary Mathematics
3–5	Engineering Design

even though her whole life it *has* been the right way. One girl can let another know that what she does, how she dresses, or how she behaves is babyish, boyish, or another label that is surely not meant to be good or acceptable.

Why talk about this in a book about math and science? Because our goal in writing this book is to help parents raise girls who are strong, confident, creative beings who feel that there are no restraints on what they can achieve. And building communities of young girls who care about each other, who have each other's backs, results in strong communities of women ready to problem-solve together. There are many girls who are sweet and kind and who treat other girls with care. These are the girls that have your daughter's back, and these are the girls you want influencing her. Friends and older role models like these will help protect your daughter's sense of self and help her build empathy.

Related Career Examples

Atmospheric Science, Aerospace Engineer
(satellites for studying climate)

Electrical Engineer, Petroleum Engineer

Electrical Engineer, Physicist, Computer Scientist

Chemical Engineer, Materials Engineer (mimicry)

Civil Engineer (erosion prevention)

Materials Engineer

Nuclear Engineer, Petroleum Engineer, Fire Protection Engineer

Astronomer, Physicist, Geologist, Aerospace Engineer

Petroleum Engineer

Computer Scientist, Software Engineer, Financial Analyst,
Actuary

Human Factors Engineer

This age group can have difficulty distinguishing between purposeful meanness and legitimate disagreements. Being intentionally mean is not OK. But disagreements are an unavoidable part of life and *are* OK. We all want girls to be comfortable standing up for themselves. Being a thoughtful, considerate leader or friend sometimes means disagreeing with others. This can be hard for children to understand.

As girls reach the end of elementary school, parents can't help but wonder and even fear what is waiting for them around the corner. Middle school can bring with it some hefty obstacles, and, more than ever, parents are becoming spectators. As girls reach this age, they begin to pull away from their parents—which is exactly what they should be doing. They will begin to seek opinions and advice from peers and media first—and parents will become less involved in their daily lives. Girls will feel the pressures of conformity, sexuality and body changes, and even dating. They will take risks. They will wonder where they fall in the social sphere and ruthlessly compare themselves to others. These issues may take center stage for a while. Schoolwork may suffer.

Lay the groundwork throughout elementary school in preparation for turbulent times ahead. Develop those traits that are going to help her handle anything middle school might throw at her.

Putting It into Practice

- **Involve her in sports.** Sports develop self-esteem as well as promote the body as a strong, powerful, healthy machine. All sports—team and individual, common and not so common—give girls a sense of belonging and contribution.

- **Increase her media literacy and digital literacy.** Build her protective shield so that she can navigate the world of media on her own, especially online. Give her the tools she needs to navigate digital spaces safely.

- **Build her sense of self.** Encourage her to try different activities, and respect her opinions about what is "her" and what is "not her." Do the same with clothes and accessories—let her develop an identity that reflects her own spirit and that is not wholly based on what others around her are wearing. Encourage her to select friends because they share similar interests, a similar sense of humor, or similar passions, and because they are kind to others.

- **Provide an outlet.** An activity that she loves and that she can retreat to can be a saving grace when hard times hit and she needs some alone time. This could be reading, singing, art, or playing catch in the yard. What calms your daughter? What can you do to provide that soothing space for her when she needs it?

- **Give her the gift of language.** Teach her short impactful phrases for dealing with difficult situations. (American Girl's *Stand Up for Yourself & Your Friends* offers many suggestions.) Encourage her to build a group of friends who are comfortable standing up for each other. Let them handle their own situations to an extent in grade school so that they can gain confidence and handle similar situations in the future.

 Be a role model. Parents, grandparents, educators, all adults can remember that children are always watching and learning from us. Think about your own values, priorities, and friendships. Reflect on your own media usage. Model a positive problem-solving attitude in your own daily setbacks: "We'll handle this."

 Contain social media. Set social media limits for everyone in the family so that you can prevent overdependence. In a world where tweens and teens have basically quantified popularity through the counting of Likes and Shares, make sure those external factors do not control her.

 Be there for her.

Middle School: Don't Give Up!

Look at what's happening in middle school and it's easy to see why so many girls lose interest in STEM—or even school in general—during these turbulent years:

 Girls may begin to pay particular attention to their physical appearance. Body image, hair and makeup, and clothes become increasingly important.

 They may begin to show an interest in dating and may wonder what others find attractive in a girl.

 They may begin to more actively consider and inhabit traditional gender norms as a way of "growing up."

 They may pull back from their parents and begin to look to peers for acceptance, identity, and influence.

 They may experience sadness or depression.

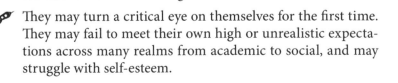 They experience puberty—bodies develop, menstruation starts, and hormonal changes cause moodiness.

They may turn a critical eye on themselves for the first time. They may fail to meet their own high or unrealistic expectations across many realms from academic to social, and may struggle with self-esteem.

Higher expectations, increased academic difficulty, and greater emphasis on executive functioning and personal responsibility may lead girls to have higher levels of stress and lower confidence at school.

 They are starting to understand that people might view the world differently than they do. But they're not quite there yet.

While some girls will glide through these years with relative ease, others will struggle to find acceptance and validation. Some use all their time and energy to focus on social challenges. Through our work, we've talked to sixth-grade girls who have been frozen out by their friends, girls of all ages who have been shamed and bullied on social media. Others struggle in school for the first time and begin to internalize the idea that they are not as talented or accomplished as their peers. Some are hesitant to move ahead with interests that they fear will differentiate them. In particular, they fear that interest in STEM labels them as unfeminine. In extreme cases, some girls are in distress and need love and support to handle large and complex issues.

In early and middle childhood, parents face very little resistance when they want to spend time with their children. You work and play with them, take them on excursions, bring them outdoors, and help them with school projects. They more or less enjoy your company. Encouraging them in STEM was likely easier in those days than it will ever be again. It figures that this period is followed by what may be the most difficult and trying time. How should you approach these years?

More middle school boys than girls participate in STEM extracurricular activities today. Those participation rates could be improved by modifying the programs so that they appeal to all children in a way that more accurately reflects the many paths in today's STEM world. But just attracting more girls to STEM activities and classes misses the big, complex picture. What about the girls who have no interest in taking such classes? For those girls, you will likely need to adjust course. You may even need to tread water for a while. But just giving up and saying, "Oh well, STEM just isn't for her" is a surefire way to lose your girl's participation for good.

So don't give up! There are steps you can take to hold the STEM door open for your middle school daughter as she makes her way through the serious business of figuring out exactly who she is:

Build her self-esteem by enforcing that failure and mistakes are OK, and celebrate her uniqueness.

 Continue to challenge the gender stereotypes that constrain and limit her.

 Introduce her to role models she can relate to while continuing to talk to her about a variety of engaging STEM careers.

 Provide her with a private space where she can let down her facade and be herself.

 Support her academic needs.

 Ensure that STEM opportunities in her school are exciting and welcoming to all students.

 Most important, just be there for her. Nothing can take the place of making your daughter feel that she has a fully supportive home she can retreat to and where she can be herself.

Self-Esteem Is the Cornerstone

Min Chen excelled at math as a child and always had the support and encouragement of her parents. They weren't wealthy. In fact, when they emigrated to Panama from China when Min was only a few years old, her father, an engineer, took many freelance projects as employment was not available to immigrants. He was talented at repairing all sorts of machinery and found work where he could, often bringing Min along with him to watch. Meanwhile, her mother made games and toys for her at home out of cardboard boxes and other recyclable materials.

Although Min began preschool not knowing a word of Spanish, she excelled in math even from that young age. She studied computer engineering in college. She didn't enjoy repetitive tasks and rote work, so designing computer programs to take the place of this work sounded like a good fit. After years of working in programming and project management, though, she saw a lot of wasted time and effort in the building of computer systems—and she knew she could do better. She left her job for a master's degree in software engineering to learn how to do software projects the right way. After the master's program, she started her own business helping other companies run successful projects.

Min is friendly, confident, and passionate. She is also introspective and articulate. When asked what advice she would give to young women, she said she wished she had better understood the subtle difference between self-confidence and self-esteem when she was younger.

"Since I remember, I've always been confident. I knew if I was willing to work hard and put enough time in, I could achieve anything. I was also one of the kids with the highest grades and so I never thought that there was something else called self-esteem that was not self-confidence," she says. She had to figure out the difference for herself once she was an adult—and she'd like to change this for younger women.

So, what is the difference, and why is it important that girls understand it from a young age?

Your self-confidence may be rooted in your ability to succeed in certain areas—to win awards, complete projects successfully, earn good grades, make friends, put together nice outfits and hairstyles, speak before audiences, or succeed at a sport. Confidence is compartmentalized—high confidence in one area does not guarantee confidence in others.

Self-esteem, on the other hand, is your measure of yourself—your happiness with who you are beneath the surface. In a world void of awards, compliments, trophies, and grades, are you still content with who you have become?

Those with high self-esteem are resilient because external factors such as a social slight or a failure at work or school do not define them. A girl with high confidence may feel secure that she will score well on a physics exam, for example, and a good grade may bolster her self-confidence, but without adequate self-esteem, that feeling is ephemeral. Quite quickly, she may feel undeserving. She may say, "Well, this test was super easy," "Everyone did well this time," or even, "I bet most of the other kids got perfect scores." She may feel that those around her are smarter, better, and in possession of attributes—beauty, brains, social graces—that she is not. Or she may already be looking ahead to the next award, the next external validation of her worth, in order to keep the feeling alive.

As a parent, it can seem that if a child is doing well in school and athletics, if she has a group of friends and a social life, then everything is good, but that's not always the case. Even high achievers can draw their self-worth not from their talents but from external, subjective factors such as looks, grades, popularity, and, perhaps most of all, the approval of others, be they peers, teachers, or parents. They may not be skilled at standing up for themselves, and they can be unwilling to remove themselves from negative or even toxic relationships in their personal lives.

It was a male friend who first pointed out the difference to Min: "He couldn't give me all these examples that I can give now as a woman—but when he pointed out that there was a difference, there was a curiosity for me. I know I'm self-confident, but do I have high self-esteem? And then I realized—why do I put up with a person who thinks that I know less because I am a woman? Why do I have to be with that person? Do I need that person? Do I have to deal with that person in my professional life or not? In most cases, no—so why do I do that?"

Organizations like Girls Inc. and the Girl Scouts place great value on building self-esteem along with STEM skills. Low self-esteem can lead girls away from their true interests as they seek external validation. A girl with an interest in STEM in middle school can find herself locked in an internal struggle between popularity and following her passion, and male and female middle schoolers are still well aware that girls are perceived to be "not as naturally good" at math and science.

Luckily, self-esteem has high plasticity, which means it can change no matter one's age. Change begins with understanding and valuing who you are, and parents have enormous influence over a daughter's ability to do this. Start talking to your daughter now about self-esteem—here's what middle school girls need to know:

I Deserve This

Healthy self-esteem isn't about doling out participation trophies. It's about encouraging girls to take credit for their hard-earned accomplishments. In fact, it's the opposite of the everyone-wins-a-trophy mentality. Kids deserve accolades and compliments precisely *because* they worked hard for them! (As Min puts it, "You've worked hard, you've got the charisma that got you noticed—that is your accomplishment!") Tell your daughter: Own it. No humblebragging, no hiding in the back—sit in the front row where everyone can see you; then be gracious and accept that honor. You earned it.

That's the easy part. Parents also need to teach girls to go for what they deserve—which means turning away from what, and whom, they don't. Poor self-esteem often plays out in relationships through a girl's questionable choices of friends and partners. Teach your girl that she deserves better than to remain in situations where, as Min puts it, "your whole being is not being appreciated."

I Am a Nice Person, but I Don't Have to Be Nice at This Moment

"Why is it OK if I go into a room to a table full of guys and I say hi and they don't say hi back? Why is that OK? It's not OK. I'm as important as you are in this. If I say hi you should say hi, and if you don't it's rude," Min says, and she's right.

Accommodating, nice, kind, and gentle—these are wonderful attributes. But sometimes a girl's got to roar and stand up for herself or others. Let your daughter know that it's OK to flex her muscles, to live with the mantra that "I am as important as you are."

People love an accommodating person. Why wouldn't they! And that can make a person feel good—to be liked in that way. But tell your daughter, "Too much accommodation at your expense is not healthy. You shouldn't always be the person taking one for the team." In middle school this behavior might manifest as a young girl who completes a group project entirely on her own because her partners tell her she's "so smart, and thank you so much, and you're the best!" She might think she's gaining friendships by letting others, male or female, use her to cut in line or to have access to something she has that they want.

Let her know when she gives away her negotiating power too often, it can become a habit. Even Min struggles with this sometimes, like the time she agreed to help a friend out, and then let him set the time and place for their meeting. Min went along with this even though she had to go out of her way. "Later this bothered me," she says. "I've had to learn to listen to my emotions and instincts. . . . Something was bothering me. Why? I am the one sort of doing the favor but I let my friend set the time and place and everything. I gave away my negotiating power. I asked my friend can we move this half an hour earlier because it would be easier for me. He said that would be fine."

"All these little things," Min muses. "Even today I have to be really conscious of it."

I Have Legs and Code

When the Nerd Girls first kicked off, Karen brought her original group of Nerd Girls out to California for a photo shoot. They got the full treatment—hair, makeup, clothes—and the pictures were used on the Nerd Girls website. Some people wrote to Karen to ask why the Nerd Girls were styled that way—wasn't this behavior setting women back decades?

It's time to change this conversation. It sets girls up for a logical fallacy, a great either-or. There is nothing wrong with a young woman wanting to dress in a way that makes her feel good inside. There is nothing wrong with girlfriends who like to shop together, get their nails done, or get dressed up for a nice night on the town. These things don't set feminism back.

Many young women studying STEM in college have confided that they "dress down" so as to not draw attention to themselves. They want to blend in. But in doing so, they're suppressing who they really are—and this can be destructive in the long run. Min says she used to do this in high school. She didn't want the fact that she was a young woman to give her any perceived advantage. She was working hard and doing well in her classes—she wouldn't give anyone the chance to assume her good grades were the result of her wearing a skirt that showed off her legs.

She's over this now. "I dress the way I want," she says. "I dress the way that makes me feel comfortable. Not just comfort-wise . . . I like to look good. Why don't I deserve to look good? Just because I have good grades, I don't deserve to look like an attractive woman?

"I hope I don't sound arrogant," she says with a laugh. Of course she doesn't, but there it is, the awareness of that hard-to-tread line between self-esteem and arrogance, even for accomplished women.

Min changed her style a few years back. "Panama is so hot. The whole world is getting hotter, right?" she says. "I stopped wearing suits and started wearing dresses. It was a practical decision, but actually, dresses look better on me because of my body shape. I was dating someone back then, and a friend said, 'Oh you look really nice. Someone's going to get a treat.' And I said no. I am dressing nice for myself. I am not dressing nice for *that* guy. I am the first one who is benefiting from this."

This is something that middle school girls need to hear. As they start caring more about their appearance, they need to believe in this message: "I am the first one who is benefiting from this."

Min would like to say that she doesn't care what other people think, but of course she knows that's not true. We do care what other people think of us—middle school girls more than most. So the task becomes teaching your daughter to be concerned with how she projects herself to the world, never what a particular person will think of her. When she does this, she remains in control of the narrative. She'll dress for herself.

"I want to project myself as a woman who has it all," Min says. "What does it mean that I have it all? I am a happy person. I am intelligent. I have achievement. I am attractive. I am a whole woman. That is what I want to project to people. I'm conscious about how I do that in how I dress, how I walk, what my body language says about me. These things are important to me now. They weren't important to me in the past. I thought they were superficial things. 'You don't just judge a book by its cover,' we say, but yes you do, everyone does."

This mindset can be freeing. "If people are looking at me, now I don't feel that they are judging me. Even if I know someone somewhere might be doing that, I don't care," Min says. "Yes, I have legs, and they are really good, and I can also code. How amazing! I have legs and I have code."

Give Your Daughter Space

As middle school kids become more aware of who "fits in" and who doesn't, it takes work and patience to raise a daughter who stays true to herself and her own interests. Giving your middle schooler the physical and mental space to be herself will help her maintain her authenticity so that she can continue to develop her natural talents at a time when peer pressure is high and girls especially are encouraged to turn away from math and science.

In 1994 psychologist Mary Pipher's book *Reviving Ophelia* stayed on the *New York Times* bestseller list for months, making Pipher one of the most sought-after speakers in the country. In *Ophelia* Pipher explained

MODEL SELF-ESTEEM

It's hard for young girls to say "This is what I'm good at." Female role models in particular—whether mothers, step-mothers, grandmothers, older sisters—need to model this. Say something positive about yourself each day. Be proud of the work you do, the dinner you put on the table, the way you face a particular challenge. When your little one sees you getting ready and tells you that you look pretty, respond with something more like "Thanks! This outfit makes me happy!" than "Ugh. Look at that stomach."

that in adolescence girls "become 'female impersonators' who fit their whole selves into small, crowded spaces."

How can girls maintain their own identities? Just when they are beginning to figure out who they are, they are receiving confusing and often conflicting messages from media, peers, and family about who they are supposed to be.

If adolescence, as Pipher wrote, "is when girls experience social pressure to put aside their authentic selves and to display only a small portion of their gifts," what kinds of gifts does your girl have, and what are you doing to make sure that societal pressures don't force your daughter to give up what she loves? Much more is at stake here than an interest in science and math; a girl may question her whole self-identity and may wonder if the activities she loved in preadolescence—playing with dolls, dressing in sweats and kicking soccer balls, or keeping up with any boy when it came to questions about robots or machines or math—are still acceptable.

Parents can start by reinforcing how much they enjoy watching their daughter develop her own interests and talents. They can express admiration for the friends in her life, young and old, who are secure and self-aware enough to follow their own paths. They can gently guide their daughter if she ridicules those around her for being different.

At the end of the day, though, as much as you may want your daughter not to care what her friends think of her, she will. It's not enjoyable to be made fun of, no matter what age you are, and middle schoolers love to tease. These tips will help you and your daughter navigate:

- Help her out by giving her a space of her own. Here she can keep all the toys and projects that mean something to her without feeling pressure to explain or defend them in front of friends or even family who may think they are too childish, too nerdy, too boyish, or too weird.

- If she wants to drop out of a once-loved activity, such as violin or karate, you have the challenge of figuring out why. Have her interests changed? Is she embarrassed? Is it no longer fun? Does she want to focus on something else, or does she want to join an activity where she'll be with her friends? Then you have the added challenge of figuring out if quitting is the right decision. Years of violin lessons don't necessarily need to be tossed aside, but you may decide it's time for fewer lessons or a new teacher. Michelle Obama encouraged her daughters to play tennis because it's a lifelong sport that she knew would teach her girls hard work, discipline, and teamwork. If you decide not to let your child quit, be clear and consistent in explaining your reasons.

🚀 Reflect on your own reaction to societal pressures. Do you have interests that you pursue because they make you happy? Do you worry about what other people will think of you? Are you accepting of people in your community who are different?

A Media Conversation

Once they reach middle school, girls will begin to turn to peers and the media for validation and identity. And while today's teens may be watching less television than prior generations, they are spending much more of their time consuming media online, often through video and social media sites.

While this can make it more difficult to see what kids are watching and reading, parents are still needed to help young girls successfully deflect all the messages that objectify women and box them into feminine stereotypes. Middle school is the necessary time to ramp up this battle, as this age coincides with the gender-intensification period described by Riki Wilchins thusly: "interest in traditional feminine norms begins to accelerate and belief in them starts to solidify."

This means that your daughter is now at an age where you should have more in-depth discussions about media, especially the idea that all media is a construction. If you introduced media literacy when your daughter was younger, she will already be familiar with what it means to be an *active participant* in what she watches, reads, and listens to. As opposed to sitting back and letting media create her reality, she questions its intent and works to understand and critique the position from which it was created.

Talk in particular about the role of advertising in the media. Television networks, cable channels, magazines, newspapers, and radio stations can make it or break it based on their advertising revenue. Those companies not only sell advertising spots but may also make decisions about programming and content according to what an advertiser prefers. Just as importantly, though, advertising reaches teens today through hybrid methods that can be harder to spot. Individuals with YouTube channels and social media influencers make a living off peddling products online, often in ways that are meant to seem personal and authentic. Help your daughter understand the financial motivation behind such methods.

Mother-Daughter Book and Movie Clubs

As daughters become readers of more sophisticated material, mother-daughter book clubs are a way to connect with your daughter, build media literacy, help her build relationships with her friends, invite her into the world where women gather to discuss relevant topics, and find her voice through reading and discussing notable works. Lori Day's book *Her Next Chapter* is a nice introduction to mother-daughter book clubs. A few options for this age group might be the following:

- *Graceling* by Kristin Cashore
- *If You Come Softly* by Jacqueline Woodson
- *Stargirl* by Jerry Spinelli
- *Speak* by Laurie Halse Anderson
- *The Lions of Little Rock* by Kristen Levine

Parents can help daughters learn to think critically about media not just by watching movies together but also by discussing them afterward. The following films might be a good place to start:

- *The Princess Bride*
- *A League of Her Own*
- *Akeelah and the Bee*
- *Star Wars: A New Hope*
- *Star Wars: The Force Awakens*
- *The Hunger Games*
- *The Spectacular Now*
- *Election*

- *Bend It Like Beckham*
- *Billy Elliot*
- *Legally Blonde*
- *The Help*
- *Joy*

What issues do you see in these films? How are the characters portrayed? Are they cardboard characters that follow typical stereotypes? If not, what makes them complex? Do you like the characters? What surprised you about the film? Did you like the setting? If you had to pick a different actor to play a certain role, who would it be? Is there diversity in this film? Does the story line have any faults or biases?

Peer-to-Peer Social Media

Building self-esteem in a digital age has its particular challenges. The internet and celebrity culture both build an unrealistic set of expectations for children, and middle schoolers—with their busy developing brains—might not be mature enough to handle all that social media throws at them. It's a time of life when developmentally they are focused on themselves, when they are risk-takers without impulse control and reasoning, and when they are working very hard on figuring out who they are and how they fit in. It's also a time of life when their experiences play a role in building those brains. Tweens may have taken over social media, but social media was not created with their development in mind.

The following resources might help:

- *American Girls: Social Media and the Secret Lives of Teenagers* by Nancy Jo Sales
- *Irresistible: The Rise of Addictive Technology and the Business of Keeping Us Hooked* by Adam Alter
- *It's Complicated: The Social Lives of Networked Teens* by danah boyd
- *Screenagers*: In this documentary, filmmaker and physician Delaney Ruston tackles concerns with excessive screen time in a positive manner. The corresponding website (www.

screenagersmovie.com) is a jumping-off point for other content, including screen-time contracts and links to up-to-date research at institutions like the MIT Media Lab and the Center on Media and Child Health.

 Screen-Smart Parenting: How to Find Balance and Benefit in Your Child's Use of Social Media, Apps, and Digital Devices by Jodi Gold

Harness the Power of Media

Digital literacy isn't all about patrolling and looking for danger. Teach your middle schooler how social media can be used for social change and she will be more than critical of the media she consumes—she'll be thoughtful and responsible about the media that she creates.

Social media especially has given citizens so much power. As with all power, it is up to us how we use it. Social media has brought about remarkable changes in the areas of disaster response, citizen journalism, and public awareness campaigns.

In events like the devastating 8.9 magnitude earthquake that hit Japan in 2011, social media sites such as Twitter have been used to alert residents to dangers, spread the word about where to find shelter and how to access emergency phone lines, reach family members, and help search-and-rescue teams coordinate efforts in real time.

Citizen journalism has also been called "democratic" and "street" journalism. The internet brings power to the people to share images and words with the entire world in the click of a button. Whenever something is happening, someone with a camera and video is close by, meaning that anyone can collect, report, and disseminate information to a wide audience.

Some citizen journalists are "accidental journalists"—they happen to be recording video or taking pictures in a spot when an event happens. Today, after a large-scale event hundreds if not thousands of people send video footage to news outlets. Compare this with the Zapruder film—the silent color home video of the 1963 assassination of John F. Kennedy that turned Abraham Zapruder into an accidental journalist.

Social media allows people to organize for a cause and to show their support. Hashtags such as #BlackLivesMatter, #MeToo, #RefugeesWelcome, and #NeverAgain have connected people around the world with a cause. There are online petitions for almost any issue, some more effective than others. One that was effective? During the 2012 US presidential elections three teenage girls from New Jersey learned that it had been twenty years since a female had moderated a presidential debate. Their petition requesting that the Commission on Presidential Debates (an all-male committee) add a woman moderator gathered over 120,000 signatures. Candy Crowley moderated the second debate, although this decision was never attributed specifically to the petition. Still, when social media catches wind of a petition and it becomes a trending issue, it tends to spur action.

Putting It into Practice

 Online, it's important what you see, but what you don't see is just as important. Teach your daughter to think about who isn't being represented—and why.

 Understanding the technical aspect of what you see online is one component of media literacy. This could mean understanding the ways in which photographs can be altered, how marketers use your personal information to send you targeted ads, or how web management tools allow anyone to create professional-looking sites.

THINK OUTSIDE THE BOX

Challenge tweens and teens to create sets of images—one that shows a "perfect" or enhanced close-up view of a situation, and another that pans out to show that the situation in the frame is actually fake.

Next-Level Mentors

Twelve-year-old Anna is bright and inquisitive. She has just started as a seventh grader at one of the top public schools in the country. In her school the students receive a separate grade in declamation each term, and she has just performed her first one. It was difficult, but she did well and is proud of herself. Still, she hopes to get better—as good as some of the high schoolers. She's seen them in action, so she knows what she wants. One day her entire grade was brought to the auditorium to listen to a declamation competition at the high school. She was inspired by a young woman who gave a remarkable and inspiring declamation from *Catcher in the Rye*.

Anna would like to be a doctor, maybe a pediatrician. She'd like to work with children, and she definitely doesn't want to sit at a desk all day. "I want to be moving around," she says. Many of Anna's friends want to be surgeons because of the way they are glamorized on shows like *Gray's Anatomy*.

She doesn't know any specific types of engineers, and she has a vague sense of engineers as people who build things. She tells a story about her nine-year-old brother who wanted to be an engineer because he thought they blew things up, which seemed to her to be the opposite of what they actually do. When he learned that engineers build bridges and cars, though, that still appealed to him. Like many girls, however, neither the prospect of blowing things up nor of building things particularly inspired Anna.

What would inspire Anna and her friends to maintain their STEM interest in medicine? What if young women in high school or college mentored middle school girls in STEM? Middle school girls respond to these next-level role models, and they'll often turn to them for advice when they won't listen to their own parents. In fact, the Girl Talk program shows the impact high school mentors can have on helping middle schoolers navigate the drama years of middle school. In the STEM world, high school girls are in a unique position to be able to educate middle school girls and introduce them to some of the cool STEM opportunities awaiting them in high school. For a young girl who has shown no interest in STEM, a next-level mentor might provide that initial spark. For a middle schooler having a difficult time maintaining her interest in the face of peer pressure, a high school– or college-aged young women can be the light at the end of a long middle school tunnel, a beacon of sorts for better things to come.

Those of us who work with girls and STEM often talk about a STEM pipeline. In fact, the lack of girls and women in STEM is often referred to as a "leaky pipeline," as if girls of all sorts are dripping out here and there along the way. The so-called STEM pipeline is very much at the service of industry—how can we fix the leaks, we ask, so that we can get more girls to stay in the pipes? Maybe it's better to think of it as a pathway at the service of the girls themselves. This pathway has twists and turns, varied terrains and obstacles, and many decision points. It can be difficult for many middle schoolers to care about what comes at the end of this pathway. That first job is an eternity away. They are, however, encouraged and excited when the pathway is enjoyable and filled with friendly and familiar faces guiding them along the way.

Middle School Math

If there is one subject that gets a lot of scrutiny in middle school, it's math. As one middle school principal remarked, parents are intense about math. They tend to see it as a gatekeeper of sorts—those who excel at this age will be placed in advanced courses and will therefore be on the path to taking calculus in high school, which they see as necessary for getting into a good college. Beyond that, and arguably the bigger issue, math concepts build on each other, so a bad experience one year can cause pain that lasts long into the future.

Your daughter may be worried enough about math class without thinking about the future, though. It is very likely that over the course of her middle school years, your daughter will, at times, not understand her homework, perform poorly on an assessment, or complain that math is stupid, difficult, or useless. She may cry over her homework, or she may decide she doesn't care to do it. Middle school may be the time that she is either selected for an honors math class or not selected for one, which both may present challenges. It may be the beginning of honor roll, which may be publicly listed in the town paper. Not making the honor roll can have an impact on a child, but—believe it or not—so can *making* it and the subsequent stress of making it again.

Stay grounded through any ups and downs in math class. Your daughter needs to focus on the here and now, not spend time worrying that something she did yesterday has doomed her entire future.

Math Struggles

Peggy Orenstein writes in *Schoolgirls: Young Women, Self Esteem, and the Confidence Gap* that "a loss of confidence in math usually precedes a drop in achievement, rather than vice versa." If so, our first step as parents is to continue to build mathematical confidence—and one way to do that is by defining perfection as unattainable and reassuring girls that failures (wrong answers, poor test scores) are momentary setbacks that do not indicate overall achievement. Such setbacks are a signal that we may need to work harder in a particular area.

Continue to emphasize this need to dig in and increase effort, as opposed to confirming a girl's suspicion that math is too difficult by (possibly to her great relief) lowering expectations. Unfortunately, we tend to give up on girls easier, perhaps unsure ourselves whether they are actually capable.

With confidence must come grit. Angela Duckworth spent a number of years studying grit. Her interest was piqued because she found herself in an environment where grit was on full display—she was teaching math to low-income middle schoolers. This is one of the experiences that really opened Duckworth's eyes to the importance of perseverance, a quality that she would go on to argue was more important than talent. If she had come into this particular classroom thinking that the students who scored well at the beginning of the course would be the same ones at the top of the heap by the end of the year, she was mistaken: "During the next several years of teaching, I grew less and less convinced that talent was destiny and more and more intrigued by the returns generated by effort," she writes. Luckily for all of us, grit is just one more part of our makeup that is changeable, and a failed math test presents an opportunity to assess our child's grit and coach her in perseverance. Most kids—especially those who have, for the most part, sailed through with good grades—have never had to learn this, and although it may not seem so at the time, it is a gift to learn how to deal with this issue before high school and college.

Besides memorization, many middle schoolers haven't really studied before, especially for a subject like math. Effort means putting in the work—studying. Praising effort over talent gives girls a growth mindset (develops grit) and keeps the praise internal as opposed to external (develops self-esteem). For a child who is struggling, remind her that she's in it for the long haul, that grades are short-term indicators of progress at a particular spot in time and that their primary purpose is to serve as a warning sign and mark of progress. Put grades aside as you work together on establishing these three skills:

 A student must be able to recognize (and perhaps admit) when she doesn't understand something. This may seem straight-forward, but it represents an ability to self-reflect on her own learning so that she can then take meaningful action. If this is the first time math class has challenged your daughter, this may be a new skill. ("Let's look at your notes from class. Walk me through what your teacher explained to you and let's see if we can pinpoint where you got lost.")

 In addition, a student must have a clear understanding of the material that will be on a test. Teachers often send this infor-mation home or post it online, but a student who hasn't had to study before may not have learned how to use this informa-tion and will leave it sitting in her locker. As your daughter becomes increasingly responsible for material that may not have been covered extensively in class, this starts to matter more.

 She should begin to develop the skills of a proactive and resourceful learner. She should know that there are many methods to obtaining information, and she should not always rely on parents and teachers to explain concepts.

Clear away all the noise and instruct your daughter to play the long game by focusing on the above skills. These will turn her into an active learner in charge of her own education. (These skills will also serve her well throughout her lifetime and will make her a coveted employee one day!)

Of course, there remains one important question: What does your child do once she realizes she doesn't understand something? Some chil-dren, afraid to ask for help, will spin their wheels and end up even more frustrated.

In class it can be hard for kids to speak up when they don't under-stand something. Sometimes adults are uncomfortable speaking up in meetings, and in those situations we're fairly confident no one is going to laugh at us or tease us overtly. If there's one time in life where raising your hand to admit you don't understand something fills you with dread, it's likely middle school.

Teaching your daughter to be comfortable asking questions is admittedly easier said than done. Even if you had a precocious question asker in elementary school, she may have morphed into a more silent type. Besides, we've all been told that there is no such thing as a dumb question, but that adage is not always helpful. Surely, there *is* such a thing as a dumb question, kids tell us, before proceeding to rattle off a dozen examples.

"I didn't follow that" is an acceptable remark that places the blame on neither teacher nor self, as is "Could you explain that another way?" Having the right words does make it easier for a student to register her confusion, although a student might be worried that once she is in the teacher's crosshairs she will be called on for follow-up questions.

Technology helps with this. Some schools use apps that allow students to ask questions anonymously in class. Others use apps to ask students questions in real time so that teachers can gauge how many students actually understand the material, no matter how many say that they do.

If the above aren't options, there are many backup plans. Does she want to get to school early, stay late, or visit a teacher during lunch or a study period? Does she prefer to come home and work on a problem on her own before going in the next day with her questions? Does she want to email the teacher? She may be hesitant to let the teacher know that she is struggling, and here she will need your encouragement. Remind her that communicating with the teacher is important. It alerts the teacher to potential issues, and it also demonstrates that your daughter is conscientious and diligent. If she is having difficulties, they are not for lack of effort.

If your daughter is struggling with homework, encourage her to start assignments early in the day so that she has time to do any of the following:

 Email the teacher a question if there is something she doesn't understand

 Get together with a friend to review homework together

 Go in early or stay late for help

 Use internet resources like Khan Academy

🚀 Video-chat with a friend to work through a homework problem together

What's scary about failure for children (and adults, too, for that matter) is the potential that even after we put all this time in studying, after we commit so strongly to caring—we might perform just as poorly on the next test. A daughter who pushes back on this action plan isn't necessarily being lazy—she's scared that another failure is embarrassing and defining. Think back to middle school. Remember what it was like when the teacher picked up a stack of graded papers and began to hand them out. Everyone wants to know how you did, and they don't take no for an answer. That failure can be very public.

|||||||||||||||||||||||||||||||||||||||||||||||||||||||||||||||||||||||||||||||||||||||||||||||||||||||||||||||||||||||||||

Putting It into Practice

⚛ Don't compare your child to another sibling or peer. "Why can't you do it? Sarah can do it, and you're just as smart as she is. You must not be trying hard enough."

⚛ The "careless mistakes" comment is hurtful. A child who adds incorrectly on tests might not be careless—she could be stressed about the test conditions and time limits.

⚛ Preteens and teens can react fairly dramatically, so their initial reaction to a poor score will likely be strong and negative. That's OK.

⚛ It becomes increasingly necessary to study. Make sure your child knows how.

⚛ Questions are a large part of the learning process.

⚛ Teach your daughter a backup plan for when she doesn't want to raise a hand in class.

⚛ Don't assume you know what's going on inside her head.

|||||||||||||||||||||||||||||||||||||||||||||||||||||||||||||||||||||||||||||||||||||||||||||||||||||||||||||||||||||||||||

Science

A presentation slide credited to Jaime Casap, Google's global education evangelist, gives the following career advice for the twenty-first century: "Don't ask kids what they want to be when they grow up but what problems do they want to solve." It's great advice, and to do their part in following through, parents need to ensure that they are opening up the world to kids in a way that shows them the problems that are out there waiting for them.

In middle school science, students will investigate a range of different concepts across biology, chemistry, and physics. They will study the cell, states of matter, the earth's layers, tectonic plates, weather and climate, the periodic table, chemical and physical reactions, types of rocks, and so on. A strong science program will not only make these subjects engaging through hands-on activities but will also show strong connections to real-world problems.

Take the cell phone, for example. Middle school children are definitely enthusiastic cell phone consumers—many children get their first cell phone during these years. Some classes allow students to use their personal devices to work on projects, research, and participate in activities like Quizlet, but the cell phone is a teaching tool in so many other ways:

- Tracking cell phone usage gives middle school children an interesting look into the world of data collection. Students can track their own usage for a week, or they can monitor from a particular safe area outside the school to count those who drive while on their cell phones. They can review studies like the one from Louisiana State University on "The Distracting Effects of a Ringing Cell Phone" and then make up their own studies to prove or disprove this theory.

- If you look at a periodic table, you see two rows of elements that don't quite fit. These may be elements that you more or less ignored in high school chemistry (to most of us, they seemed unimportant, squeezed out of the actual table as they were) and yet, they are key to much of the technology we have today. They're called the rare earth elements, and they have difficult names like lanthanum and yttrium. This is where the famed europium sits. A number of these elements are what make the color in your cell phone screen. Others combine to give you that glass screen that is so polished and smooth. It's magnetic neodymium that sits behind those tiny high-quality speakers, and it is that same magnetic quality that enables neodymium to make our phones vibrate. Ask middle schoolers how they think their cell phones vibrate—have they ever thought about what materials and what algorithms are used?

But there's much more to the story. Rare earth elements are really hard to extract. Refining the ore is difficult, expensive, and leads to a lot of toxic waste. How do we build a clean and sustainable future when almost all our technologies—including electronic cars and wind turbines—require these rare earth elements? Read about the tailings pond that sits about six miles away from the Yellow River in Baotou, China, and about Molycorp, the only rare earth element mine and processor in the United States.

There's even more to the story. A German market research firm estimated global smartphone sales in 2014 at 1.2 billion units. In our quest for the newest technology, Americans alone throw away 130 million cell phones a year. That e-waste can include toxic lead, mercury, cadmium, and nickel. What does this mean?

Students can take a look at the cell phone apps that are being created to solve problems. If so many people have cell phones, what does that open to us, from the simple to the complex?

+ By adding attachments to cell phones, we can use them as mobile computers—you've likely seen small businesses attach credit-card swipers to their phones and tablets. In similar fashion, researchers are developing disposable biosensors based on a SIM card platform. Doctors in rural areas will attach the biosensor to their cell phones in order to test for malaria.

+ Wondering how the internet knows what the traffic is like out there? It's thanks to the cell phone data of unsuspecting drivers already on the road. Cell phone companies always know where you are, often from the cell phone towers you are triangulating off of and your phone's GPS capabilities. They crowdsource this data, build a complex algorithm to take into account different anomalies (delivery trucks, low amounts of cars on the road, the mailman) and pass along what roads are backed up. Ask your middle schooler what anomalies could wreak havoc on a traffic algorithm.

How do cell phones work to begin with? Lots and lots of physics. They transmit radio waves across a series of antennae. They emit electromagnetic radiation. Their energy comes from batteries that engineers work to make smaller and to last longer.

The following chart shows what your middle schooler may study in science and math if using a curriculum similar to the Next Generation Science Standards. Use this chart to connect her to some of the careers that use these skills:

Concept	Related Career Example
Structure and Properties of Matter	Nuclear Engineer Physicist
Chemical Reactions	Materials Engineer Chemist
Forces and Interactions	Aeronautical Engineer Mechanical Engineer Civil Engineer
Energy	Petroleum Engineer Power and Energy Engineer
Waves and Electromagnetic Radiation	Electrical Engineer Electronics Engineer
Structure, Function, and Information Processing	Biologist Chemist

continued on next page . . .

Concept	Related Career Example
Growth, Development, and Reproduction of Organisms	Biomedical Engineer
Matter and Energy in Organisms and Ecosystems	Biologist Biotechnology Engineer
Interdependent Relationships in Ecosystems	Civil Engineer
Natural Selection and Adaptations	Wildlife Biologist
Space Systems	Astronomer Aerospace Engineer Physicist
History of Earth	Geologist
Earth's Systems	Civil Drafter
Weather and Climate	Atmospheric Scientist
Human Impacts	Petroleum Engineer Civil Engineer
Engineering Design	Computer Scientist Computer Engineer
Elementary and Middle School Math	Computer Analyst Financial Analyst Actuary

Bring on the STEM Classes

Many middle schools are working to offer STEM courses. Some require them, and others offer them as electives. These courses vary greatly from school to school, but the best will offer engaging hands-on opportunities that build spatial awareness, computational thinking, and digital literacy while also discussing timely and relevant challenges and discoveries. This can be difficult to achieve, though—schools need both expertise and money to introduce STEM in the right way.

Project Lead the Way (PLTW) is an example of a successful nonprofit program that seeks to help schools with both constraints. PLTW offers a full curriculum for kindergarten through high school classes in programming, engineering, and biomedical science. And extensive teacher training is part of the package.

PLTW provides the curriculum at no charge. Schools pay for teachers to attend professional development at an affiliated university (eighty hours for high school teachers, forty hours for middle school teachers), the materials needed for the course, and an annual fee for such costs as software licenses, ongoing teacher training, and access to the PLTW Learning Management System. Many low-income schools qualify for grants to help cover these costs.

In the most successful schools, STEM becomes part of a culture. STEM concepts become integrated into other courses, and the entire community comes together to celebrate STEM through events like STEM Family Nights and student Maker Faires. Implementing a program like PLTW helps drive this excitement. Teachers are prepared and inspired to teach STEM content, and this affects how they teach their other courses as well.

All this doesn't mean that girls are automatically engaged, though, and educators need to be prepared for some obstacles. Katianne once had the opportunity to lead a PLTW robotics unit. It was a struggle to inspire the small group of girls that shared a single table in the back of the room. This was an interactive workshop-style class, as it should be, but that dynamic meant that boys were loud and took up the majority of space in the room. They were out of their seats the entire time. They even preferred to work standing up. The ones who weren't actively building were playing with spare parts—constructing things or spinning wheels or making the world's largest tread. The girls tended to stay in their area. The one time the girls took charge was when it became time to organize the equipment cart. The boys halfheartedly pitched in for the most part. Some worked diligently for a few minutes and then had had enough. The girls saw it through. They were always responsible—listening during lessons, cleaning up their area without being told, pushing in their chairs when class ended. One of the girls was very interested in robotics because of an older brother, but the others seemed unsure why they were in the class, and they didn't take initiative to problem-solve and create. Teacher training in STEM doesn't ensure that teachers will be able to motivate.

In addition, even with training, there are a number of ways in which STEM classes might not work like you hope they will:

 Many schools cannot afford to hire full-time STEM teachers. In that case, a STEM elective is taught by a math or science teacher who might already have a full schedule. This means STEM can become just one more thing on a busy teacher's plate—and, since it is only an elective, it can fall low on the priority list, which will fail to create the inspirational atmosphere middle schoolers need.

 Teachers of STEM courses can rely on self-teaching through computer modules and trial and error because engineering "is about figuring it out for yourself." This type of course serves the children who already have a foothold in STEM—those children who already feel capable and confident, whether they are boys or girls. They make strides in their problem-solving autonomy because, usually through their own personal interests, they have already developed a solid STEM foundation. These will be the kids who are already designated by their peers as the "smart kids," the "math and science geeks," and "the nerds," and they will often band together. They are often male, often bold and boastful about their talents, ribbing each other and challenging each other's knowledge because this is their domain. The rest of the class struggles to learn the basics and sees this as confirmation that they lack the skill and talent to catch up.

 A pure focus on group work can leave some feeling lost and left out. If the STEM course is project based, very likely it is also group based, and the same collaboration issues that can exist in other classrooms can certainly exist here. This experience does not benefit all children. Children who might otherwise shine are held back because of introversion, uncertainty, or because they are ostracized by peers.

 Sometimes the equipment available leaves students more frustrated than excited. Many public schools have trouble keeping up with expensive, constantly changing technology. Middle schoolers can be rough on equipment, and if too many crucial parts disappear or break, the students are limited. Schools are forced to come up with plans for sharing equipment between classes or for continuing to run unsupported software. Any teacher who has worked in science or STEM has likely encountered scenarios where student groups have had to share at a time when sharing is difficult and frustrating (how do you share an axle?) or have had to make groups larger than ideal because there are not enough parts to go around. This can be frustrating to teachers and students alike. And, of course, students will easily draw the connections between this frustrating experience and a STEM career. They need to be challenged but not frustrated. Their successes and failures should be tied to surmounting obstacles in trial and error and in design within the project—not in the lack of equipment.

STEM Classes for All

Stereotypical images of robotics can be misleading. When you picture a robot, you picture something android-like, perhaps, something that walks or rolls. You might think about shows like *Robot Wars* or *Battle-Bots* where contestants build robots that fight to the "death." Girls who hear the word *robotics* may not necessarily imagine anything that might interest them. This is a problem! Robotics has and will continue to have a profound impact on all aspects of our lives, across all disciplines and interests:

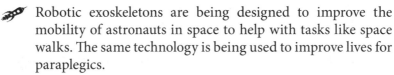 There are robots to vacuum your house, mow your lawn, and clear your gutters.

Robotic exoskeletons are being designed to improve the mobility of astronauts in space to help with tasks like space walks. The same technology is being used to improve lives for paraplegics.

People with quadriplegia may don a cap that captures brain activity and eye movement without the need for implants or messy gel applied to the scalp. This information is sent to a tablet, which then sends instructions to a robotic hand that helps users perform everyday tasks like drinking and eating.

Magnetic microbots are tiny robots that are designed to travel inside the human body to diagnose and treat various conditions. Instead of having moving mechanical parts, these robots are made of special materials that can be manipulated by external electromagnetic fields to move the robot in any direction. These microbots can deliver medicine, position cameras internally, or perform intricate and delicate tasks in hard-to-reach areas, like clear up blocked blood vessels in the retina that have been causing blindness.

Why not bring robotics into art, literature, music, theater, and dance? Health, physical education, and sports? And instead of always having a competition, make it project-based and provide students with a way to showcase their work, such as an art exhibit.

Say the assignment is to build a simple four-wheeled platform car. Must a race follow, to see whose car is fastest? If a student, girl or boy, is turned off by that environment and seems to be hanging back, can the teacher offer a creative option? Why not provide options other than a car? Turn the four-wheeled platform into a parade float or a robot for a haunted house. There are many different ways to test students' skill at problem-solving, coding, and precision. Teachers should provide options and showcase the students' creations. More children will be invested. With artistic vision in hand, designing and programming the robot becomes not the task and end goal but just one of the steps in the creative process.

The STEM program isn't just for gearheads. It's for those who love theater, art, video games, music, or sports. In other words, the robotics package is the tool. Let boys and girls use it to make something that is of interest to them.

It's All in the Packaging

Marketing matters. This means that what schools name STEM courses and how those courses are described can have an impact on who signs up to take the course. How the courses are taught matters even more. Circuit theory is the number-one course that drives women away from electrical engineering because of the traditional way it's taught with an emphasis on tools and not the big picture.

For a success story, look at Harvey Mudd College, which saw its number of female computer science majors jump from 10 percent to

40 percent when it implemented a three-step strategy to attract more women. It started with changing the introductory computer science class from Introduction to Programming in Java to Creative Approaches to Problem Solving in Science and Engineering Using Python. The switch from Java to Python, the emphasis on meaningful projects with real-world applications, and new yearly trips to the Grace Hopper Celebration of Women in Computing all made the class more inviting and accessible to women.

The Makerspace

Just like it did in grade school, the middle school makerspace provides an important physical space for children that facilitates much more than STEM work. As girls find their way through middle school, a makerspace is a place to go where they can be themselves, where they can shine, or where they can de-stress, hang out, and deepen relationships with friends.

The middle school makerspace can have similar materials to an elementary school makerspace. If budget allows, it might include the addition of a few more expensive and sophisticated pieces of machinery like laser cutters or 3-D printers. Don't be surprised, though, when teens and tweens still enjoy working on low-tech projects.

The successful makerspaces tend to be ones where students have ownership—where they view the space as theirs and work to keep it clean and orderly. The space itself becomes a resource for those working on projects for their classes. It will sometimes be a place of connection and collaboration for high-energy groups, while other times students who need to decompress in the middle of a long day will appreciate a quiet space.

High School: Keeping the Door to STEM Open

Mother: "You got an A in math!"
Daughter: "Just because it was geometry, and geometry is easy."

For all the difficulties of middle school, many girls move into high school and begin to find their place. Their sense of self grows, and typically, high schoolers begin to be more accepting of different personalities and interests in their peers. The obstacles change:

- College looms on the horizon, and that's exciting but also scary.

- Young women still interested in math and science may continue to feel the pressure of gender differences from peers, parents, or teachers and guidance counselors.

- Math and science courses become more difficult.

- STEM seems too limiting to girls who want to make an impact on the world.

- Late bloomers feel it is too late to pick up skills such as programming.

A High School Perspective

In the summer of 2016 Katianne traveled to a suburb of Ann Arbor, Michigan, to have coffee with a group of girls while picking their brains on their STEM experiences so far. There was a range of ages—a few high school juniors, incoming freshmen, and a middle schooler.

She asked them what they want to be. Kaitlyn, a junior, said, "I have no idea. My interests are constantly changing, so I don't really know. I thought I'd be playing volleyball in college, but now I'm not. How can I decide what I want to do after college when I don't even know what I want to do *in* college?"

There was angst about decisions. They surprised each other with their answers. What they want to be when they grow up—this isn't something kids this age talk about all that much.

Meagan, whose father is a mechanical engineer, said, "Engineering. Maybe aerospace, but I probably won't get a job, so maybe something more general."

The thought of space travel made her younger sister Ellie perk up. "We should send you to the moon. Do you need a permission slip to go to the moon?"

These girls don't fit the narrative of young women dissuaded from STEM because of gender, and much of the conversation didn't even revolve around the fact that everyone at the table was female and was there to discuss what it means to be a girl. Rather, they talked in general about what it's like to be a public-school kid today.

None of the girls was exactly sure what STEM means. They've heard it before, sort of. Maybe the *S* is for science? Is the *M* for math? They made guesses at the rest of the acronym. Despite STEM being everywhere in educational literature, parenting magazines, and even politics, the girls hadn't been introduced. This isn't to say they haven't had STEM classes—they have, they just haven't been called that.

Once everyone was clear on what STEM stands for, Katianne asked the girls what kinds of STEM careers they knew about. The table went quiet, and then they laughed. Finally, one said, "Biologist." "Marine biologist," another piped up. Katianne found out later that one of the most beloved teachers in the school teaches biology.

Silence.

"Civil engineer!" Kaitlyn said.

"Great! What does a civil engineer do?"

"I don't know. I just know that's what my dad was going to do in college but then didn't . . ."

Much of the conversation was like this. The girls seemed to be in unfamiliar territory, being asked questions they hadn't really been asked before, and their answers were tentative and uncertain.

Katianne asked Meagan what her father does.

"I have no idea," she said right away, although that wasn't true. She followed that up with what she does know: "He designs parts for engines. A company will call him and say, 'Can you help us make this new engine?' or, 'Can you help us make this engine better?'" She's interested in this work, she said.

Katianne had expected the older girls to be more aware of STEM occupations—they've taken honors courses in both math and science, and she expected that teachers were talking up these careers. "How often do they stop class and say, 'You might use this in this particular field . . .'?" she asked.

"Never."

"Well, not never," Meagan interjected. "There was one time last year. Something to do with statistics. Our teacher stopped class and said, 'They use this in insurance companies, and that job makes a lot of money.'"

"Actuary?"

"Yes!"

"OK," Katianne said. "That's a start!" So she moved on to math.

"She's taking precalc this year—may she rest in peace—" Kaitlyn said, nodding in Meagan's direction.

"I've heard it's not that bad—"

"I'm doing stats. I'm excited for stats," Kaitlyn said.

Kaitlyn's "done with advanced math." She made it through Algebra 2 thanks to "this girl sitting next to me," she said, poking Meagan. Kaitlyn started hating math in fifth grade and has never changed course. She's moved around—she left Michigan to spend fifth grade in Minnesota, then returned to Michigan the following year. She lamented that she missed out on a year that had some really great teachers, but something else happened during that transition—the math curriculums were different in each state, and so she got a little lost. "All I think of when I think of fifth grade is learning that I actually really hate math. I walked into math class thinking, 'I love story problems!' Then I realized I wasn't good at math. . . . Then I realized I hated math."

For all these girls, whether they love or hate a course—and by extension, the subject—often comes down to the teacher. The girls didn't mince words. They've spent a lot of time in classrooms and they don't feel they've had many good teachers since that boon that was fifth grade. Everything seemed to change in middle school.

"I feel like a lot of the teachers we've disliked—they do a lot of the online notes stuff. Like go to this website, learn this, and then you'll be tested on it, and if you don't understand it, it's your own fault," Kaitlyn said. The rest of the girls agreed.

The good teachers, they observed, make smart use of the online materials: "They do the online stuff because it's fun—but they don't only do that. They do regular notes first, then send us to an online simulation that maybe reflects our notes."

This is the one striking characteristic of their favorite teachers—they simply "got up in front of the class."

"I disliked science until this year," Kaitlyn said. "Math and science were tied as my least favorite subjects. Then biology this year really changed that. We had touched on bio in ninth grade and I had hated it, but I had to take it this year. So I took regular, not advanced. The first day I remember my teacher telling me, 'If you didn't like biology you will by the end of the year,' and me going, 'Yeah, right.' Then I fell in love with it." She took a sip of her drink and sighed. "She was the only science teacher I ever liked," she said.

If they're not too keen on their teachers, then they're certainly not going to go to them for extra help. If they're stuck on homework they start with their friends in their classes. If that doesn't help they look online. ("Like how to memorize the unit circle," Meagan remembered. "That video saved my life.") Sarah calls her aunt. Meagan asks her father—but "he's usually wrong," she joked.

"So no one asks the teacher?"

Groans all around, and then a long discussion about a particularly unhelpful math teacher. He's well known for being impatient or unhelpful. "Kids would go and ask for help, and he'd say, 'If you don't know it by now, there's nothing I can do for you.'"

He's not the only teacher these young women find unapproachable. "I hate how at the very beginning of the semester teachers are all like, 'You can always come up to me.' So we all watch as someone actually goes up to the teacher, and it becomes a negative experience. None of us want to come up to you now. It doesn't matter how many times you tell us we can," Kaitlyn said.

She played with the straw in her drink. "We don't really like the way our school system is set up. I feel like that just needs to be stated. I didn't used to hate school. I don't know what it is exactly that makes me hate it now. I just don't think any of us genuinely enjoy school anymore."

"A lot of it has to do with us never knowing what's going on. You couldn't ask us what to expect in eighth grade because it's all changed," someone said.

What they meant by this is that their school system, like so many in the country, has spent years trying to figure out how to teach math better. While the school system works to enhance its math offerings, those actually in the school can't help but feel the effects of the constant shuffle. They're bewildered by the idea that geometry has been moved around so much that both eighth graders and tenth graders end up taking the class at the same time. The high schoolers can't believe that their younger siblings can now actually test out of a year of math, and that it's possible to be studying the same coursework as someone younger. Lauren talked about being involved in a bewildering pilot program for half a year of math in middle school—"self-learning," she thought it was called, or maybe it was "personalized learning." The students weren't told about the pilot, she said, so everyone was confused. They'd take packets home and wouldn't know how to do the material in them. She felt that this method taught her nothing. "I missed things in math—like how to factor. Sarah had to teach me," she said, nodding toward her younger sister.

"Whatever they're doing in the younger grades today must be working," Kaitlyn said, "because it's making us high schoolers feel stupid."

"Why don't they motivate us with food?" someone said as the conversation drew to a close. "Instead of motivating us with 'Do well so you don't have to take this class again,' or 'Do well so you can get into college,' why not food?"

At first the mention of food seemed like a funny, random thing to say, but the girls quickly began reminiscing back to a time when everything came down to a Popsicle stick jar or a sticker chart, days when they were very often incentivized with the promise of ice cream sundae parties.

For all this, gender bias is more or less out of the picture. They don't see a difference in how boys and girls are treated in the classroom. Someone pointed out that there is a Women in Science Club at the high school, but no Men in Science Club. "What's it trying to equal out?" Kaitlyn wondered out loud. "It doesn't really seem to equalize anything."

Science Is a Place for Women

Pam Laquidera is an expert in women's studies who taught for years at Bunker Hill Community College in Charlestown, Boston. "Much of science originated as an off-shoot of magic. Science as magic, magic as entertainment for the bourgeoisie in Europe," she says. "The people entertaining were women in parlors performing basic science. Really, women were at the cutting edge. Who observed stars in the sky? Much was done by women. Botany? A lot can be traced back to women. Catching butterflies, etymology? Women. Women shared in all these pursuits in the twelve hundreds, thirteen hundreds, all the way up to the Enlightenment."

During the Enlightenment, women were excluded from universities, which means, Pam says, that "men took science, molded it in a way that was authentic for men, and in doing so, two hundred years later when women did have access to universities, science was foreign to them, less appealing, and the gap just got bigger."

Today, women are finding their place at the table, and as they do society is reaping the benefits. Diversity brings new perspectives and ideas, but there's more to it than that. The scientific community is also starting to acknowledge that, as Pam puts it, there's room for feelings in science. Emotion, empathy, communication—as scientists turn these talents on some of the world's most pressing scientific problems and most exciting technological advances, they find themselves conducting studies and inventing solutions that are more, not less, successful.

Jane Goodall is a striking early example of this. In 1960 when Goodall arrived at Tanzania's Gombe National Park to study chimpanzees, she had no college degree—just a passion to live among African animals that had begun when she was a child, thanks in part to the adventure stories of Tarzan and Doctor Dolittle. She found her way to Kenya as a twenty-something where she was persistent in establishing a relationship with well-known anthropologist Louis Leakey. He took her on as an assistant and encouraged her research into chimpanzees. Her techniques were unorthodox and many scientists of the time were critical of her methods. Instead of numbering her subjects, for example, she named them—this was one of the ways in which she established an intimacy that many viewed as unscientific. Over time, she became accepted by the chimpanzees, and her window into this world over a period of years showed us that chimpanzees are highly intelligent, have complex social structures, make and use tools, and experience a range of emotions. Not only is her research still used today, but Gombe changed her—her experiences led her to become a lifelong advocate for chimpanzees. She established multiple chimpanzee refuges in Africa and has traveled the world speaking out against the use of chimpanzees in scientific research and medical studies.

Many of us have a sterile masculinized view of science—lone men in lab coats. We have a pedantic pencil-and-paper view of mathematics as opposed to seeing it as a playful, creative art. We have an outdated view of technology and engineering that paints it as rigid and unfeeling. These views ignore that today interdisciplinary research is paramount. No one wants to work in a silo. There's room for feeling in science.

Take the issue of the decimation of the African elephant from poaching. The newly formed Tufts Elephant Alliance brings together at least one member from every school in the university. Members have backgrounds in law and diplomacy, medicine, dentistry, economics, veterinary science, and more. Only when they come together can this group paint a full picture of the issues that have created the race to extinction of the African elephant today: deforestation for wood and charcoal, landgrabs by foreign investors, poverty, mercenary armies and terrorist groups, international law, pass-through countries with negligible penalties for smuggling, the long-roaming distances of elephants, the cultural acceptance of ivory, and more. Then, their expertise can be put to work on different solutions: medical access in poor areas, strengthening laws, identifying smuggling routes. From an engineering standpoint, the group considers what tools can be developed to help these different endeavors. How can digital imaging be used to help track roaming elephant populations, for example? STEM is at the service of those who seek solutions. What problem are you trying to solve? Let's see how STEM can help you.

What Is She Learning in Science Class and What's It Got to Do with Anything?

A high school science course may just seem like one more step toward graduation. What's the point of biology, chemistry, or physics? Parents can help their daughters connect the dots between these fields of study and some of the advancements going on in the world today.

Biology

Biology relies on an understanding of both chemistry and physics. For example, all living matter is made up of a certain set of elements—you can't get much closer to chemistry than that.

The foods we eat are broken down into the chemical substances that then nourish the body. There would be no life without water. We know this. But why is water so important? What is it about that water molecule that makes it so remarkable? All living elements share one common element: carbon. How have humans changed the delicate balance of carbon in our atmosphere, and what is that, in turn, doing to other species? Are those species adapting—or are they threatened with extinction?

Mix some physics in too. The human brain functions thanks to both electrical signals and chemical messengers. We see because light reacts with chemicals in our eyes, but we can start the story by using physics to explain the existence of light waves in the first place.

Some biologists are interested in the larger (literally) questions of biology. Beyond water, what else does the Earth provide that has created the perfect environment to support life? Those who study the Earth from this global scope often have to look at the planet from a distance (via satellite proxy) to get a clear view of what might be going on. Some biologists are interested in life beyond Earth. What are scientists looking for when they look for other life-supporting planets? How would a human fare in a different environment like, say, Mars? Biologists help answer those questions.

Other biologists study a particular ecosystem on our planet. They may be drawn to the rain forest, or how development is affecting ecosystems right in their own backyard.

Biologists like E. O. Wilson are passionate about a particular organism. A whole lifetime on ants? But remember that Wilson's study of ants overlapped with his study of sociobiology. What's the genetic basis behind the social behaviors of an animal? It turns out there is much to be learned from ant colonies.

Other biologists study the mosquito in order to understand how diseases like encephalitis, West Nile virus, and Zika are spread—but they need to join forces with scientists who study the global climate (including climate change) and its impact on the length of the mosquito-breeding season.

The more biologists study other animals, the more they realize how little we know. Biologists are able to learn so much more now that they can use sophisticated technologies like tracking devices to monitor the behaviors of other animals. Then they can use technology to imitate those behaviors. Take the elephants mentioned earlier—how do they communicate with each other across vast distances? Now that scientists are figuring that out, can humans mimic that behavior in a way that will help us save them?

Biologists who study the human body and its systems may search for cures or create vaccines for diseases. Engineers help these initiatives by building models. Electrical engineering professor Alice Parker and her doctoral students are working on a very long-term project—simulating the human brain. Although this project will likely never be completed, the mere attempt is leading to fascinating discoveries.

Still other biologists zoom in closer to study genetics and the manipulation of DNA within organisms. What are the pros and cons of the genetically modified organisms we are likely buying from supermarkets? It's not all supervegetables. The field of genetics holds great promise for personalized medicine.

An example of biology's place in engineering? When the Zakim Bridge was built in Boston, civil engineers made modifications to the bridge in order to ensure that enough sunlight could still reach the migratory fish below. In this way, civil engineering is not just about safety, structure, and capacity; it is also about inclusion—human structures must live in synergy with the environment.

Physics

Physics and chemistry are both about the study of matter and energy. Some say chemistry is the base—or bridge—science, as it provides the relationship between physics and biology, while others say that chemistry is a subscience of physics. In any case, the fields overlap in industry: physicists and chemists often work together.

Physics includes such subjects as the study of the atom, mechanics (machines, starting with simple pulleys, levers, etc.), heat, radiation (including light), sound, electricity, and magnetism. Physics explains sound and light—both travel as waves. Physics is the flow of electricity that allows humans to power everything in their world. It is also magnets, whether of the toy variety or the giant kind that is Earth. Physics is gravity. It explains how fast a skydiver accelerates when free-falling

MUSIC + STEM = MENTAL HEALTH SOLUTION?

Could electrical engineering and jazz lead to a better understanding of schizophrenia? Alice Parker is an electrical engineering professor at the University of Southern California. When one of her undergraduate students came to her with an idea that would combine his love of jazz with electrical engineering, she was all in. Jazz is full of variations, these improvisations arranged in a certain way. "Whether music, images, or speech patterns, your brain is predicting what will come next," Alice says. "If what comes next isn't what your brain predicted, it can be very enjoyable or it can be very jarring, so this prediction mechanism is the key."

Alice and her students attempted to build neural networks in software and in electronic circuits that would emulate this prediction mechanism in the brain, and they've had success: "Our understanding of how the brain works seems to be sound because electrical circuits seem to be doing the same thing. We're validating the little pieces that neuroscientists are discovering," Alice says. "A lot of what we do that's fun and amusing is also interesting because it leads to questions about disorders." In this case, that disorder is schizophrenia, a debilitating brain disorder that destroys cognitive ability. This same predictive behavior is believed to show up in schizophrenia, which is part of the reason why those with symptoms can hear voices that aren't there.

"They're probably hearing those voices because their prediction circuitry is getting kicked off erroneously," Alice explains. "They're hearing something they've heard before. A regular churchgoer might hear a biblical phrase. Or they see images, and their brain is trying to recognize the image because it's seen it before. The thing is, you're not really seeing anything. It is cells that aren't well."

from an airplane, and then explains what happens (thankfully) when the diver opens the parachute. Physics is behind the effects of temperature, heat transfer, and changes of phase that students and scientists may study within biology, engineering, or many other fields.

Many of the machines used in the medical field owe their existence to the research of medical physicists. X-rays are high-frequency electromagnetic waves that can penetrate flesh—which is why bones can be seen through the images they produce. But X-rays have been around for a long time. Think about the combination of medical physics and nanotechnology and what that might mean for the treatment of cancer as scientists are finding new ways to send targeted therapies only to the cells that need them. They are able to increase concentrations of therapeutic agents in the cancerous cells while at the same time minimizing buildup of these agents in surrounding healthy cells.

Rocket scientists are, of course, masters of physics. Take the satellite NASA uses to study the biosphere. Physics allows it to launch and to break through the atmosphere, and physics again ensures that after it's launched the satellite doesn't fall back to Earth. Physics also gets that satellite to stay in orbit at a constant speed and, if necessary, gets it to stay at the same point above Earth. Engineers who build the satellite rely on principles of physics. They use what they know about electricity and mechanics to build the tools that are onboard the satellite. A power source is needed. If it is solar panels, for example, then the solar energy needs to be stored and converted to electricity.

Physics sits at the helm of the breakthroughs being made in renewable energy—not only in the transformation of wind, sunlight, or waves into energy but also in the operation of the machines that do this work, which requires cranks, levers, gears, and so on.

Chemistry

Understanding the basic building blocks of chemistry opens up an investigation into the chemical makeup of anything around us. Chemistry is behind many of the items we depend on, including those we use for food, medicine, and shelter. Materials scientists use their knowledge of chemistry to create custom materials to fit certain criteria. They may, for example, be involved in the design of integrated circuits for a technology company, or prosthetics and implants for the biomedical field.

Flowers and plants need certain chemicals in the atmosphere and in the soil. Photosynthesis and respiration are both complicated sequences of chemical reactions. Oil and natural gas are fossil fuels—meaning they come from decayed microorganisms like plankton and algae that lived millions of years ago. How does this plankton and algae give us the energy that has powered our societies? They died and sank to the ocean floor, where they were buried under layers of sediment and subjected to great pressure. These organisms have energy trapped in their hydrocarbons (thanks to their photosynthesis days of living on the ocean's surface) and combustion releases that energy.

Environmental scientists measure concentrations of chemicals in water or in the air. They study the environmental effects of using catalysts in manufacturing.

Chemistry is used in mining to separate the rare earth metals needed for pretty much every piece of technology that exists today—every cell phone, every laptop. But toxic by-products are buried or left in tailings ponds. Is there a better way? Some scientists are looking back to biology—namely, bacteria—to find out if there's a less toxic path to retrieving these valuable elements.

It's Never Too Late to Program

Even when parents and educators do all they can to remove the filters and stigmas of who can succeed in STEM fields and who can't, too often girls get to high school and think they aren't smart enough for computer science or that they are too far behind their zealous peers who eat, live, and breathe programming. On top of that, some young women don't want to be that entrenched but believe that's the sacrifice one makes to be in computing fields like computer science.

If your high schooler is contemplating signing up for a programming class, even AP Computer Science, let her know that it's never too late to learn:

> The majority of peers who have been programming have been working with basic programming, although possibly at a skill level that helps them create some complex programs. Programmers can get pretty far using logical if-then statements, loops, variables, and functions. It's likely that they haven't yet moved on to the more complex ideas of pointers and recursion that a student will encounter in a computer science class.

🚀 Many peers who boast about their programming skills are exaggerating. Boasting adds a bit of competition, the same way it does on the athletic field—it's a way of asserting dominance in the classroom. Much of it isn't true or is irrelevant.

🚀 A newbie who walks into a programming class can easily be overwhelmed by all the jargon, but this jargon doesn't necessarily matter. If some of the students in the class are the type who eat, sleep, and breathe not just programming but technology in general, they may like to talk in specs—numbers and letters that string together to name processors, processor speeds, hard-drive capacities, and so on. If that's your girl's thing, great. If not, it's OK. It won't affect her ability to write code.

🚀 Give a high school student with no programming experience one year to catch up with the majority of her peers.

🚀 There are a few different AP Computer Science courses offered today. The newer AP Computer Science Principles were introduced in 2016 and have a focus on creative problem-solving and multidisciplinary endeavors. It's meant to be widely accessible (no prior experience necessary) and is not language-specific—high school teachers can choose what language they'd like to teach. The older AP Computer Science uses Java at the moment and is similar to a first course in computer science at many universities.

Today, every job relies heavily on knowing how to use technology, regardless of one's discipline. We use technology to do everything from conceptualizing and visualizing ideas, to making purchasing decisions, to collecting and analyzing data. Computer science helps individuals learn to use logic to structure thought processes. More important, it helps us to consider all possible scenarios and to appropriately use solutions that anticipate proper use—and misuse—of technology.

Ideally, computer science classes will move toward including more real-world projects that have an impact on society. Such courses are very successful. They help students see the big picture of how their skills can benefit humanity, and this ultimately improves student retention rates. This opens up more opportunities for teamwork on interdisciplinary projects. The days of computer scientists in their own little bubble are fading. Today, everything is about teamwork and understanding how to apply computer science skills to solving problems across disciplines.

Here's an example: Students from Tamil Nadu, India, saw a high rate of autism and blindness among young girls in their villages. They approached the local government officials and were told that there was no data to substantiate their observations. The students partnered with medical professionals from NGOs to visit households in the villages to gather the data using an app they created. The data was then uploaded to the cloud and the statistics overwhelmingly proved their case. Furthermore, data mining showed some indicators for the causes of these afflictions. Armed with this data, policy makers took action and provided support to the communities to address the issues.

Thinking about Careers

Sarah is a graduate student in mechanical engineering at Ohio State University. She remembers the moment in high school when she realized that her interests aligned with engineering. When Sarah was a junior in high school, she took AP Physics. She was not only the only junior in the class but also the only girl. Every boy in that class was going into engineering (most planned to go to Purdue) and they were, as Sarah says, "very much on this path." The boys jokingly tried to talk her into engineering, but she didn't take them seriously. She liked physics and calculus, but she hadn't considered the future too much. She didn't have her career figured out yet, but she knew that she was interested in alternative energy.

One day, the teacher took the class to a conference room where they joined a video chat with other students and engineers. There were a few engineers who were working in alternative energy, and it sounded to Sarah like something that fit what she wanted to do. As Sarah puts it, until this point she had an angle but not a path. This is typical of many girls, and it highlights the two main entry points to becoming an engineer or a scientist. Either the student is inspired by the science and technology itself, despite not necessarily having a particular problem she wants to solve, or she is inspired by a problem—and then someone shows her the STEM career path that will allow her to focus in that area.

Not surprisingly, the first entry point is much easier, as it requires only a general inclination toward a particular subject and leaves the specifics to be sorted out later. The second entry point, though, requires that a student not only develop this fairly specific "overarching principle" at an early age but that she then be able to link this principle to a STEM career. This is where parents and educators come in. It's not always easy to see the possibilities, and even enterprising students may not be able to achieve this on their own.

How many adults, upon hearing of Sarah's interest in alternative energy, would have suggested the pathway of mechanical engineering? The more exposure a girl has to actual careers, the better, and this shouldn't be relegated only to the AP classroom. Use the stories in this book to inspire your daughter, but always be on the lookout for new stories. Here are a few resources:

- The website Spark 101 has a series of short STEM videos that show STEM professionals working on a variety of problems, including bone density loss in space, concussions in youth football, and capturing wind energy in New York City.

- Contact local universities to see if they have STEM outreach groups that visit schools. Women in Engineering is one such organization, and many engineering schools have a WIE chapter. Minority Engineering Program ambassadors are college engineering students at Purdue University who visit schools in the Lafayette, Indiana, area.

- Look for programs like the chat event hosted by UK website I'm an Engineer, Get Me Out of Here. This chat is also a competition—and students are the judges. Classes book a half-hour chat session with engineers in which they can ask any questions they like. Students then vote for their favorite engineer—and that person wins a small purse of prize money to continue outreach efforts.

So, easy enough? If today there is too much inaction, if today girls are wandering through the halls of high school not knowing that their interest in recycling means that they might one day thrive as chemical engineers, then, OK, we adults can educate ourselves so that we are better positioned to help them, right? But there's another component in Sarah's story that is worth pointing out: even before the webinar she had the support and encouragement of her physics teacher and her male classmates.

In 2013 writer Eileen Pollack wrote a piece for the *New York Times* titled "Why Are There Still So Few Women in Science?" In 1978 Pollack and a classmate became the first two women to earn bachelor of science degrees in physics from Yale. Physics was Pollack's dream—but she left the field because of a lack of encouragement. Years later, after Lawrence Summers wondered at that Harvard luncheon why there weren't more tenured women professors in the sciences, a curious Pollack returned to Yale to host a tea in order to get at just that. She imagined things in the encouragement and support department had improved—after all, women's participation numbers in the sciences are much higher today than in 1978, so they had a much stronger network. Organizers of the event wondered if women would even bother to attend, but the room was packed with "80 young women (and three curious men)," many eager to share their stories.

Many of these bright Yale women had faced bias and even ridicule in high school science classrooms where they were only one of a handful of girls or, like Sarah, were the only female in the room. Imagine a class full of boys jokingly telling you your entire gender can't do physics while a male teacher refuses to stand up for you, or a teacher who jokes about grading your test on a different, easier curve—"the girl curve." These are some of the stories Pollack heard that day.

Compare this to Sarah's experience, where the joke wasn't "Why are you here?"—it was "Come on! Don't you want to be an engineer like us?"

The Positive Cancels the Negative

Sometimes, as in Alice's case, positive reinforcement is necessary to cancel out the negative. When Alice was a junior in high school, she, like Sarah, wasn't sure what she wanted to do or what universities she wanted to apply to. She went to visit the guidance counselor, who was the first person to look at Alice's math and science grades and recommend that Alice consider engineering. "That made so much sense," Alice says, "I don't know why I didn't think of it."

Alice struggled through a computer science course that year (she received a D one quarter), but she worked hard and scored a 4 out of 5 on the AP exam. "This gave me hope that I could survive engineering school," Alice says.

During her senior year in high school, Alice's Chinese teacher told her that girls should not be engineers. In Alice's case this only solidified her desire to "go against the norm." She enrolled at Tufts University and majored in computer engineering. While in college, a cousin-in-law had the same reaction, but by then, Alice says, it was too late to change her mind.

Engineer for a Week

Many colleges and universities offer programs that allow high school students to learn more about STEM opportunities. This is especially important for engineering since high schoolers apply directly to most engineering schools. Once a student has expressed interest in an engineering career, these programs can help cement that interest. They can also help a student narrow down a field of study. A good program will excite your daughter. She will meet other young women with similar interests, experience a bit of college life, and see the breadth of engineering opportunities available to her.

There are many different programs, and each has its own unique culture and focus. Make sure to assess its competitiveness and workload—if you are looking for something that will be fun, exciting, and eye-opening, you don't want your daughter to end up in an intense and challenging, even cutthroat program. Here's a sampling of the many programs out there:

- Prep for college admissions. **Purdue's Multiethnic Introduction to Engineering Academic Boot Camp** is a five-week program focused on engineering but also on preparing students for college through emphasis on boosting SAT scores.

- Get ready to be a freshman. The **University of Washington's WiSE Up Summer Bridge** is a four-and-a-half-week program for young women who will be entering the university's engineering program the following fall.

- Stay on campus for a week. **WiE Rise at Ohio State University** is a weeklong program for young women who are either sophomores or juniors in high school. There are social and recreational activities in the evening, on-campus presentations and activities, and off-campus field trips during the days.

- Be a day camper. The **University of Cincinnati** holds a one-week summer day camp for women interested in engineering and applied science. Learn about the different engineering departments, work on projects, and go on field trips to different corporate engineering plants in the Cincinnati area.

Don't Try to Engineer Her Success

With college looming on the horizon, parents can get a little nervous. Even those who were really good about letting their child find her own way early on can let stress about the future get the best of them when the kid is in high school and the stakes suddenly seem much higher. You may believe you're acting in her best interest, but if you're trying to engineer her success by micromanaging, you're not.

There are so many paths to a happy, productive future, and your daughter has to find her own way. In the interest of college applications, parents try to route their children along one particular path or another. Perhaps a girl should quit singing, because even though she loves it, it's still just a hobby, or she should forgo an art elective to make room for something more serious. Getting into college is a big deal, but the bumps on the road to adulthood can be a much bigger deal. If your daughter enjoys singing in a choir or expresses herself through her art, don't steal that (and her confidence) from her.

This applies to coursework as well. Some parents encourage their child not to take classes that will be too difficult, as a bad grade will adversely affect the student's GPA, or they encourage the child to drop out of courses in which she's not succeeding. This can happen if parents don't understand the future utility of more difficult math and science coursework, or if they don't truly believe that their daughter is capable. Push her to achieve. The difficulty and stress of higher-level trigonometry and calculus can make young women feel like failures if they are not empowered with the drive, determination, and confidence necessary to push through the challenging times, and so it's time to believe in them and point them toward future goals.

You want your child to find success, so instead of limiting her with micromanaging and a lack of career creativity, broaden her career knowledge and work with her to discover how to best put her talents and passions to use.

Face Your Own Fears

It's possible that even if you've spent the last fifteen or so years encouraging your daughter to embrace STEM in all sorts of wonderful ways, right now you've decided that maybe that's not what you really want for her. This likely isn't the kind of thought you are willing to share—but there it is.

Adults can spend a lot of time talking about gender stereotypes and the disparaging and hurtful remarks people can make, and can assume that these detractors must be awful people who don't want to see women succeed. But the truth is—sometimes these people are parents, and they're not awful people at all! Parents want their daughters to succeed so much that they worry about them—constantly. They worry that their daughter will pick the wrong major at the wrong college that will then lead to the wrong career. These worries can lead to subtle or not-so-subtle remarks and messages that doubt or discourage their girl.

What are some of the things they might worry about? Well, where to start?

Will the workload be too much? What the heck is "Orgo"? Will her professors be biased against her because she's a woman? Will she miss out on the college experience because she's holed up in a lab? What if she doesn't like her program? How will her classmates treat her? What if she fails a class? What if she's lost in her coursework and I can't help? What if she develops anxiety or depression? What if she can't make any friends because she's working so hard and her classmates are all antisocial guys who play *Halo* day and night?

Then there's the prospect of a job. Will the hours be too long? Will the work be too difficult? Is she smart enough? How will she meet a romantic partner if she's married to her job? What if she has children and wants to stay home with them? What if she needs to work part-time? Will she like working in such a male environment? Will she have to fight to be heard and to get promoted? Will she be happy? Will she wish one day that she had taken a less intense and more traditionally female job? Will she wish she had summers off?

You can't know what your daughter's future will bring, and no matter how hard you try to clear the path for her she will have her difficult times. Don't let your own fears, opinions, and perhaps even misperceptions hold her back from pursuing a dream career. Offer your support and your ear for listening. Help her make informed decisions. Learn more about her goals in order to allay some of your own concerns.

Careers

As your daughter advances through her high school coursework, she will deep-dive into some topics that will hopefully be of great interest to her. Discuss these careers with her as they align with her high school curriculum:

Concept	Related Career Example
Chemical Reactions	Forensic Science Technologist Chemical Engineer Chemist Biotechnology Engineer
Structure and Properties of Matter	Physicist Chemical Engineer Materials Engineer
Waves and Electromagnetic Radiation	Sound or Recording Engineer Electrical Engineer
Forces and Interactions	Aerospace Engineer Marine Engineer
Energy	Nuclear Engineer Petroleum Engineer Wind Energy Engineer Mechanical Engineer Electrical Engineer
Structure and Function	Biologist Biochemical Engineer Bioinformatics Technician
Matter and Energy in Organisms and Ecosystems	Zoologist Biologist Biochemical Engineer Electrical Engineer (brain model)

continued on next page . . .

Concept	Related Career Example
Interdependent Relationships in Ecosystems	Civil Engineer Environmental Engineer
Inheritance and Variation in Traits	Geneticist Molecular or Cellular Biologist Medical Physicist
Natural Selection and Evolution	Epidemiologist
Space Systems	Physicist
History of Earth	Mining and Geological Engineers
Earth's Systems	Geophysicist
Weather and Climate	Meteorologist Marine Engineer Atmospheric and Space Scientist
Human Sustainability	Humanitarian Engineer Atmospheric Scientist Electrical Engineer
Engineering Design	Industrial Engineer Human Factors Engineer UX Designer
Geometry	Mechanical Engineer Civil Drafter Architect Civil Engineer

continued on next page . . .

Concept	Related Career Example
Probability and Statistics	Actuary Statistician Cybersecurity Analyst
Algebra	Software Engineer
Trigonometry	Mechanical Engineer Architect
Calculus	Electrical Engineer

The College Search

A student considering a STEM career has much to think about as the college search begins. At the top of this list is deciding what type of school she wants to attend.

There are many institutes of technology (such as Rensselaer Institute of Technology, Worcester Polytechnic Institute, or Massachusetts Institute of Technology) that offer a chance to spend time with others who are also passionate about science and technology.

A student may want to spend her college days with a greater variety of people, or she may know that she wants to be able to take classes, or even double-major, in the humanities. In this case, she may be more interested in a large university with various specialized schools.

She may be in search of a more personalized opportunity. She may be attracted to the liberal arts or fine arts but may also want the advantage of creating her own interdisciplinary program that blends, for example, art and computer science. Such programs do exist, but they are unique to certain schools.

Community colleges have been ramping up their offerings in order to give students a more affordable pathway to a STEM degree. Students can earn an associate's degree or can transfer their credits to a four-year college or university.

Having an idea—or a few ideas—about what she might like to study will help her narrow her options down.

What Will She Study?

Many students investigate career options on the internet but are passive about their research approach. This "read only" type of individual will only read about topics but won't ask questions or interact with someone who truly knows what it means to be in that career. This approach usually leaves the searcher with a very binary view: *I will love it or hate it.* As a result, the whole story may not be portrayed accurately.

This can be especially true of STEM-oriented careers, which can at first blush sound overtechnical or dry. Say that she performs a quick internet search on "computer engineering." She'll be led to believe that computer engineers put parts together. This makes computer engineers sound like assembly-line workers. As a computer engineer, she might, like Karen, write programs to develop simulators, design microcontrollers to control robots to go to places humans cannot, and create image-processing algorithms for detecting cancers as well as finding threat objects in baggage at airports.

The most popular tech fields for women are biomedical, chemical engineering, and environmental engineering. Why? Because developing cures for diseases, providing clean water and sustainable energy, or helping disabled individuals regain their independence are really appealing careers that have a huge social impact. Most students are not aware of the social impact of the field of electrical engineering. Many, for example, do not know that electrical engineers are heavily involved in the development of renewable energy solutions.

Electrical engineering is not the only field with an image problem. By this point you will hopefully have spent time with your daughter talking about the many different ways STEM fields affect humans, animals, and the planet. Ideally, she also sees that today STEM fields intersect with each other as well as the arts and humanities in countless ways. If so, as your daughter reads that a computer engineer puts parts together, an electrical engineer solders circuits, and a civil engineer builds bridges, she will see the limitations in these definitions.

As an example, look at a few of the projects that the Nerd Girls have worked on:

> **Harvard Program in Refugee Trauma:** Refugees have suffered traumatic experiences that affect their health, but if medical professionals don't know the survivor's full trauma

history they may not treat them properly. For example, refugees may have symptoms of PTSD and depression, but those conditions might also mask an underlying condition such as a serious brain injury. The Harvard Program in Refugee Trauma asked the Nerd Girls to develop a technology that would help patients tell their trauma stories. The Nerd Girls worked with RFID tags—these tags are inexpensive, water resistant, and aren't of much use to a hacker without the corresponding reader. With RFID tags to store their stories, refugees would need to fill out a medical questionnaire only one time. This way, if a survivor met with a new doctor or faced a language barrier, he or she would be able to easily and accurately share personal history.

- **UAV Technology for Search and Rescue in Human Trafficking:** This project researched the use of unmanned aerial vehicles in search-and-rescue efforts in human trafficking.

- **Thacher Island Renewable Energy Project:** Thacher Island sits off the coast of Rockport, Massachusetts. On it sit the last operating twin lighthouses in the United States. The Nerd Girls were tasked with implementing alternative energy solutions on the island that would power the lighthouses and other buildings. The team worked with the EPA because the island is home to a bird sanctuary. They also worked with historians and preservationists to ensure that their work would allow the lighthouse to maintain its historical designation.

Clearing Up Misconceptions

The college selection process is daunting, and everyone will have an opinion. Sort through all the well-intentioned advice and help your daughter stay on track by keeping the following in mind:

- A school with a reputation for a prestigious professional program (such as a medical school) does not necessarily have the same quality of undergraduate education in all majors. Look carefully at the rankings for particular programs.

- Your daughter may get to rub elbows with renowned faculty right away, or she may not. It will depend on the school, and it doesn't necessarily come down to research institutions versus liberal arts colleges. At MIT, for example, all undergraduate courses—even introductory classes—are taught by professors. At some other schools, on the other hand, upwards of 20 percent of undergraduate courses might have a graduate teaching assistant as the primary instructor. (Keep in mind that this isn't necessarily a negative, though—a 2016 study asserts that undergraduates are more likely to stay with a major if the introductory course is taught by a graduate student!)

It wasn't that long ago that undergraduates conducting research was rare. Now it's common, and those who plan to go to graduate school, especially, will want research experience on their undergraduate résumé. But research work isn't guaranteed at most schools. Landing a position in a lab requires the same diligence, perseverance, and networking as landing a job. In fact, most of the time, lab positions aren't posted. Students need to take the initiative to visit labs, find out what work is being done, and make their own connections.

The bigger-name school isn't always the best choice. You want your daughter to be challenged but able to succeed. Most important, you want her to be happy. Successful STEM women come from a wide range of colleges and universities. Young women may find that cutting-edge research in their particular area of interest just happens to be taking place at a smaller, lesser-known school. This can lead to great opportunities.

How to Get the Most out of a College Visit

College tours are often led by outgoing, personable student volunteers. These tours are designed to sell the school to you and your child. They are, in effect, a type of marketing. Come prepared with questions—yours and your daughter's—so that you can all get the most out of your tour. Or, if she is taking the tour on her own, help her brainstorm a list of questions before she goes. There will be many questions that the tour guide won't be able to answer, but with any luck he or she can point her in the right direction when the tour is over. Once that acceptance letter is in hand, you and your daughter will have even more questions.

Make your questions specific. For example, don't ask how many women are studying "engineering" in general—the numbers will vary greatly from degree to degree. Chemical and biochemical engineering will have higher numbers of women, which will inflate the numbers across engineering as a whole. If your daughter is thinking about becoming an electrical engineer, she'll want to ask the percentage of women specifically in the electrical engineering department.

Here are some other questions your daughter might want to ask that are particularly relevant to young women considering STEM and STEM-related majors:

- *Can we see a classroom, lab, or the building that houses classes in the major I'm interested in?* A college tour may include a look at a classroom or lab, but it will likely be in one of the newest, flashiest buildings, and your daughter may never set foot there once she's a student. You and your daughter want to see where she'll be spending her time.

- *Where do the students in this major get internships and summer jobs?* Employers will be looking for work experience. Some schools are fantastic at helping students find summer jobs and internships, others not so much.

- *How many full tenured professors are there in this major?*

- *How many full tenured female professors are there in this major?*

- *Where can I read about or meet the professors in this major?*

- *Can I see your exit survey data? How many students have job offers, and where are they going?* You are not looking for flashy marketing brochures with pictures of students gathered in circles on the lawn. You want to see actual data.

- *Is cross-collaboration encouraged between departments, and can you give some examples?*

- *What are any extra costs associated with this major?*

- *What are the technology requirements for this major?*

- *Are students guaranteed to get into classes?* At some schools, popular classes can have long waiting lists, and each school will have its own class-selection policy that may prioritize students by seniority or major. Courses that require the use of particular equipment such as editing machines may be especially restrictive.

Do I apply directly to the engineering school or do I apply to the program after I'm enrolled at the university?

 How many students drop out of this major in their freshman year? Why? What is the process for transferring between schools (if, for example, I decide to switch from the engineering school to the liberal arts school)?

 If applying directly to an engineering school, what are the liberal arts requirements?

 How much opportunity is there for me to take electives in non-engineering interests?

 What are the study abroad opportunities?

 What is your policy on students being treated as adults? In other words, will a parent be sent critical correspondence, such as financial bills?

 What are the options available to help students return safely to their rooms when they are out late at night? Depending on her major, your daughter will likely spend a lot of time in labs.

 What is the incidence of sexual misconduct cases at this school?

 What is the incidence of violent crime and sexual assault at this school?

 What is the school's procedure for handling sexual assault allegations?

The Skinny on Co-ops and Internships in STEM Fields

STEM employers want to see that even entry-level job seekers have some experience under their belts, and opportunities such as cooperative education programs (co-ops) and internships build résumés. In this way, they help drive more equal access to the workforce and level the playing field for students who do not have a strong network such as family connections to draw upon. And the experience alone is worth so much. Work experience at a particular company helps a college student figure out not just what she wants out of a career but also what kind of company culture she prefers.

Internships generally take place over the summer or as a part-time job during the school year. While they offer flexibility, this part-time status can make it harder for a student to deep-dive into a project, and some students report that this means that they don't feel "as much a part of the team." Still, internships are a great way to test the waters with no commitment. Depending on the company or institution offering the internship, pay can vary from great to none at all.

Michelle, a mechanical engineer at Ohio State University (OSU), used three internships to figure out what she wanted to do when she graduated. OSU doesn't have a mandatory co-op program, but the career service center actively brings in many companies to hire students. When she was a sophomore she interned at a major car manufacturer. She did two rotations with a company that makes minimally invasive surgery devices, and, finally, she networked at a Society of Women Engineers event to land an internship at a food-manufacturing plant.

A co-op, on the other hand, is generally a full-time temporary work assignment. Instead of taking classes for a semester, for example, a student will report to her co-op position. There is often an established relationship between the company and the school, and the co-op is usually listed on a student's transcript with a pass-fail grade. These co-ops are often paid positions and provide the benefit of a longer duration and a more strategic investment in the student. Students in co-ops might find themselves with more responsibility and a bigger chunk of an actual project than they would have during an internship.

Northeastern University in Boston is a popular choice among STEM-oriented students because of its well-known co-op program. The engineering co-op program includes a co-op course, and through this course a coordinator helps students pick a co-op that best suits their career goals, skills, and interests. Part of the experience includes self-reflection. Co-ops last for a full semester, and students can complete either two co-ops in a four-year program or up to three co-ops in a five-year program.

If your daughter is interested in a co-op program, make sure to investigate the financial impacts fully. It's unusual to charge tuition during the co-op semester, but you would continue to pay room and board if she still lives on campus. Ask about the impact of the co-op period on a family's financial commitment, and ask for a full picture of the bookkeeping around the co-op semester and the subsequent return to coursework, including financial aid, meal plans, and housing.

If Her Test Scores Aren't up to Par

In the United States, the hallmark of college admissions has long been the SAT, a test owned by the nonprofit College Board. It has undergone several incarnations, the latest in 2016, which brought the SAT back to its original 1,600-point scale but now with an optional essay component. Over the last decades, the ACT has been gaining in popularity. The test was long used mainly at midwestern colleges, but many colleges now accept ACT scores in lieu of SAT scores. Other schools are more test-flexible, meaning that students may submit scores from tests such as AP tests or the International Baccalaureate.

A criticism of these tests is that they give an advantage to higher-income students, and deans of admission at many schools are taking notice. Right now, many schools in America are ditching or downplaying tests as admissions criteria. Smith College made tests optional after research showed correlations between testing and race, testing and parental educational attainment, and, most significant of all, testing and family income. Many lower-income students don't have the means to pay for special test-prep courses or to retake exams multiple times.

It's hard to imagine applying to a STEM program without that all-important math SAT score, and as you might guess, test-optional admissions policies are more likely to be found at liberal arts colleges. Still, in 2007, Worcester Polytechnic Institute became the first nationally ranked science and engineering university to follow suit.

Your daughter might want to consider withholding test scores if she feels that they do not paint a realistic picture of her abilities. If so, she will want to ensure that the other parts of her application go above and beyond in demonstrating who she is and what she is capable of achieving. Grades continue to be an important admissions factor, and stellar teacher recommendations will go a long way in speaking to a student's work ethic, general attitude, and potential. Many test-optional schools encourage students to differentiate themselves by supplementing applications with art and design portfolios or descriptions of individual research projects and work experience. A student who institutes a litter clean-up day at her school, for example, will be able to use that experience to demonstrate her leadership and passion for the environment.

There are currently roughly eighty schools that are test optional or that are piloting test-optional programs. If your daughter struggles with testing, you may want to investigate some of these schools that look beyond scores, but be sure to inquire if going test-free will affect grants and scholarships. (Follow up with a search online, as this list is constantly growing and changing):

- Bates College, ME
- Bryn Mawr College, PA
- Smith College, MA
- University of Massachusetts Lowell
- Wake Forest University, NC
- Wesleyan College, CT
- Worcester Polytechnic Institute, MA

Finally, a word about the inevitable. There's a good chance your daughter will receive a rejection letter from one or more schools she applies to. See your role as cheerleader for your girl through to the finish line. You encouraged her to hold fast to her love of both American Girl dolls *and* science experiments in elementary school; you didn't let her become discouraged from joining that mostly boys robotics club in middle school; you cheered her on when that B in algebra almost got her down; so don't let a college rejection, even one from her top-choice school, derail her dreams.

Remind her that colleges reject undergraduate students for all sorts of reasons that have nothing at all to do with skills and intellect, including their need to achieve a balance of students from various geographic and socioeconomic backgrounds, a balance between genders, and so on.

Be prepared to inspire your daughter with examples of scrappy women who fought for everything they got or people who turned their lives around after disappointment. Here's one: College didn't exactly work out the way Karen planned. She dreamed about going to Tufts University, but she didn't get in. Her father told her that "they'd want her one day." He was right: years later she became a professor in Tufts' Department of Electrical and Computer Engineering.

College:
Getting Strategic

As your daughter heads off to college, you will be parenting from a distance, but your role as supporter and encourager is still critical. College presents new opportunities but also new challenges. Not only can coursework be more difficult, but also the stakes can seem much higher. Some students, like chemical engineer Kara, who had graduated at the top of her high school class, face the surprise of "not being the smartest person in the room." Women in some majors will find that there are not many other women in the room, and this can leave them feeling isolated. For students who aren't sure that they "belong" in STEM to begin with, switching fields can be tempting. Your relationship with your daughter may have changed, but your positive attitude, your belief in her, and your willingness to talk about the good and the bad will still go a long way toward helping her combine her talents with STEM.

Major Decisions

Many students spend their freshman year without declaring a major. Before making that decision, your daughter can investigate a field in the following ways:

 Take advantage of a great resource on campus—professors and upperclassmen.

Meet people who hold the degree she is considering. Many professional organizations are eager for students to attend their meetings. They understand that their members' experiences can inspire youth to find careers that not only provide financial independence but also will create future technologies to benefit humanity. The Institute of Electrical and Electronics Engineers is a great example. By meeting IEEE members, students get experience, find mentors, and interact with the famous individuals doing the dream jobs that are changing the world and stimulating the economy. These interactions could be via webinars, mentor networks, or local chapters all around the world.

Network within student chapters of professional societies such as the Association for Women in Mathematics, the Society of Women Engineers, the Institute of Electrical and Electronics Engineers, Women in Engineering, the Association for Women in Science, and the American Medical Women's Association.

Look at job postings to see what kind of skills, experience, and degrees employers are seeking in candidates.

Joan Lampert has spent over two decades coaching people through all sorts of career transitions. She has one more suggestion for students deciding which major to choose: talk to adults. Encourage your

RESEARCH WISELY

The Resources section at the end of this book provides websites that are helpful for researching different fields. The websites of professional organizations, university science and engineering programs, and government agencies provide a more detailed look into the real world of STEM applications than a less targeted internet search can provide.

daughter to talk to your friends and relatives to find out what they do and whether that sounds interesting. "She should start to do this lovely kind of research and make some nice friends along the way," Lampert says.

What kind of questions should a student ask?

- What's it like to be a . . . ?
- What's the field like?
- How hard is it?
- How do women fare in this field?
- What do you do every day?
- What do you like best about your role?
- What do you like least?
- What qualifications would I need to succeed?

What to Expect in STEM Majors

The remarkable advances in science and technology over the last few decades have made college STEM courses much more interesting and accessible than they used to be. Real-world projects and research opportunities are easier to come by, and sophisticated digital tools have opened up new ways of learning.

Today, computer science concentrations are available in areas such as artificial intelligence, bioinformatics, and data mining, and computer science has a strong interdisciplinary focus across some campuses. Electrical and computer engineering courses may have the same fundamentals, but advances in robotics and other hands-on learning methods make even introductory college courses a lot more exciting and fun. College makerspaces stocked with equipment such as 3-D printers let even first- and second-year students easily prototype designs. In terms of opportunity, it's a great time to be a college student. Below is a brief look at what your student may expect in different STEM majors.

Science and Math

Her major will likely reside within a college of arts and sciences. There, she will likely need to satisfy a distribution requirement, meaning that the courses she takes will spread across humanities, arts, social sciences, natural sciences, and mathematics. Different colleges and universities will have different requirements.

A science major will take a number of courses in her particular discipline, as well as a number of electives in the other sciences that interest her. She will likely have the option to specialize in a subdiscipline or a cross-disciplinary area and may be able to take courses in engineering, computer science, or law that will help her reach future goals.

Math graduates have a number of career options available to them across a variety of fields. With this in mind, she may choose a standard math major in which she'll study calculus, linear algebra, differential equations, and more, or she may choose an applied math major.

Applied math allows a student to put math to work in other fields such as engineering, economics, or science, or even social sciences, languages, or history. For example, it was Stanley Milgram from Harvard who studied human social networks to give us the idea of six degrees of separation. Core courses for the first year or so will likely be the same as a standard math major.

Engineering

A future engineer will likely apply directly to the engineering school, but she may not need to declare a major her freshman year. This is because her first year will consist of a set of core courses. She'll probably take a writing course, a math course, a science, and introductory engineering courses related to technology and the engineering design process. These will give her a taste of the engineering program, but she should still use this year to get to know upperclassmen or professors in various majors so she can explore potential disciplines.

Her second year will likely continue on with next-level core courses. For example, even chemical engineers will take a foundational course in electrical systems. Once an upperclassman, her days will be full of concentration courses and labs in her major. She will have some leeway, but there are still many required courses.

Over the course of her undergraduate days, she will have some electives to fill. When her days are full of science and math, electives can provide an opportunity to study other interests such as creative writing, psychology, art, or history. You never know how these might blend one day with her engineering degree. Or she can take business and communications classes to position herself for a specific career.

"I came to college knowing I wanted to study engineering but was unsure which discipline. From my physics mechanics course and interest in robotics, I decided to pursue mechanical engineering and began those core classes sophomore year, including calculus 3, linear algebra, and differential equations. I had never excelled in math, but I knew that to become an engineer I would have to push through these courses. The biggest piece of advice I have is to take advantage of school tutoring centers, office hours, and to try to form study groups with friends. College is also a time for exploration, and I have been able to incorporate my interest in computer science, art, the environment, and writing through elective courses." —Laura, *mechanical engineering student at the University of Pittsburgh*

Information Science and Technology

The field of information science and technology is incredibly broad. What is it? Is it working for a big consulting firm designing custom software, or is it working behind the scenes to strengthen networks and stop hackers? It can be either, and a lot more. Take a deep look into the programs offered at different universities (or even within the same university) to see the many flavors of IST specialties.

At George Mason University in Fairfax, Virginia, an undergraduate can apply to the Department of Information Sciences and Technology, which sits within the Volgenau School of Engineering, and receive a bachelor of science in information technology. This student will take courses with professors who specialize in such areas as cybersecurity, learning analytics, and data mining, and she may choose a concentration in information security, networking and telecommunications, web development and multimedia, database technology and programming, health IT, or information technology entrepreneurship.

Computer Science

Computer science courses may be housed in either liberal arts or engineering colleges. Some schools offer the degree in both places, and it will be up to your daughter to choose whether she wants a liberal arts or an engineering education. Some programs offer research opportunities for students, and undergrads can sometimes apply to be teaching assistants working in computer labs.

A student majoring in computer science may combine her major with another interest. For example, Brown University offers concentrations in computational biology, math–computer science, and computer science–economics.

Some traditional liberal arts colleges that have not previously offered any type of computer science major are planning to add new programs. These schools aren't necessarily interested in traditional comp sci, though. Take, for example, Union College in New York. Union has successfully built up an interdisciplinary computing program that serves the needs of its liberal arts students. Through this program, students can combine computer science courses with almost any other major— be it art or psychology—to create an interdepartmental major.

> *"I knew nothing about computer science until my first day of class freshman year, so my worries were astronomical. Each year I've learned many new aspects about computers and programming languages I didn't know existed. The coursework gets tougher and more time consuming, but at some point you realize there are plenty of people who also struggle and are willing to help you, and then you worry less and everything is OK." —Savanh L., computer science student at Embry–Riddle Aeronautical University*

Endless Possibilities

If a student chooses her school carefully, she may have the chance to augment her liberal arts or fine arts degree with STEM coursework that is relevant and interesting to her. As higher education changes in response to the STEM needs of the twenty-first century, many schools are moving toward multidisciplinary teaching and cross-collaboration, but they are doing this in different ways. Certain schools like Lafayette College in Pennsylvania and Harvey Mudd College in California are at the forefront of liberal arts institutions that are blending liberal arts with science and engineering to provide students with a well-rounded education that prepares them to tackle real-world problems.

At large universities, a student should have the chance to put together a suitable double major. A student interested in becoming an art conservator might combine majors in art history and chemistry. One interested in working abroad might combine a STEM degree with a foreign language. A journalism major who also has a background in biology or technology, for example, will be better positioned to develop a nice writing niche that could also lead to corporate work or expert status in a field, as journalism major Sally French did when she combined her degree and her love of drones into the highly successful *Drone Girl* blog. A psychology major might consider a minor in human factors engineering.

If a young woman pursuing a degree in the fine arts chooses a school that also offers STEM degrees, she might relish the opportunity to combine her interests with a minor or double major in a STEM subject. An artist might find that a science degree leads to opportunities to work in scientific animation, or she may find that a major in engineering design is a satisfying way to incorporate art into her career.

Building Personal and Social Skills

Networking. Negotiating. Self-promoting. These three skills can be difficult for women. In fact, many women prefer to let their hard work speak for itself. It won't seem particularly fair, though, when a savvy self-promoter beats your daughter and her hard work out of a promotion. The good news is that these skills are built on the same habits of self-esteem, perseverance, creativity, and sense of self that you have been reinforcing for years, and even a young woman who doesn't enjoy employing these skills can stand up for herself when it counts. It just takes knowledge, practice, and preparation.

Refining these skills in college can help a young woman develop relationships with mentors and role models, make contacts within academia and in her chosen industry, and even seize opportunities like internships, research positions, conferences, and competitions.

Networking Isn't Awful

Networking doesn't need to be about false personae and schmoozing at cocktail parties, and it's not always about getting the job. In fact, it relies heavily on the same traits that make someone a good friend and an organized student. Looked at from this angle, many young women should be confident about their networking ability.

A STEM student will be rewarded if she builds strong networks with her peers. Much of the coursework is collaborative, and so a student capable of building a strong team will be positioned for success. Those who hope to work in a science research lab or obtain an internship will also need to do some serious networking with professors and industry professionals. Career counselor Joan Lampert has this advice to help students develop the networking skills that are authentic to them:

- **Networks need maintaining.** It's a continuous event. A student shouldn't drop in on someone, request a favor, and then disappear. Networks are relationships that happen to be based on the idea that when we help each other, we all benefit. Your daughter's network should be a community of people with different skills and connections. Homework assignments in many STEM courses are problem sets—and professors *expect* students to form groups to work on these assignments together. Networking is practically a necessity. Look at it this way: a student can jump the hurdles herself, or she can surround herself with others who can help. A strong, lasting study group will have students who excel in different areas.

- **Networking is about organization.** Your daughter should maintain a spreadsheet that lists whom she talked to, when she talked to them, and what they talked about with the understanding that she'll keep a conversation going. Maybe she reads an article that relates to something they discussed, so she forwards it in an email.

- **It's not too early to start.** A student's networking skills may be less polished, but seeking people out for advice and doing so in a way that says, "I can help you, too. I want to do my part," is nice. College students shouldn't let inexperience stop them. Professionals love hearing from students, and they grant them a lot of leeway.

- **Networking happens everywhere.** She should network with parents of friends and friends of parents. She should start building networks with current classmates. It may be hard to envision now, but as years pass and classmates become established in different areas, those connections will be important.

 Use professors in a similar way. Your daughter should have career conversations with her professors. Who should she reach out to? What should she be reading? What are the professors working on? Students looking for research opportunities will be in a better position if they've already established relationships, and professors may just think of them when an internship opportunity comes up.

 Go to events. Your daughter should join professional societies like IEEE and attend the young professional activities on campus or in the area.

Prepare to Self-Promote

Many suggest that talking about achievements doesn't come as naturally to women as it does to men in part because it's not received as well— by both men and women. Unfortunately, other women can be a tough crowd. Self-promotion runs counter to the stereotypical female traits of modesty and passivity. Not only that, but making others feel good about themselves through flattery has long been seen as a feminine skill. Because of this, women who want to appear confident are often worried about instead being seen as show-offs.

In addition, women studying STEM fields can face particular challenges. Subtle biases can erode confidence. A Hispanic woman engineering student recalls walking the halls of her department at Stanford and being asked if perhaps she was lost. A physics student remembers male classmates doubting her calculations. A woman at MIT says she was once asked if she thought she had been admitted "because she was a woman." Instances like these can make a young woman feel like she doesn't belong.

Being prepared to self-promote will help young women with their confidence, and when a professor is looking for a student to join a research team, or when your daughter is called upon to deliver a pitch for a business idea, it will be easier for her to talk about herself. The following tips will help your daughter speak up for herself in a thoughtful and natural way that widens her network and brings opportunity:

 Write and memorize an elevator pitch. If your daughter is not a particularly confident extemporaneous speaker, recommend that she memorize a short introduction that she can use to get a conversation off on the right foot. "I've been interested in microbiology since high school, and they have such a great program here," is a much better answer to "How'd you end up at this school?" than "It's a good school." It might lead to a deeper and more memorable conversation, which is what networking is all about. Self-promotion doesn't mean she's bragging about her award-winning high school science fair project every chance she gets—she's letting someone know who she is and what she's interested in.

🐾 **Write and memorize a second elevator pitch.** This pitch should speak more to her accomplishments and goals. This way, when someone asks her to expand on her work and interests, she'll have a polished and confident reply: "I'm working in Dr. Panetta's lab. I've been learning about digital imaging, and I'm looking forward to working on a project with a graduate student next fall. Her name's Lindsay. Do you know her?" Speaking up about her accomplishments is really just a natural way of conversing and getting to know someone.

🐾 **Develop a culture of promoting others.** When women combine their talents, everyone wins. Promoting others helps build a community.

🐾 **Know your strengths.** A young woman who has spent time in middle school and high school considering her strengths and weaknesses will be better prepared to naturally self-promote. She should believe in herself and her ability to do a job as well as anyone else.

🐾 **Speak up in the interest of helping others.** "I'd love to help with the project you were talking about earlier. I have three years of programming under my belt, and I see a lot of overlap between what you need and the experiences I had interning last summer."

Negotiation Is a Skill

If young women build their negotiating skills over time, they'll be more confident when it comes time to negotiate the big deals like salary, research projects, and job benefits. And college can offer plenty of opportunities for practice. Consider this example, which many women in male-dominated STEM courses are familiar with: the group project where they are given the role of note-taker or presentation designer instead of the more technical or analytical role they would prefer.

- **Mind-set is number one in negotiating.** No one is doing her any favors. She is doing them a favor. Confidence and the belief that she deserves something as much as another person is key in recognizing that she is in a negotiating situation to begin with.
- **View negotiating as problem-solving.** She is not being demanding or greedy in asking for something that seems fair.
- **Be prepared.** What is she asking for? Why does she want it? Who benefits? Why does she deserve it?
- **Seek out opportunities to practice.** Remind her not to strive only to make other people happy but to find fair and reasonable situations in her personal as well as in her academic life.

College Challenges

Gender bias and fear of failure go hand in hand as two of the top challenges that a young woman pursuing a STEM degree will face.

Gender Bias

Say that you surveyed seventeen hundred biology students (where numbers are fairly equally split between male and female) to nominate the "stars" in their introductory biology course. Who do they think is doing exceptionally well? As the men would tell it, other men are. This isn't just about first impressions, either. Females with high grades and strong class participation couldn't catch a break relative to males with high grades and strong class participation, leading this study's authors to determine that "being male is a prerequisite for celebrity status."

The point of the study was to examine why women leave the sciences at a higher rate than men. Perhaps a student's confidence is influenced by her peers. As the authors point out, it's not so much outright discrimination as it is an accumulation of small events that can make a woman feel unwelcome or undeserving, and can have an effect on her especially when she is wading into her major and wondering if she made the right choice.

Columbia University's Graduate School of Arts and Sciences Teaching Center noted that males tend to talk in the classroom in order to assert their status, and they can take a more argumentative tone. Women are less likely to want to share ideas so that they may be evaluated by classmates. Males give longer answers and speak more often without raising their hands. Females answer in more tentative terms ("I think . . ." and "I guess . . ."), are interrupted more frequently, including by other women, and don't talk for long. Perhaps because of these differences, professors tend to call on male students (and to call them by name) more often.

Such behavior is not necessarily confined to STEM college lecture halls—your daughter will likely find the same dynamic in a history or economics course—but add in stereotype threat, and it can make a young woman lose confidence and question whether she should be in this course. This is especially damaging to freshmen and sophomores who are still adjusting to college. They may already be wondering if they have what it takes. They may have felt comfortable in a high school setting with familiar classmates and teachers and now may feel adrift. It can help to be aware that these situations are often more common in the first years of college as students jockey to impress each other and faculty. A student will not feel as alone, and will be more apt to see these as temporary obstacles if she knows others feel the same uncertainty. She may find that as she gets deeper into her major and classes get smaller, the tone shifts as camaraderie builds and friendships develop.

> *"While I am lucky enough to go to a college with a lot of women in the computer science major, I do face some bias at times. I find that men often speak over women who are answering questions in class, or they make insensitive remarks. It can be aggravating, but surrounding myself with awesome women in the major has made it a lot more bearable." —Hannah, computer science and biomedical engineering student at Tufts University*

Fear of Failure

Too often a lack of mathematical confidence, not of ability, turns girls away from STEM. But your daughter has made it this far, and now here she is in college where perhaps she has chosen a STEM field of study. Unfortunately, lack of confidence could still be her undoing.

If your daughter has moved along the STEM pathway with general ease, suddenly hitting upon a difficult math course such as Calculus I in college can make her doubt her ability to succeed in a STEM career. This may be her first big failure moment, which is unfortunate because there's a good chance Calculus I isn't going to make or break her career.

Here's a secret of Calculus I at most universities: most students sitting in that classroom have taken this course already. If your daughter is taking calculus for the first time, she may look around the room and think that everyone else is smarter than she is—they're all *getting* this so quickly. Of course they are! They've seen it before!

> *"I was really good at math in high school, receiving As with minimal studying. But college calculus was an entirely different story. During my first quarter of undergrad, I got a 0 percent on my first three calculus quizzes. I was completely distraught, and I remember calling my mom to tell her I was going to fail out of engineering. Thankfully, that didn't happen! I realized I needed to change my study habits and work harder in this class, so I did. The hard work definitely did pay off—I recovered my grade to an A–. Failure is hard, but it can lead you to making positive changes." —Sarah W., mechanical engineering graduate student at Ohio State University*

A Degree Is a Tool

In 2014 engineer Courtney Gras was named one of Forbes 30 Under 30 in the area of energy, but she's modest about it. "It's not that I'm some incredible person with incredible talents who was able to blaze my own path," she says. "That's not it at all! I was certainly not a straight-A student; I'm not the best at everything."

Courtney's secret is that she spent time understanding not just what she was good at but also what her natural strengths and interests were. From there, she worked strategically to find a career that suited her. In doing so, she had to make the difficult decision to leave what she had always thought was her dream job as an electrical engineer at NASA.

Trying to be good at everything is exhausting—and it doesn't work. In fact, in trying to be good at everything, a young woman risks never discovering and fully embracing her best self. Many bright and ambitious young women learn this late in life, if ever, as they strive to fulfill expectations that may not truly be their own.

Through self-reflection, Courtney determined that communication, organization, and leadership were her key strengths. She may have been at NASA, but she knew that what she really wanted was to run her own energy start-up.

Understanding one's skills and talents makes key decisions more obvious, thus allowing a young woman to breeze more easily through life's setbacks. "Who cares if I'm not the best at this task?" she gets to say. "My strengths are elsewhere."

What to do about those tasks that are not her strong suit? Courtney's advice is this: "Focus on your strengths and build a team around you that will compensate for your weaknesses." She explained, "I realized that I'm not the best analytical engineering type person, so I'll be most effective in my organization if I can surround myself with people who are really great engineers so I can focus on my strengths."

If Courtney had it to do over again, would she major in business, or marketing, perhaps, instead of electrical engineering? Not at all. Courtney grew up fascinated by NASA and video games. She loved her courses at the University of Akron, and without those courses she wouldn't be where she is today. She loved her time at NASA, where she worked with the smartest, friendliest, most supportive team. She is able to successfully run an engineering firm because she has a solid engineering background. A young college student should think of her major as one part of the whole package, and she should choose her major and even a first job deliberately for the way in which it will round out her skill set.

Having Fun

Don't worry—joining the ranks of young women in STEM majors doesn't mean your daughter will be subjected to one long stand against gender bias throughout college, or four long years of impossibly difficult courses. There are bumps, to be sure, as young adults figure out some truly vexing questions, compare themselves to others, lose out on opportunities, and persevere over decisions that seem life altering.

But in there, too, should be excitement and fun. Hopefully, your daughter has chosen a major that she enjoys. Perhaps she has a plan for the future, or maybe not yet, but if she continues to advance by taking small steps and forays into different classes and research projects and summer jobs, she will find her way.

> "Some of my favorite memories come from hackathons—thirty-six- to forty-eight-hour events dedicated to working with a team to develop, prototype, code, and pitch a new application or product. Traveling to hackathons at MIT, University of Michigan, and University of Pennsylvania, I was able to meet students passionate to solve a certain problem, and we would form a team. I enjoyed the collaborative spirit of the hackathons. Female participation in hackathons is low, and a speculated reason for this is that hackathons promote a 'bro culture.' So, I partnered with the computer science, engineering, and business departments at my university to cofound She Innovates, an exclusive all-women's hackathon. I am proud of She Innovates, now in its third year, which helps provide a collaborative building environment, tech talks, and mentoring for women to team up and develop awesome applications." —Laura, mechanical engineering student at the University of Pittsburgh

What the Future Brings

After college your daughter will embark on either a first career or a graduate degree. Whatever her version of success may be, you have done her a remarkable service by not only being engaged in her education but also allowing her to discover and nurture her authentic self. She will have ups and downs in her career, but this combination of self-knowledge and STEM confidence will give her the passion and perseverance to reach her goals.

But is it enough to cheer only for our own daughters? In the United States, it is easy to take girls' access to education for granted. Around the world, many girls have no such access, and the results are tragic. Education can be a matter of life and death. Educated mothers have much lower rates of infant and maternal mortality. They are able to provide more nutritious food and give appropriate medical attention to their children. Women who are educated better understand their rights and experience greater freedom.

Inspiration can be found in stories like that of a young Jordanian woman named Ayat Amr. When Ayat was offered an internship at Microsoft in Germany, her father told her that she would not be able to go. In Jordanian culture young women are not permitted to travel alone. Undeterred, Ayat secured partial funding so that her father could accompany her as her chaperone. Today, Ayat's father is one of her biggest supporters in her mission to change the way women are viewed in Jordanian society. Ayat has done much work to bring STEM training to the women and children of Jordan, knowing that the benefits go far beyond the technical skills they learn, and she has held well-received events for both men and women where she encourages men to support their sisters, wives, and daughters in doing what they love.

Then there is Salma Abbasi. Salma is a technologist, philanthropist, and social activist. She helps countries around the world develop information technology solutions in the areas of security as well as sustainable social, economic, and environmental development. She cares greatly about the treatment of women and works to find innovative solutions to long-standing problems. In 2007 Salma turned her focus to bringing OB-GYN services to a rural area of Pakistan where women were dying because of the lack of medical care. The pure-IT solution—setting up telemedicine sites across the rural area—did nothing to help the problem: internet service and electricity at the sites were both spotty at best; there was no one to troubleshoot technical problems; and on top of all that, no one bothered to show up.

Salma talked to the men and the village elders. She discovered that the women were not allowed to travel alone, and that the men just couldn't take time off from their farming to walk the fifteen and a half miles to the site with the hope that the connections would be working that day. This is where Salma's problem-solving shines. She made the space multifunctional, thereby giving men more reasons to make the trip. While the women receive lifesaving medical treatments, the men now can not only buy fertilizer and seeds from a fertilizer company but also discuss farming practices. They can get their National Pakistani ID cards at kiosks set up at the facility. They can even receive computer training thanks to the internet capability.

As we look to the many challenges that we face globally—climate change, poverty, access to clean water, bringing aid to the many affected by conflict—we hope to inspire young women to take on these challenges, and we are optimistic that, with all of our help, the next generation will be one that doesn't just tolerate diversity but celebrates and honors it. The world's problems will be solved by involving as many perspectives as we can.

By raising a daughter who is fearless about tackling new STEM challenges while also remaining true to her authentic self, you have raised a daughter who will, in her own way, change the world. We wish her well!

ACKNOWLEDGMENTS

Thank you to my mother and father, Rita and Ralph Panetta, who are always there to support everything I do. Thank you to electrical engineering role model and brilliant technology CEO Suja Ramnath for her friendship and support.

This book would not have been possible if my coauthor, Katianne Williams, had not excelled at extracting years of STEM and Nerd Girl life experiences from my brain to help me put it all in writing.

My colleagues at IEEE (the Institute of Electrical and Electronics Engineers) have helped support and build my career through invaluable mentorship, professional development, and leadership training from my student days and continue to support me to this day.

I have been fortunate to have traveled around the world to meet thousands of young aspiring students. Their energy and passion has inspired me throughout the years to continue this STEM outreach work. Watching students grow and flourish into strong, confident professionals has been my reward, and I thank them for letting me know that my work has had an impact on their lives.

Thank you to my Tufts University students, my research team, and longtime research partner, Dr. Sos Agaian, for helping me innovate technology to change the world.

Thank you to Keyana Tennant, Dr. Arthur Winston, and Dr. Sinaia Nathanson.

A special thanks to my Nerd Girl partners Paola di Florio and Karen Johnson for their years of collaborations. Thank you to my K&L Gates legal team Christopher Centurelli and Phi Lan Tinsley for their advice and guidance.

Finally, thank you to the first ladies of "magic," Barbara Eden, the late Elizabeth Montgomery, and Emma Watson, who perhaps without knowing it, have inspired me and millions of other girls and women to use our imagination and engineering skills to make the magic real.

—KAREN

Thank you, Brian, for supporting me through the writing of this book. You say the right things at the right time, and you have given me the space and time to follow this particular dream, as well as so many others.

I could not possibly name all the people who responded to my request for an interview with an immediate and enthusiastic yes. Your reactions truly amazed me. From friends, relatives, and previous interviewees, to those I hunted down over LinkedIn or through webpage contact forms, I can honestly say that the community of women in STEM is a strong, supportive group that cares greatly about helping future generations of women. I especially want to acknowledge the many students who shared their stories; the young girls at Girls, Inc., in Lynn, Massachusetts, for their conversation; and the teachers and students in New Bedford, Massachusetts, who invited me and my daughter to their STEAM night.

My many coffee-shop conversations with Karen provided not only the material for this book but also welcome mentorship. Karen's energy and dream-big attitude is always uplifting.

My years at *IEEE Women in Engineering Magazine* have given me the opportunity to meet so many wonderful people and to study so many interesting topics. These stories have changed the way I view the world, and they fill me with such optimism. Every day, the men and women of science are making remarkable achievements.

To my family, for their continued support: Brian, Lucas, Lily, but also my parents, John and Kathy, and of course Amy, Mia, Sam, Dave, Nancy, Phil, Angie, Meagan, Ellie, Cam, and Sue. I couldn't ask for more.

Finally, to the team at Chicago Review Press, thank you for the great care that you have all given this book. I have enjoyed learning from and working with each of you. I send a special note of gratitude to our wonderful editor, Lisa Reardon. I cannot think of a change you suggested that I didn't immediately think, *Well, of course!* Thank you for shepherding us through the process and for caring so much about our project.

—KATIANNE

STEM JOB DESCRIPTIONS

|||||||||||||||||||||||||||||||||||||||||||||||||||||||||||||||||||||

There are many more jobs that use STEM skills than we could possibly cover here. Share this section with your daughter and consider it just a starting point for the conversations you will have together. The careers we have selected represent established as well as growing disciplines and are meant to cover a variety of interests.

Actuary

Like stats? Actuaries are the financial forecasters and trusted advisers of the business world. If a business understands the chances of certain events happening in the future (like the odds of a hurricane, fluctuations in the stock market, or population shifts), that business can make appropriate financial decisions. Actuaries use their mathematics, statistics, and financial know-how (and computer programs!) to model these different types of risk.

That's just part of the job, though. Actuaries are problem solvers. They are instrumental in helping their clients figure out innovative ways to mitigate this risk. Their goal is to reduce the chances of negative events happening in the first place but also to find ways to lessen the impact of any events.

Actuaries are widely associated with the insurance industry, which makes sense, as the insurance industry is already in the business of forecasting. But the insurance industry is far from the only industry that employs actuaries. Investment companies need actuaries, as do any companies that maintain retirement funds. Corporations hire actuaries to help them evaluate strategic decisions they may be thinking of regarding expansion, staffing, or downsizing. Banks need actuaries to help manage assets and liabilities.

In order to achieve professional status, actuaries take a series of exams—but an actuary doesn't have to complete the exams in order to begin work. Exams are part of the actuary culture—companies typically grant study time and pay for the exams—and a passing grade may mean a raise.

Aerospace Engineer

NASA's Cassini spacecraft began a seven-year journey to Saturn back in 1997. It orbited the planet for years, sending back amazing images, before beginning what the Jet Propulsion Laboratory termed the grand finale in November 2016—it ventured closer to Saturn than ever before, made twenty-two loops between Saturn and its rings, then suicide-plunged into the planet. The Mars Curiosity rover deployed a very special kind of parachute as it barreled toward Mars at nine hundred miles per hour. Unmanned aerial vehicles (drones) aren't just used for military reconnaissance and attack—they're used in scientific studies and in inspections of areas too small, dangerous, or inaccessible. They're useful in firefighting, search and rescue, and in the studies of animal habitats. Wind turbines, deeply entrenched in terra firma, harness the power of the wind. Complex flight simulators train pilots to land on aircraft carriers long before they actually have to do so.

Missiles, aircraft, helicopters, cutting-edge spacecraft, any satellite in the sky today, pretty much anything that might benefit from some attention to aerodynamics—aerospace engineers play a part in all of these.

Aerospace engineers spend time at their computers performing calculations and creating mathematical models for their projects. They build computer models that they then run through complex simulations. They create prototypes that are then heavily tested. They research and test in wind tunnels to determine how a craft responds as air flows around it, and, finally, they sometimes take test flights.

AEROSPACE AND AERONAUTICAL: WHAT'S THE DIFFERENCE?

Aerospace engineers develop both spacecraft and aircraft. Aeronautical engineers are those within aerospace who work specifically on aircraft such as airplanes and helicopters—aircraft that move within Earth's atmosphere.

An aerospace engineer will usually specialize in a certain area. For example, the structural design of an aircraft—what you may first think of when you think aerospace—is just one piece of any project. There's also guidance, navigation, and control—guidance systems determine the trajectory we need to follow to get to where we want to go, navigation systems let us know where we are right now, while control systems employ thrusters and the like create the force that will actually make us move.

Architect

An architect designs buildings and oversees their construction. Architecture can be rewarding in many ways—each new project is a chance to design a structure that will bring beauty and purpose to the people who inhabit it. Every measurement must be precise, and architects are trained to pay attention to the details.

An architect with an eye to sustainability and green building will challenge herself to reduce the building's carbon footprint and minimize any impact to the surroundings, whether in a city or forest. Architects use many methods to design low-energy buildings. These can range from the decidedly low-tech and passive—the thoughtful placement and number of windows, the size of rooms—to high-tech features like the large wings on the side of the Milwaukee Art Museum's Quadracci Pavilion that open to shade the building from the sun.

It's not all drawing at a drafting table. Architects use drafting programs for architectural drawings and designs, spend a fair amount of time writing reports and communications, and spend a lot of time listening to clients' needs and working with other experts. Because designing buildings requires a heavy focus on safety and public health, licensure is very important.

Art Conservator

Art conservator Tiarna Doherty and her team use their understanding of chemistry to restore works of art. When they need to clean a surface or use an adhesive to repair damage, they understand what chemicals they can use that won't alter the original surface or material. In addition, it is important that any changes can easily be "undone" in the future. Besides chemistry, art conservators need a strong background in art history and studio art. Art history, Doherty says, "informs aesthetic decision-making and helps one understand the artist's intent." When combined with chemistry, art history also guides the conservator in determining an object's original material. Hand skills are very important in this specialized career.

Astronomer and Astrophysicist

The Hubble telescope has sat in low Earth orbit since 1990. The first telescope in space, it sends us unobstructed pictures of the universe. No fog. No light pollution. The Hubble is no longer serviced by astronauts but will keep running until the power goes out, which is expected to be sometime in the 2030s. Hubble observations have allowed astronomers to discover far-reaching galaxies, capture the collision of a comet with Jupiter, and study Pluto.

Astronomy is a small field but grows at an average pace relative to other careers, and while you may think of astronomy as stargazing, it involves a good deal of physics. In fact, the terms *astronomy* and *astrophysics* are often used interchangeably. Both involve studying celestial bodies—planets, stars, comets, asteroids, galaxies near and far, black holes, and so much more.

Astronomy is an ancient natural science, and today an astronomer may be a theoretical or an observational astronomer. She may study the chemistry of celestial objects, or work to explain the motion of these objects. Astrophysicists use their knowledge in subjects such as particle physics, nuclear physics, and thermodynamics to study how properties such as chemical composition, density, mass, or temperature make celestial bodies behave the way they do.

Atmospheric Scientist

Clouds reflect the sun's energy back into space to help cool the planet, and without clouds we'd have no water cycle. So they're pretty important! You'd think we know all there is to know about clouds, but the truth is, we don't. Clouds hold lots of secrets, and we're anxious to unlock them.

CLOUD WATCHERS

Pedro Falcon is an outreach coordinator at the Jet Propulsion Laboratory. One of the projects that he works on is Cloud-Sat—an experimental satellite that observes clouds and precipitation from space. It orbits Earth as part of the A-train constellation of satellites. Citizen scientists from around the world, often elementary school children, record their own cloud observations when CloudSat is in the sky above them. They send their results to NASA so that NASA can compare their notes with what CloudSat reported, and this data helps improve CloudSat.

Our atmosphere is fragile, and very thin. If you pick up a globe, the atmosphere around that Earth would be no thicker than a layer of varnish. The field of atmospheric science brings together physics and chemistry in the study of this atmosphere. An atmospheric scientist might study the affect oceans have on the atmosphere, or the chemical composition of the atmosphere. She will study such things as clouds, gases, and the airborne particles called aerosols (these might be sea salt or dust or smoke particles) that are often necessary for cloud formation (the water droplets collect around these small solids—NASA calls them tiny "seeds"). How do different aerosols affect cloud creation? What impact does human activity have on clouds, and what does that mean to our future?

An atmospheric scientist will likely work for the government at organizations like the EPA, NASA, or the National Weather Service. She might also work for television stations, airlines, aircraft manufacturers, or commercial airlines. At NASA members of the Atmospheric Sciences research group might work with instruments to gather data, analyze and model the data, or work in laboratories to replicate atmospheric conditions.

Biochemist

What are the chemical reactions happening inside all of us at the molecular level, and how do these reactions set the stage for all biological processes? Biochemistry helps us understand the causes of diseases in humans, animals, and plants. That research often yields methods that can cure or prevent diseases.

A biochemist might find work in medicine, agriculture, biotechnology, molecular genetics, or bioengineering, and will often find her job intersecting with technology and chemical engineering. She may develop brain-imaging techniques or gene therapies that treat diseases through the addition of genetic material. She may work with teams to create sensors that use biological matter such as enzymes or antibodies to test for a certain disease.

Bioinformaticist

Bioinformatics is a combination of biology and information—it's about developing the software and methods for understanding all this biology data that we can now collect. In this way, it combines biology, computer science, engineering, and math, particularly statistics. It blends interest in biology with computational skills such as developing algorithms to understand or identify parts of a biological system and then to analyze that data.

It's a fairly new field—the need for it grew out of the great strides we have made in computer processing speeds and storage capacity, as it is this increase in computing performance that has allowed us to sequence DNA.

Biologist

There are so many types of biologists, but they do have one thing in common—they study living organisms. A biologist may work in medicine, agriculture, industry, or the environmental sector. Biologists may work indoors in a laboratory or outside in the field in all sorts of conditions.

A biologist who works in the private sector may be hired by a company looking to develop a particular product. She might work for a pharmaceutical company; she might perform medical research. Then there are environmental conservation NGOs and government jobs, zoos and aquariums, and consulting firms that help develop environmental management plans.

A botanist studies plants and their environments; a zoologist studies animals, their behavior, and their environments. Then, with the remarkable advances that have been made in biotechnology and genetics, there are many fields that explore biology at the tiniest level. A microbiologist studies microscopic organisms. Think bacteria, algae, and fungi. A cellular biologist studies the cell—the building block of life! How does it function? How does it respond to different stimuli? Understand the cell and you have a better understanding of the tissues and organisms it makes up. A molecular biologist studies biology at the molecular level, so, not surprisingly, this field shares a close relationship with biochemistry. Like a cellular biologist, she is still involved in the study of the cell, but in a different way and to a different end. A molecular biologist is concerned with how the cell acts at that molecular level—what is happening within the molecules of a cell, for example, that makes DNA replicate, or a gene turn off and on?

Biomedical Engineer

A biomedical engineer applies engineering and technology to human biology and, as such, usually concentrates on human medicine and health. Biomedical engineers have a hand in the development of things like artificial joints and heart valves. These engineers need a deep understanding of biomechanics, which can take the basic engineering principles of mechanics and apply them to the human body to show how blood flows and how the heart pumps, how a cell works, or how the human body moves. Bioengineers also work in the area of diagnostics, developing imaging systems (think CT and MRI) and dialysis machines, while others focus on biomaterials—what materials will be safe and strong enough to implant in a human body?

Biomedical engineering is very popular. You could say it is the new computer engineering because of the way in which it blends many different fields of study to create one advanced, specific field. It is a combination of robotics, medicine, chemical engineering, materials engineering, computing, electronics, anatomy, simulation, and many more. Many working in the bio-medical field have PhDs.

Biotechnology Engineer

Biotech sounds new but it's been around for about ten thousand years. When we combine tiny biological organisms and technology, we can make some useful materials. The use of fermentation to make wine, beer, cheese, yogurt, and bread is an example of this.

Biotechnology is applied to many different areas. Biotechnology engineers might work on biological sources for renewable energy. The development of biosensors is a biotechnology. Disease-resistant plants, or any genetically modified plant, for that matter—is a biotechnology. A biotechnology engineer might also work to develop biological control agents—an agricultural pest-control method that relies on natural microorganisms and insect predators to control another organism. This can decrease reliance on synthetic pesticides. In New Zealand, for example, the small red spider mites eat enough of the prickly invasive gorse weed to keep it under control.

Business Analyst

A business analyst is the bridge between the technical team and the users in a software development project. These two groups can sometimes seem to be speaking different languages, and it's the business analyst who discovers what the user really wants and translates that information into software requirements. She then works with the technical team to make sure that what gets delivered fits the client's needs.

You don't need a degree in business analysis—they aren't really offered—but if you have strong communication skills, a technical degree will fill up your toolbox.

Chemical Engineer

We have a limited supply of resources on this earth. Everything we know of is made of some combination of elements that we find in the periodic table. We combine elements together to make new materials. We experiment with chemistry to make things stronger, to make things less toxic, and to cure or halt diseases. The American Institute of Chemical Engineers breaks chemical engineering into the following specialties: chemicals and materials, sustainability and the environment, biological engineering, and energy.

Chemical engineers figure out innovative ways to recycle more things more efficiently. When acid rain from factory pollution is an issue, chemical engineers develop wet scrubbers that sit in the flues and smokestacks to neutralize those acids and remove the by-products. Julie Sygiel was a chemical engineering student at Brown University when she began testing out different materials for what would become Dear Kates—all-fabric period underwear that wicks away and traps moisture while also being breathable, stain releasing, and antimicrobial.

A chemical engineer may work in research and development trying to create new materials that fit certain criteria. She may test how this material holds up under different stresses, such as tension or heat. She might develop methods that model and simulate how drugs react in a human body to replace certain animal tests. A chemical engineer might even study the brain, developing models to increase understanding of things like cell generation and neural networks.

Chemist

A chemist investigates substances at the molecular level. She may work to create an entirely new substance. She may work in industry using chemistry to test materials. A forensics chemist will analyze crime scenes to help create a picture of events. An environmental chemist might head out of the lab to collect water samples, and then bring them back to analyze them for pollutants.

Civil Drafter

If you've ever looked at a topographic or relief map, you've looked at the work of a civil drafter. A civil drafter takes the information that has been gathered during land surveys—elevations, contours, structures, even formations that exist under the surface—and represents them in maps that are used in all sorts of civil engineering projects, including the construction of bridges, pipelines, dams, roadways, and parks.

Civil Engineer

The parking lots at a large theme park were designed to filter runoff from rainfall and reuse it to water the grounds. An elementary school in Washington that sits on the Cascadia subduction zone has a gymnasium built to withstand an earthquake, and the high points of the school are designed to provide students and residents safe refuge from a tsunami.

A civil engineer may walk around a construction site in a hard hat and work boots. The work she does may protect citizens from natural disasters through the design of dams and storm surge barriers and through earthquake engineering. She may travel to developing countries to design wells or to develop and implement systems for purifying drinking water. She may

CIVIL ENGINEERING MEETS THE BRA?

The women-led Trusst Lingerie company combined 3-D printing, nanotechnology, product design, and engineering to rethink bra construction, especially for larger-busted women. Their new bra is "a patent-pending technology that is packed with supportive contours, luxurious fabrics, beautiful patterns, and the highest quality craftsmanship." They wanted to shift the support to a woman's core—and they looked to bridges to accomplish this. Taking inspiration from the truss of a bridge (hence the name), they did away with the underwire and replaced it with something that actually can distribute the load along the core, making the job of the shoulder straps much easier.

design bridges, roadways, tunnels, and buildings, or she may work with architects and landscape designers to envision beautiful works of functional art.

A civil engineer may focus on the environment. She may have the opportunity to positively affect communities around the world by curbing air pollution, cleaning contaminated soils and groundwater, or studying the effects of pollutants on the environment.

Computer Engineer

A computer engineer, trained in both computer science and electrical engineering, may develop computer software, much like a computer scientist, or she may develop computer hardware. She may specialize by working in aircraft design, health care, or wireless networks. She may develop operating systems or the hardware for mobile devices. She may work in consulting or for a semiconductor company. Like Karen, she may write programs to develop simulators, design microcontrollers to control robots to go to places humans cannot, or create image-processing algorithms for detecting cancers as well as finding threat objects in baggage at airports.

Computer Scientist and Software Engineer

Computer programs analyze health-care results, send satellites into space, and decode human genomes. Computer models are built to predict weather patterns, financial information, even traffic flow.

WHAT'S IN A NAME?

What is the difference between a computer scientist and a software engineer major? Computer science coursework can be more theoretical and can delve into the development of operating systems, the real nuts and bolts of how computers work. Software engineering coursework will focus more on designing and building software, including the process of gathering requirements, software architecting, testing, and deploying the programs.

On Wall Street computer scientists are needed to design and build the software that will model markets and help make predictions by looking for patterns. Computer scientists are also needed to keep these and other systems secure.

Programmers create simulators to model and conduct experiments that would be too costly to do in a laboratory, create databases that can quickly be searched for pertinent information, or use algorithms to transform information into more useful or entertaining forms. Examples of these include manipulating digital images, creating more lifelike animations of people and natural phenomena like fire and waves for the entertainment industry, or finding ways to help athletes improve their performance.

Cybersecurity Analyst

A cybersecurity analyst safeguards an organization's data by preventing, detecting, and responding to threats. Preventing threats means more than protecting a company's network—those working in cybersecurity may develop new methods of using biometrics to authenticate users, or may focus on enhancing cryptography for the secure transfer of sensitive information.

Cybersecurity experts work with governments and industry to improve defenses around power grids and other critical infrastructure. They work with the financial and retail industries to defend against breaches. The healthcare industry, with its large amounts of electronic patient records, is a frequent target of cybercrime. In preparing for the future, Sonia Arista, former chief information security officer at a major medical center, says that ransomware incidents, where encrypted data is held until a hospital pays, are a potential threat, as is the ability of outsiders to hack into and manipulate medical devices.

Electrical Engineer

Electrical engineering is a wide field and, like mechanical engineering, can be broken down into many different specialties, including power, control, telecommunications, computer, signal processing, instrumentation, and electronics.

Electrical engineers have a hand in everything from self-driving cars and drones to consumer appliances and cameras. They bring their expertise to smartphones, satellites, and the instrumentation on aircraft. They work on speech recognition and are involved in creating the sensors, algorithms, and embedded systems for augmented and virtual reality.

Electrical engineering encompasses any type of renewable energy. You're not getting far with hydropower or wind power without the electrical components to harness those elements and turn them into renewable energy.

Environmental Engineer

Clothes today can do some remarkable things, thanks to nanoparticles. Silver nanoparticles kill bacteria and fungi so our socks and exercise shirts don't stink. Nanoparticles of silica can block stains and make clothing waterproof. Nanoparticles of titanium dioxide and zinc oxide add sun protection to your bathing suits. We can't see these nanoparticles, but as they flake off our clothing and end up in our soil and streams, will they harm the environment, maybe even affect our food and water supply? Environmental engineers are studying just this.

Environmental engineers develop and implement solutions to issues like air pollution, water pollution, and waste disposal. They may also have a focus in sustainability and work in renewable energy. They work to improve recycling. And they aim to keep the public healthy.

An environmental engineer might have a background in a field such as civil engineering. She might be at a construction site, in an office, or dealing with lawmakers. She might find herself out at a wind farm. She might investigate situations like the Flint water crisis or travel to developing nations to help implement water projects or clean-energy projects.

Epidemiologist

As soon as the Zika virus was first reported, epidemiologists set out to study the infectious disease. One of their first priorities was identifying which mosquito was transferring the disease (it turned out to be the *Aedes aegypti* and *Ae. albopictus*). Infected mosquitos transmit the disease through bites, but Zika can also be transmitted from human to human through pregnancy, infected blood products, or sexual contact. Epidemiologists set out to study how long humans have the virus and how long they are capable of transmitting it.

An epidemiologist studies disease outbreaks in order to treat existing outbreaks and to prevent them from happening again. She might perform research either in a lab or in the field, and may be responsible for educating the public. She may help drive public health discussions and set public health policies. She may work for a pharmaceutical company developing new drugs and vaccines, or for hospitals, research institutions, or the government. Epidemiologists seek to decentralize health care so it is easier, cheaper, and more efficient to bring health services to rural areas, underserved populations, and disaster areas.

This is one more field that stands to benefit from the digital age and big data, but epidemiology also sees social media as a useful tool. Google Flu Trends, for example, is thought to be the first well-known example of digital epidemiology. In 2008 this program tried to use search queries to map flu outbreaks—it knows if you searched "What are flu symptoms" or "how to take care of someone with flu" and it knows where you searched from and has tried to create a map showing those trends.

For someone interested in computers and epidemiology, there could be lots of opportunity for innovation. Apps that allow people to diagnose themselves using their phones and small attachments can turn any place into a clinic for treating infectious diseases.

Financial Adviser and Certified Financial Planner

Financial advisers are certified professionals who help their clients invest. They meet with clients in order to develop a clear understanding of their goals—do they have college bills on the horizon or do they want to retire early? They need to be able to get to the heart of the matter and be comfortable talking to clients about something we don't often want to talk about—money. From there, they draw up an investment plan. Besides putting assets to work, financial advisers may advise on tax laws, insurance, and budgeting.

A financial adviser can become a certified financial planner through work experience and testing.

Fire Protection Engineer

What materials should buildings be made out of? How can you design and build an accurate fire simulation? How can you design and build a computer model that will simulate fire conditions?

What does a fire look and act like if it happens in space? What would we do if a fire were to occur on the International Space Station? Come back to

Earth and think small but valuable—what can we design that will protect valuable paintings and documents like the US Constitution? A fire engineer will consider these types of questions.

She may work for companies that design and manufacture firefighting equipment, or work as part of an architectural team in the design of high-rises to determine how they should be built, what materials should be used, and where stairs and exits should be located. She may do similar design work for boats or oil rigs, she may work for the insurance industry, or she may have a career in forensics investigations.

A fire protection engineer may design fire suppression systems like firefighting foams and automatic sprinklers. Is there a better, less costly method than using water to put out a fire that threatens a computer server room? Fire protection engineers are developing gaseous fire-extinguishing systems that can put out a fire while saving as many valuable contents as possible.

Geneticist

A geneticist is a biologist who studies genes and heredity. The field of genetics is linked to information sciences and big data that allows us to study genes. Many geneticists go into research. They may work with patients, testing for genetic markers and counseling them in determining a plan of action.

A geneticist might study the role genetics plays in certain diseases. She may look for genetic markers that can indicate an increased risk for diseases such as Parkinson's and breast cancer. This work may lead to new tests that will help prevent disease. Nanotechnology promises to help deliver gene therapies right where they're needed within the human body, but are the materials toxic to lungs? And if so, what can be done?

An environmental geneticist or ecogeneticist is interested in the link between genes and environmental factors—in other words, how do our genes change in response to the environment around us in ways that make us age or that make us sick? You may have the gene for a certain condition but can an environmental factor such as stress or pollution switch that gene on?

The human genome is the complete instruction set for building a human. It's a full set of human DNA, including all the little typos that make you you. It's so incredibly complex that the first human genome took fifteen years and around $3 billion to sequence. Today, we can sequence anyone's particular genome in about a week for under $10,000. In fact, we can sequence a genome in twenty-six hours if we're using a special processor alongside specially optimized software.

This matters for infants. The leading cause of newborn death is genetic disease. Time—and we mean minutes—is critical in diagnosing genetic conditions in newborns. If we can make it possible to quickly, accurately, and (fairly) cheaply diagnose genetic diseases—that is, if we can make it scalable for all hospitals—we will save lives.

Geophysicist

Geophysicists study the features of the Earth, even below the surface. The geophysicist can use noninvasive methods that take advantage of gravity, magnetism, and the electrical and seismic properties of different materials. They use these techniques to gather data, use that data to create a model, and then interpret the model.

Geophysicists can help industries such as oil and gas. They might use their skills to help locate minerals such as iron and copper. They can use their expertise to help determine safe places to build bridges, dams, or other human features. They can work in groundwater exploration—finding aquifers, estimating their thickness, and determining the best locations for well placement for a water supply.

A geophysicist may be a consultant who brings her knowledge to different construction projects. An oil or mining company may hire her. She may work at a university as a researcher, or for a government agency studying environmental impacts.

Human Factors Engineer

When we design something, we need to make sure that it is—well—useful and usable. We may design the most brilliant car dashboard, but if we can't reach one of those buttons from the driver's seat, what good is it? If the buttons are confusing, hard to flip, or difficult to reach, they could even be dangerous. We have to take the machine design and marry it with both human tendencies and limitations.

Human factors engineers may be called in to help with the design of machines and tools, but they also might work to design environments and entire systems. A system could be, for example, a health care system where medical staff coming on and off shift log what they have done in a way that is easy to understand and follow so that records are accurate and patients are safe.

Think about the words themselves: human factors. In trying to do a good, safe job, how can we organize a workplace to best eliminate any of the mistakes that might be made by humans? What are all the external factors that play on this machine or process once we introduce people into the mix? How can we prevent humans from picking up the wrong medicine bottle, flipping the wrong switch in the cockpit, or getting hurt while moving about an office or a factory? How can we improve productivity and efficiency, and how can we prevent repetitive stress injuries?

Human factors can include UX (user experience) design. UX designers work within software and website design. They consider the end user and help the team ensure that the experience that user has from start to finish is a positive one. A UX designer working on a website for a retail store will ensure that the website is intuitive, easy to navigate, and visually pleasing.

Humanitarian Engineer

Humanitarian engineers strive to improve living conditions for poor and marginalized communities at home or abroad. Much of the work involves bringing clean energy, clean water, and cleaner waste disposal to these areas. A humanitarian engineer may be an expert not just in engineering but also in entrepreneurship, history, politics, economics, or sociology, as the projects she works on will likely draw on these areas.

Humanitarian engineers may be trained in mechanical, electrical, civil or other types of engineering. They may have a minor in humanitarian engineering, or perhaps they trained in humanitarian engineering as part of a capstone course. Oftentimes, humanitarian engineering projects are incorporated into a university student's coursework, such as at Dartmouth College, where students have built rocket stoves and sanitary latrines.

Humanitarian engineers must devise sustainable solutions. In this context, this means that we are looking to hire local people to use local supplies to build something that can then be maintained and perhaps even replicated by locals. In other words, once the humanitarian aid is out of the picture, the project lives on and the people in the community have developed skills and taken on new jobs.

Working in underserved areas can present a unique set of challenges for engineers. There can be cultural and language barriers, unstable political conditions, and difficulties in getting needed funding and supplies. It can be hard to obtain permits for work, and it can take extra effort to achieve buy-in from a community that may be resistant to change.

Industrial Engineer

Industrial engineers might take a look at a particular process—say, for example, a diaper plant. They study the process and decide how to improve it. What can be done to lower the production costs? What can be done to make way for a new type of diaper? How can production be optimized? In other words, industrial engineers design ways to maximize both profit and quality while ensuring safety.

Industrial engineers might put these ideas together and present a plan. They may work in-house for a particular company, or they may be hired as consultants. They may provide forecasts that explain to a production company how much of a particular product they should produce, and when.

There's a human side, too. If machine efficiency is not your thing, consider industrial engineering from another angle. Theme parks hire industrial engineers to design attractions where lines flow smoothly and wait times are minimal.

Information Technology Specialist

Information technology specialists are the individuals who use computing technology and software to establish the communication and computer networks for a business or institution. These individuals are oftentimes called IT experts. They use security software and computing-services software to ensure that your network is running smoothly and efficiently. They monitor the performance of the network for illegal access and are responsible for ensuring the data on the network is backed up for fast retrieval. They understand how to diagnose network failures and malfunctioning networking hardware. They can provide a variety of media services, including setting up a video network with all the appropriate hardware and software and assisting users in the setup and installation of appropriate software. IT professionals are well-versed in cloud computing and data warehouses.

An IT specialist would learn how to implement a network of computers, share services for many users of the network, and distribute the computing workload (cloud computing), and understand the environmental factors that could affect the operation of the physical networking hardware, such as the room being too hot or creating a fail-safe shutdown of a portion of the network that is transparent to users.

Some IT professionals focus on the business side, working in what is known as management information systems. These professionals spend a lot of time working with their users to understand the needs of the new system (the requirements) and then designing the best way to handle all these requirements. Trade-offs must often be made between price and size and efficiency. Many IT professionals work as consultants.

Marine Engineer

A marine engineer designs ships—maybe aircraft carriers, submarines, sailboats, ferries, or large container ships. That's not all. There are speedboats, luxury yachts, oil platforms, and submergible autonomous vehicles.

She understands how water flows around a hull, the behaviors of waves, fluid mechanics, the hydrodynamics of a propeller, and hydrostatics. She's interested in way more than what the vessel will look like and how its design will affect the load it can carry, how fast it can go, and how impressive it looks—a marine engineer might specialize in designing propulsion systems, electrical systems, or steering systems.

She'll consider how to design these systems in an environmentally friendly, sustainable way. She'll spend much of her time in an office working on a computer with different software packages, but there's a good chance she will also get to take to the seas to test or troubleshoot her designs.

Materials Engineer

What materials should be used to make an airplane wing? Or a cell phone screen? How about a golf club or tennis racket? Materials engineers study the compositions of different materials to see how they will stand up to different stresses they may be subjected to—will they have to withstand high temperatures, low temperatures? Will they be pushed and pulled a lot? It's more than that, though. What if a company needs a material that has a certain electrical composition so that it can conduct electricity? Or a certain chemical composition?

Mechanical Engineer

How can we bring cheap, sustainable light to anyone in the world? Promethean engineers developed the GravityLight—a working light that needs no battery. It provides about twenty minutes of light, and it's all mechanical—hoist a twenty-six-and-a-half-pound weight six feet up and then let go—as the weight slowly releases toward the ground, it drives a DC generator that lights an LED lamp.

Mechanical engineering is a broad field, making it an excellent choice for a major, allowing you to go into so many different areas where you will work alongside many other types of specialized engineers.

They design machines. Then they manufacture the machines and help to maintain them. They work at defense companies. They are employed by NASA and by automobile makers. They work in aerospace. But they also work on designing the mechanical components of computers—like the cooling fans. They might work on refrigerators, robots, elevators, and power tools. They might design and develop the production systems in factories—conveyor belts and automated transfer systems—that allow the mass production of some of your favorite products.

Mechanical engineering is much larger than the traditional definition of manufacturing. Mechanical engineers work in nanotechnology and robotics. They work in thermodynamics—how can systems be created that will transform heat into energy? Opto-mechanical engineers specialize in designing for optical systems—think lasers, imaging systems, holography, and spectrometry.

Medical Physicist

Very often, medical physicists work in centers helping to treat patients with cancer, but they also work with patients with heart disease and other illnesses. Any medical setting that uses radiation employs medical physicists to ensure that the machines are calibrated correctly, as well as to ensure that treatment options are correct and that treatment is planned and carried out as required. They work in large teams in which collaboration and communication are vitally important. They work with nurses, oncology doctors, radiation therapists, and technicians, to name a few.

A medical physicist will research and test new equipment and make recommendations for her clinic, or she may work in a research capacity.

Microbiologist

In Lake Erie in 2014 a toxic algae bloom led to contamination of the water supply and about four hundred thousand people around the Toledo area were unable to drink water from their taps for two days. Microbiologists began to study what makes some Lake Erie algae—caused by nutrient runoff from plants—toxic.

The boreal toad is endangered. What's more, microbiologists have long known that the survival of boreal toads is poor when raised in captivity—and now they know why. By examining the "skin microbiomes" of captive toads compared to wild ones, microbiologists determined that the skin was different—the captive toads didn't have the same expanse of bacterial strains needed to protect against a certain fungus.

Microbiologists study tiny organisms like algae, fungi, and bacteria, as well as viruses. They work across many industries, particularly those that relate to human illnesses, veterinary health, food, and pharmaceutical products. Microbiologists might track how weather events are affecting the environment—how unusual amounts of rain in an area might lead to mold that might threaten crops, for example. They might study good bacteria like probiotics in the gut, or they may work for a company to ensure that its food products are safe for consumption.

Mining Engineers

Mine engineering is a male-dominated industry, and history shows us why. Women in Western Australia weren't allowed in mines until 1986. In South Africa it was illegal for a woman to be employed in an underground mine until the 1990s. Companies facing skills shortages are working to attract women, though, and nonprofits like Women in Mining South Africa provide mentorship and support.

Mine engineers are important as we strive to balance our need for resources with our commitment to be good stewards of the Earth. Think back to the cell phone and all the materials that we need. Mining is not going anywhere. We must develop new mining technologies that are less harmful to the Earth and that produce fewer hazardous wastes.

Mining engineers may be on-site for long periods at mines that might not be too close to home and that are not likely to be found near large cities. There they will work outside, assess sites, and collaborate and communicate with communities. This collaboration is very important. In fact, the social license to operate is granted by the local community to a mining organization when they feel the organization's values align with those of the community.

At other times, a mining engineer will work in the office doing calculations and modeling, putting together collected data to figure out how profitable a new mine will be, or how to make an older mine more profitable. She may think of innovative ways to repair mines or will design the processing facility that will be built around the mine, the equipment needed to extract from the mine, or safety programs for mine operators as well as local residents.

Nuclear Engineer

When you hear the term *nuclear engineer*, you likely think of a nuclear power plant. Nuclear energy is actually one of the cleanest energies out there. Heat is produced from fission, not from the burning of fuels, so nuclear energy doesn't produce air pollution or carbon dioxide emissions. There are, however, emissions from the mining, transport, and processing of raw uranium. And there's the looming question of safety. Still, as journalist Steve Connor puts it, a "golf-ball sized lump of uranium would supply the lifetime needs of a typical person." Many nuclear engineers work to develop power plants or work at them to ensure their safety and proper maintenance.

But nuclear engineers aren't only concerned with power. They are interested in what other benefits we can derive from nuclear energy. They work in the medical field designing devices that use nuclear material, such as the PET scanner and the cyclotron, a machine that produces a high-energy proton beam that can be used to treat tumors.

Petroleum Engineer

What are new ways to drill and extract oil and natural gas? What is the safest, most efficient way to extract oil from a well? How can you stimulate an underperforming well?

A petroleum engineer might develop new technologies and oversee the installation and operation of those technologies. She'll keep an eye on yield and make changes as necessary. She must understand the geology in the area of the well so that she can make decisions. She will assess the profitability of reservoirs before a company puts money into them. A petroleum engineer might design and build a computer simulation to model the flow of petroleum through an oil field. There are many environmental concerns to people, wildlife, and the land itself. There are safety procedures and many standards and regulations, and petroleum engineers help with all of these.

Physicist

Hadiyah-Nicole Green has her PhD in physics and now is a professor in materials science and engineering at Tuskegee University in Alabama. In 2015 she was awarded a $1.1 million grant to fight cancer. The treatment she is developing is a combination of lasers and nanoparticles. This combination creates a way to target and treat only cancer cells. It works like this—the patient takes a drug that has the nanoparticles in it. These nanoparticles make the tumor glow under imaging equipment, so doctors can locate it. Then, heating these nanoparticles with a laser activates the nanoparticles to treat the tumor. The nanoparticles are nontoxic, and the laser is harmless.

A physicist may want to work at NASA studying space. She may work in health care as a medical physicist in the areas of radiation, oncology, and nuclear medicine. If she's mechanically inclined, she may work in an engineering field—pretty much any sort—to help develop sustainable energy sources and ways to store that energy, to develop satellites and spacecraft, to build vehicles and robots, or to design new medicines.

Power and Energy Engineer

The electricity that we use to power our homes, offices, and cities has to come from somewhere. It has to be generated, transmitted, and distributed across the electrical grid. The people who figure out how to do this are called power and energy engineers.

How can we make sure that a failure at one point in the grid will not turn into a failure at another point? How can we make sure that the grid is reliable and safe? How can we make sure that the grid can handle additional energy needs in the future? What is the future of energy?

Power and energy is a big deal in the twenty-first century. Once we get all this raw energy—whether from coal, oil, natural gas, wind, solar, or any other form—how does it end up powering your oven, your heater, your lightbulb, your streetlight? Today is an exciting time to be working in the power and energy field. Engineers in this field are working on discovering and implementing clean-energy solutions, and working to update older energy grids. Power and energy engineers may also focus on efficiency and electric vehicles.

We face the challenge of finding reliable and sustainable energy sources to power our future and are tasked with updating and maintaining old power grids. We must continue to design and develop the equipment needed all along the phases of energy development and distribution. This means designing transformers and generators, transmission lines and cables. We must be innovative and nimble as we look to the future, and we must protect the power grid from natural and man-made threats. How can we ensure that an event in one locale will not bring down the power grid in an entire region?

Statistician

Statistics is a high-tech field. If you think statisticians are holed up by themselves in a room, you're wrong. Statisticians are very collaborative problem solvers. They see results, too—they apply math and science to real-world problems in such diverse areas as refugee resettlement, animal migration patterns, immigration trends, weather prediction, and exposure to ozone.

Not surprisingly, this field is growing and is popular among women— it's a STEM field that has achieved gender equity. A statistician can work in many different applications—health care, business, and engineering, almost anything. The need for statisticians to help guide business decisions is growing as we have more access to greater amounts of data.

Wealth Manager

Wealth managers spend a lot of time getting to know their clients. They're there to help them meet long-term financial goals and requirements. They manage money, picking funds and investments, whether a client is saving money for college, retirement, or a new house, but they're much more than investors.

Wealth manager Alexa has a double major in math and psychology, and the small all-women firm where she works attracts many female clients who appreciate the firm's emotional approach to money management. Many clients are going through stressful life transitions such as divorce or bereavement. These transitions can be very difficult, and keeping a handle on all the financial shifts that come along as part of that transition can be especially stressful for clients who understand that wealth and emotional well-being are closely connected.

Alexa will tell you that the psychology piece is actually more challenging than the math piece. "There are so many tools to help with the math," she says. "For an emotionally upset client, though, you've got a box of Kleenex. Then what? The rest is up to you. People get really personal with you. You're like a physician. You know things no one else knows."

Wildlife Biologist

If climate change means earlier springs, what does this mean for animals that count on spring to arrive at a certain time? Reproduction is timed so that their babies are born when food is plentiful. If climate change throws that timing off, babies arrive either too early or too late for the feast. Moths and butterflies can also leave cocoons too early or too late, with dire consequences. The polar bear has become the poster animal of climate change habitat loss, but many other animals are also affected. Local extinction of the tiny rabbit-like American pika has increased precipitously in the last decade, and experts think that climate change is threatening a rare marsupial in Australia, the lemuroid ringtail possum, with extinction.

Wildlife biologists might study how climate change affects animals. How will they adapt to changes in climate? What can humans do to help? How can we make use of protected lands to facilitate animals that need to relocate to more appropriate climates?

Wildlife biologists study how animals in the wild interact with each other as well as with humans. In addition, they study the impact of human activities such as fishing, logging, hunting, and development on animal populations.

A wildlife biologist may find work in her backyard or on the other side of the world. She might work in the forestry industry to ensure that practices are in line with environmental safeguards and with safeguards such as the Endangered Species Act. She might work for a conservation organization, or perhaps in a natural park where she will check on habitats to assess quality and quantity, track populations, and make recommendations for habitat restoration.

Wind Energy Engineer

It's hard to go for a drive these days without seeing a giant wind turbine on the horizon. It represents only a small percent of the typical energy market, but there's a lot of room for growth. The US Department of Energy believes wind power could generate up to 20 percent of electricity in the United States by 2030.

There are many pathways for entry. Components need to be designed and manufactured. The wind turbines themselves have to be designed, developed, and manufactured. There is a race to make wind turbines more efficient and more powerful through engineering.

If you have a background in almost any main engineering field, you can find a job in the wind energy sector. Aerospace engineers will work to design aerodynamic blades and to locate the best site for a wind farm. Mechanical and electrical engineers might be responsible for designing, developing, and manufacturing both electrical and mechanical components, as well as designing the systems to test these components. Industrial engineers design the production processes to minimize costs. Environmental engineers assess the impact of a farm on the surrounding wildlife and humans. Materials engineers select the materials that will be able to withstand all the stresses of the system. Civil engineers design the site so that large loads can be brought in for construction and so that the turbines can withstand weather and forces of nature.

ORGANIZATIONS, WEBSITES, AND OTHER RESOURCES

|||||||||||||||||||||||||||||||||||||||||||||||||||||||||||||||

There are so many websites, clubs, teams, and organizations that provide fun, learning, and support for young girls interested in STEM. You just have to know where to look for them. There are also technologies and toys for teaching STEM skills at certain ages. This reference section lists some of these.

Apps to Teach STEM Skills

Hopscotch (7–10)
Lightbot (all ages)
Swift Playgrounds (10+)

Books

Young Readers

Ada Lovelace, Poet of Science: The First Computer Programmer by Diane Stanley

Balloons over Broadway: The True Story of the Puppeteer of Macy's Parade by Melissa Sweet

The Boy Who Loved Math: The Improbable Life of Paul Erdös by Deborah Heiligman

Emmanuel's Dream: The True Story of Emmanuel Ofosu Yeboah by Laurie Ann Thompson

If You Decide to Go to the Moon by Faith McNulty

Mae Jemison by Jodie Shepherd

Marvelous Mattie: How Margaret E. Knight Became an Inventor by Emily Arnold McCully

Me . . . Jane by Patrick McDonnell

Odd Boy Out: Young Albert Einstein by Don Brown

One Plastic Bag: Isatou Ceesay and the Recycling Women of the Gambia by Miranda Paul

Rosie Revere, Engineer by Andrea Beaty

Seeds of Change: Wangari's Gift to the World by Jen Cullerton Johnson

Small Wonders: Jean-Henri Fabre and His World of Insects by Matthew Clark Smith

Solving the Puzzle Under the Sea: Marie Tharp Maps the Ocean Floor by Robert Burleigh

Summer Birds: The Butterflies of Maria Merian by Margarita Engle

To the Stars: The First American Woman to Walk in Space by Carmella Van Vleet

Who Says Women Can't be Doctors?: The Story of Elizabeth Blackwell by Tanya Lee Stone

Middle Grade Readers

Because of Winn-Dixie by Kate DiCamillo

The Evolution of Calpurnia Tate by Jacqueline Kelly

Girls Think of Everything: Stories of Ingenious Inventions by Women by Catherine Thimmesh

I Am Malala: How One Girl Stood Up for Education and Changed the World by Malala Yousafzai

The Mighty Miss Malone by Christopher Paul Curtis

The One and Only Ivan by Katherine Applegate

Out of My Mind by Sharon Draper

Remarkable by Elizabeth Foley

Savvy by Ingrid Law

Strong Force: The Story of Physicist Shirley Ann Jackson by Dianne O'Connell

Women of Steel and Stone: 22 Inspirational Architects, Engineers, and Landscape Designers by Anna. M. Lewis

Older Readers

The Book Thief by Markus Zusak

Esperanza Rising by Pam Muñoz Ryan

Inside Out & Back Again by Thanhha Lai

A Long Walk to Water by Linda Sue Park

Career and Learning Resource Websites

MIT OpenCourseWare Highlights for High School: https://ocw.mit.edu
/high-school
O*NET OnLine: www.onetonline.org
TryComputing.org
TryEngineering.org
TryNano.org

Coding Partnerships

Black Girls Code: www.blackgirlscode.com
Code.org: www.code.org
Code.org's Hour of Code: https://hourofcode.com/us
Girls Who Code: www.girlswhocode.com

College Websites

The websites of departments or schools at different colleges and universities often have stories of the interesting research they are working on.

Purdue University Engineering: https://engineering.purdue.edu/Engr
Tufts University Engineering: http://engineering.tufts.edu
University of Michigan: www.eecs.umich.edu

Education Standards

The Next Generation Science Standards PDF: www.nextgenscience.org/sites
/ngss/files/NGSS%20DCI%20Combined%2011.6.13.pdf
Mathematics standards for the Common Core: www.corestandards.org

Engineering Organizations for Women and Minorities

American Indian Science and Engineering Society (AISES): www.aises.org
IEEE Women in Engineering (WIE): www.ieee.org/membership_services
/membership/women/index.html
National Society of Black Engineers (NSBE): www.nsbe.org
Society of Hispanic Professional Engineers (SHPE): www.shpe.org
Society of Women Engineers (SWE): http://swe.org

Gift Ideas

Elementary School

Learning Resources' Primary Science Lab Set
Magna-Tiles

Makey Makey
Qwirkle
Robot Turtles
Roominate
Sphero
Water rocket

Middle School

Lego Mindstorms
LittleBits electronics kits
Snap Circuits

High School

Acoustic guitar or piano keyboard
Digital art software such as Corel Painter or Clip Studio Paint Pro
Digital drawing tablet and pen such as Wacom Intuos
LittleBits
Arduino
Coding Kit

Government Websites

EPA: www.epa.gov/science-and-technology
NASA: www.nasa.gov
National Science Foundation: www.nsf.gov

Groups and Competitions

Destination Imagination: www.destinationimagination.org
FIRST Lego League: www.firstlegoleague.org
Future City Competition: http://futurecity.org
Girl Scouts: www.girlscouts.org
Odyssey of the Mind: www.odysseyofthemind.com
VEX Robotics: www.vexrobotics.com/competition

Informative Science Websites

MentalFloss.com
NPR: http://npr.org/sections/science/
ScienceDaily.com

Online Games to Teach STEM Skills

ASCEVille: www.asceville.org
Engineering.com/games
PBSKids.org/games/engineering
ScienceKids.co.nz/engineering.html

Professional Organizations

The websites of professional organizations often offer up articles about some of the advances being made in their respective fields. These articles are not as technical as what might be found in a scholarly journal and can therefore be easier to digest. These sites provide current real-world examples of projects that help to form a much more thorough understanding of what research and developments are actually ongoing.

American Institute of Chemical Engineers (AIChE): www.aiche.org
American Society of Agricultural and Biological Engineers (ASABE): www
   .asabe.org
American Society of Civil Engineers (ASCE): www.asce.org
American Society of Mechanical Engineers (ASME): www.asme.org
Be an Actuary: BeAnActuary.org
Institute of Electrical and Electronics Engineers (IEEE): www.ieeeusa.org
Society for Biological Engineering (SBE): www.aiche.org/sbe

Programming Languages

Python: https://python.org
Scratch: https://scratch.mit.edu
Snap: https://snap.berkeley.edu
Swift: https://swift.org
Twine: https://twinery.org

Programming Online Resources

Khan Academy: www.khanacademy.org/computing/computer
   -programming

Programs for Artists and Designers

Animation-ish: www.fablevisionlearning.com/shop
BlocksCAD: www.blockscad3d.com
HUE Animation Studio: https://huehd.com/animation
Tinkercad: www.tinkercad.com

Websites for Encouraging Girls of All Ages

Nerd Girls: www.nerdgirls.com
A Mighty Girl: www.amightygirl.com
Amy Poehler's Smart Girls: https://amysmartgirls.com
National Girls Collaborative Project: https://ngcproject.org
Engineer Girl: www.engineergirl.org

Worldwide Programs for Girls

Let Girls Learn: A United States government program worldwide launched by President Barack Obama and First Lady Michelle Obama to help adolescent girls access education. Sixty-two million girls worldwide—half of them adolescents—are not in school. www.letgirlslearn.gov #LetGirls Learn

United Nations Girls' Education Initiative: The initiative aims to improve education for girls worldwide, especially for those most underserved and marginalized. www.ungei.org

NOTES

Throughout the book, some names, especially those of children, have been changed.

Chapter 1: Maintain the Awesomeness

They bring home a salary: US Department of Commerce, Economics and Statistics Administration, "STEM: Good Jobs Now and for the Future" (ESA Issue Brief #03-11, July 2011), www.esa.doc.gov/sites/default/files/stemfinaly july14_1.pdf.

STEM fields are projected to grow: Dennis Vilorio, Bureau of Labor Statistics, *Occupational Outlook Quarterly* (Spring 2014), www.bls.gov/careeroutlook /2014/spring/art01.pdf.

Jeanne Beliveau-Dunn is CEO: Jeanne Beliveau-Dunn, *Building the Human Capital for Sustainable Cities*, Meeting of the Minds, Video Webinar, 1:00:15, http://cityminded.org/cal/human-capital-sustainable-cities.

Chapter 2: Whose Brain Is Really Better?

Victor Lavy and Edith Sand, economists from: Victor Lavy and Edith Sand, *On the Origins of Gender Human Capital Gaps: Short and Long Term Consequences of Teachers' Stereotypical Biases*, National Bureau of Economic Research Working Paper 20909, January 2015, www.nber.org/papers /w20909.pdf.

Henry Houh and Rebecca Rapoport, cofounders: Katianne Williams, "A Smarter Way to Play: Einstein's Workshop Is a Techie Community Center," *IEEE Women in Engineering Magazine* 9, no. 1 (June 2015): 23–25.

Overall, scientists reveal that young girls' brains: Michael Gurian and Kathy Stevens, "With Boys and Girls in Mind," *Educational Leadership* 62, no. 3 (November 2004): 21–26, www.ascd.org/publications/educational-leader ship/nov04/vol62/num03/With-Boys-and-Girls-in-Mind.aspx.

British neuroscientist Gina Rippon: Sarah Knapton, "Men and Women Do Not Have Different Brains, Claims Neuroscientist," *Telegraph*, March 8, 2014, www.telegraph.co.uk/news/science/science-news/10684179/Men-and -women-do-not-have-different-brains-claims-neuroscientist.html.

Researchers have tried to tackle: M. F. Shaycroft, J. T. Dailey, D. B. Orr, C. A. Neyman, and S. E. Sherman, "Project Talent: The Identification, Development, and Utilization of Human Talents. Studies of a Complete Age Group—Age 15," Cooperative Research Project No. 566 (Project Talent Office, University of Pittsburgh, Pittsburgh, PA, 1963), www.projecttalent .org/docs/Studies_of_Complete_Age_Group_-_Age_15_(1963).pdf.

Summers said in the same speech: Daniel J. Hemel, "Summers' Comments on Women and Science Draw Ire," *Harvard Crimson*, January 14, 2005, www.thecrimson.com/article/2005/1/14/summers-comments-on-women -and-science.

In 2009 Janet Hyde and Janet Mertz reported: Janet S. Hyde and Janet E. Mertz, "Gender, Culture, and Mathematics Performance," *PNAS* 106, no. 22 (June 2009), www.pnas.org/content/106/22/8801.full.

Jonathan Wai and his team: Jonathan Wai, Megan Cacchio, Martha Putallaz, and Matthew C. Makel, "Sex Differences in the Right Tail of Cognitive Abilities: A 30 Year Examination," *Intelligence*, April 26, 2010, www .psychologytoday.com/files/attachments/56143/sex-differences-in-the -right-tail-cognitive-abilities.pdf.

Chapter 3: Meet Them Where They Are

"half a dozen global studies": Katty Kay and Claire Shipman, "The Confidence Gap," *Atlantic*, May 2014, www.theatlantic.com/features/archive/2014/04 /the-confidence-gap/359815.

The blue LED is so important: Christopher Shea, "LED Lights Are a 'Transformative Technology' in the Developing World," NPR, October 13, 2014, www.npr.org/sections/goatsandsoda/2014/10/13/354845893/led-lights -are-a-transformative-technology-in-the-developing-world.

Cancer treatment relies on physics: Katianne Williams, "The Scientists Driving Cancer Care," *IEEE Women in Engineering Magazine* 2, no. 1 (June 2011): 6–8.

Daniele has traveled to more than: Katianne Williams, "Measuring the Effectiveness of Water Treatment Programs: Lantagne Focusing on Developing Countries," *IEEE Women in Engineering Magazine* 8, no. 2 (November 2014): 21–23.

Jessica keeps an eye on: Katianne Williams, "Bian Selected as the IEEE PES Wanda Reder Award Winner," *IEEE Women in Engineering Magazine* 9, no. 2 (December 2015): 18–20.

Heather is an artist: Katianne Williams, "Stranger Visions: Creating Realistic 3-D Portraits," *IEEE Women in Engineering Magazine* 10, no. 1 (June 2016): 11–14.

In her studies of high school girls: Judy Steeh, "U-M Study Helps Define Why Fewer Women Choose Math," May 22, 2003, http://ns.umich.edu /Releases/2003/May03/r052203.html.

Chapter 4: The Power of Following Her Interests

Margo Apostolos turned her love of dance: Katianne Williams, "Shall We Dance?: Entering the World of Robot Choreography," *IEEE Women in Engineering Magazine,* 11, no. 1 (June 2017): 24–25.

phenomenon of separating art from science: "Archive of NSF/RISD Bridging STEM to STEAM Workshop," STEM to STEAM, www.stemtosteam.org /archive/nsf-risd-workshop.

John Maeda . . . says that scientists and artists: John Maeda, "Artists and Scientists: More Alike than Different," *Guest Blog, Scientific American*, July 11, 2013, https://blogs.scientificamerican.com/guest-blog/artists-and -scientists-more-alike-than-different.

Michael Ruhlman has a cookbook: Jennifer Reese, "One Part Creativity: Zero Parts Recipe," *Slate*, June 2, 2009, www.slate.com/articles/life /food/2009/06/one_part_creativity_zero_parts_recipe.html.

Cooking, Crafts, and STEM activity: Developed for this book by Meredith Outwater.

Erin Winick, an undergraduate at the University of Florida: Erin Winick, interview, September 13, 2016.

Playing an instrument can actually grow your brain: Diane Cole, "Your Aging Brain Will Be in Better Shape If You Take Music Lessons," *National Geographic*, January 3, 2014, http://news.nationalgeographic.com /news/2014/01/140103-music-lessons-brain-aging-cognitive-neuroscience.

And singers rejoice: Kelsey Menehan, "Singing and the Brain," Chorus America, December 4, 2015, www.chorusamerica.org/advocacy-research /singing-and-brain.

Learning fractions is such a major benefit: Susan Joan Courey et al., "Academic Music: Music Instruction to Engage Third-Grade Students in

Learning Basic Fraction Concepts," *Educational Studies in Mathematics* 81, no. 2 (2012): 251.

Learning fractions is such a major benefit: "Getting in Rhythm Helps Children Grasp Fractions, Study Finds," *ScienceDaily*, March 22, 2012, www .sciencedaily.com/releases/2012/03/120322100209.htm.

And sometimes those programs don't come back: Prepared Remarks of US Secretary of Education Arne Duncan on the Report, "Arts Education in Public Elementary and Secondary Schools: 2009-2010," April 2, 2012, www .ed.gov/news/speeches/prepared-remarks-us-secretary-education-arne -duncan-report-arts-education-public-eleme.

John Maeda doesn't see technology flourishing: "Archive of NSF/RISD."

Chapter 5: It's Better to Create than to Consume

"Emails 'Hurt IQ More than Pot'": "E-mails 'Hurt IQ More than Pot,'" CNN .com, April 22, 2005, http://edition.cnn.com/2005/WORLD/europe/04/22 /text.iq.

A typical teen sends and receives thirty texts: Amanda Lenhart, "Teens, Social Media & Technology Overview 2015," Pew Research Center, April 9, 2015, www.pewinternet.org/2015/04/09/teens-social-media-technology-2015.

The MyBlock Education Program: "Impact," MyBlock Education Program, accessed September 23, 2016, www.myblockedu.org/impact.

It was critical to her feisty character: Bryan Alexander, "Merida's Hair in *Brave* Is an Animation Sensation," *USA Today*, June 26, 2012, http://usatoday30.usatoday.com/life/movies/news/story/2012-06-26 /brave-princess-merida-hair/55821498/1.

While video games may have a bad rap: Aviva Rutkin, "How Minecraft Is Helping Children with Autism Make New Friends," *New Scientist*, April 27, 2016, www.newscientist.com/article/mg23030713-100-how-is-help ing-children-with-autism-make-new-friends.

Chapter 6: Adults, Check Your Attitude

Even when girls are simply made aware of the stereotype: L. T. O'Brien and C. S. Crandall, "Stereotype threat and arousal: effects on women's math performance," *Personality and Social Psychology Bulletin* 29, no. 6 (June 2003): 782–89, www.ncbi.nlm.nih.gov/pubmed/15189633.

As Jean Piaget explained: Jean Piaget, *The Construction of Reality in the Child* (New York: Ballantine Books, 1971).

whether this anxiety transferred: Sian L. Beilock, Elizabeth A. Gunderson, Gerardo Ramirez, and Susan C. Levine, "Female Teacher's Math Anxiety Impacts Girls' Math Achievement," *PNAS* 107, no. 5: 1860–63, doi:10.1073 /pnas.0910967107.

While teaching biology: The AMS reprinted side by side an essay by E. O. Wilson from the *Wall Street Journal* and a response by Edward Frankel from *Slate*. American Mathematical Society, "Two Views: How Much Math Do Scientists Need?" *Notices of the American Mathematical Society*, August 2013, www.ams.org/notices/201307/rnoti-p837.pdf.

the way math is taught: Andrew Hacker, *The Math Myth: And Other STEM Delusions* (New York: New Press, 2016).

Nicole Sallak Anderson is CTO of SapientX: Nicole Sallak Anderson, "Calling All Parents: Don't Let Calculus I Be the End," *Code Like a Girl*, August 18, 2016, https://code.likeagirl.io/calling-all-parents-dont-let-calculus-i-be-the-end-6ece9cc5cc4e.

the feedback girls receive: Heidi Grant Halverson, "The Trouble with Bright Girls," *Psychology Today*, January 27, 2011, www.psychologytoday.com/blog/the-science-success/201101/the-trouble-bright-girls.

gender equality at home: "Dads Who Share the Load Bolster Daughter's Aspirations," Association for Psychological Science, May 28, 2014, www.psychologicalscience.org/index.php/news/releases/dads-who-share-the-load-bolster-daughters-aspirations.html.

wasn't raised in a gender-neutral home: Makers, "Sheryl Sandberg Honors Single Moms in This Touching Mother's Day Facebook Post," www.makers.com/moments/gender-roles-home.

Chapter 7: The Power of Role Models

when Noramay Cadena was just a year old: Katianne Williams, "Orbiting Next-Gen Technology: The Women Behind Boeing's MexSat Satellite," *IEEE Women in Engineering Magazine* 8, no. 2 (December 2014): 6–10.

Young women can identify: Sapna Cheryan, John Oliver Siy, Marissa Vichayapai, Benjamin J. Drury, Saenam Kim, "Do Female and Male Role Models Who Embody STEM Stereotypes Hinder Women's Anticipated Success in STEM?" *Social Psychological and Personality Science* 2, no. 6 (April 2011): 656-64, http://spp.sagepub.com/content/2/6/656.

On the heels of that study came another: Jared Wadley, "My Fair Physicist? Feminine Math, Science Role Models Do Not Motivate Girls," Michigan News: University of Michigan, April 24, 2012, http://ns.umich.edu/new/releases/20355-my-fair-physicist-feminine-math-science-role-models-do-not-motivate-girls.

to try to replicate anyone else's successes: Katianne Williams, "Building a Career that Works for You: Gras Writes Her Own Story," *IEEE Women in Engineering Magazine* 11, no. 1 (June 2017): 27–29.

Chapter 8: Grade School: The World of Possibilities

75 percent of the women who've made it to the executive: Nanette Fondas, "Research: More than Half of Top Female Execs Were College Athletes," *Harvard Business Review*, October 9, 2014, https://hbr.org/2014/10 /research-more-than-half-of-female-execs-were-college-athletes.

Psychoanalyst Adam Phillips writes: Adam Phillips, *On Kissing, Tickling, and Being Bored* (Cambridge, MA: Harvard University Press, 1994).

As a child, Japanese video-game designer: Jennifer deWinter, *Influential Video Game Designers: Shigeru Miyamoto* (New York: Bloomsbury Academic, 2015).

a high number of MacArthur "genius award" winners: Karen Schrock, "Imaginary Worlds Are Early Signs of Highly Creative Kids," *Scientific American*, August 7, 2009, https://blogs.scientificamerican.com/news-blog /imaginary-worlds-are-early-sign-of-2009-08-07.

took a look at roughly three hundred thousand CQ scores: Kyung Hee Kim, "The Creativity Crisis: The Decrease in Creative Thinking Scores on the Torrance Tests of Creative Thinking," *Creativity Research Journal* 23, no. 4 (2011): 285–95, http://kkim.wmwikis.net/file/view/Kim_2011_Creativity _crisis.pdf.

In 2010 Jonathan Plucker: Po Bronson and Ashley Merryman, "The Creativity Crisis," *Newsweek*, July 10, 2010, www.newsweek.com/creativity -crisis-74665.

Scott Barry Kaufman and Carolyn Gregoire write: Scott Barry Kaufman and Carolyn Gregoire, *Wired to Create: Unraveling the Mysteries of the Creative Mind* (New York: Perigee, 2015).

It's half past seven in the morning: Alex Caram, interview, September 12, 2016.

At the start of the century: National Education Association, "An Educator's Guide to the 'Four Cs,'" Accessed April 18, 2016, www.nea.org/assets /docs/A-Guide-to-Four-Cs.pdf.

have not historically been regulated: Andrew J. Rotherham and Daniel Willingham, "21st Century Skills: The Challenges Ahead," *Educational Leadership* 67, no. 1 (September 2009): 16–21, www.ascd.org/publications /educational-leadership/sept09/vol67/num01/21st-Century-Skills@-The -Challenges-Ahead.aspx.

worked for math reform: Skip Fennell, interview, October 24, 2016.

lays out five building blocks: W. Stephen Wilson, "Elementary School Mathematics Priorities," www.math.jhu.edu/~wsw/papers2/education/14b-elem -math-priorities-preferred-09.pdf.

correlate with math achievement in tenth grade: Hugues Lortie-Forgues, Jing Tian, and Robert S. Siegler, "Why Is Learning Fraction and Decimal Arithmetic So Difficult?" *Developmental Review* 38 (2015): 201–21, www .psy.cmu.edu/~siegler/2015-LF-etal.pdf.

these stereotypes may embed: Meghanna Bhatt, Johanna Blakely, Natasha Mohanty, and Rachel Payne, "How Media Shapes Perceptions of Science and Technology for Women and Girls" white paper, Fem Inc. (October 2014), https://learcenter.org/wp-content/uploads/2014/10/femSTEM.pdf.

the CS for All initiative: Megan Smith, "Computer Science for All," *White House* (blog), January 30, 2016, www.whitehouse.gov/blog/2016/01/30/computer-science-all.

activities for teaching computer science: CSUnplugged.org is a project of the CS Education Research Group at the University of Canterbury in New Zealand, and is for grades K–12.

spatial ability training helps with mathematics: Yi-Ling Cheng and Kelly S. Mix, "Spatial Training Improves Children's Mathematical Ability," *Journal of Cognition and Development* 15, no. 1 (2014): 2–11, doi.org/10.1080/15248372.2012.725186.

Spatial skills are easily learned: Society for Research in Child Development, "Gender Gap in Spatial Ability Can Be Reduced Through Training," *ScienceDaily*, September 16, 2010, www.sciencedaily.com/releases/2010/09/100915080431.htm.

Lego Friends product line: Roar Rude Trangbæk, "Lego Friends Doubled Expectations for Sales in 2012," February 21, 2013, https://wwwsecure.lego.com/en-us/aboutus/news-room/2013/february/lego-friends-doubled-expectations-for-sales-in-2012.

That percentage has gone up sharply: Jonathan Chew, "How Lego Finally Found Success with Girls," *Fortune*, December 30, 2015, http://fortune.com/2015/12/30/lego-friends-girls.

three times as many girls: Diana Kapp, "Can New Building Toys for Girls Improve Math and Science Skills?" *Wall Street Journal*, April 16, 2013, www.wsj.com/articles/SB10001424127887324504704578411194039125724.

tiny camera-carrying robot: University of Leeds, "Frog-Like Robot Will Help Surgeons," April 11, 2013, www.leeds.ac.uk/news/article/3388/frog-like_robot_will_help_surgeons.

moving to a gecko-inspired adhesive: Hannah Furlong, "Ford, P&G Looking to Gecko for Adhesive Innovations," Sustainable Brands, October 21, 2015, www.sustainablebrands.com/news_and_views/chemistry_materials/hannah_furlong/ford_pg_looking_gecko_adhesive_innovations.

working on a textured paint: Jaymi Heimbuch, "Shark Week and Biomimicry: Four Futuristic Technologies Inspired by Sharks," Treehugger, August 2, 2011, www.treehugger.com/clean-technology/shark-week-and-biomimicry-four-futuristic-technologies-inspired-by-sharks.html.

those annoying burrs: Ryan Goodrick, "Who Invented Velcro?" Live Science, May 21, 2013, www.livescience.com/34572-velcro.html.

that mimic the seal's whiskers: Heather Beem, "Seal Whiskers Inspire Marine Technology," *Oceanus Magazine*, January 27, 2016, www.whoi.edu /oceanus/feature/seal-whiskers-inspire-marine-technology.

over 40 percent first became interested: Vince M. Bertram, *One Nation Under Taught: Solving America's Science, Technology, Engineering, and Math Crisis* (New York: Beaufort Books, 2014).

so talk up the following careers: Achieve Inc., "Topic Arrangements of the Next Generation Science Standards," Next Generation Science Standards, November 2013, www.nextgenscience.org/sites/default/files/NGSS%20 Combined%20Topics%2011.8.13.pdf. The topic arrangements in this section, as well as in the middle school and high school sections, are from Archive Inc.

Chapter 9: Middle School: Don't Give Up!

excelled at math as a child: Min Chen, interview, November 10, 2016.

Pipher explained that in adolescence: Mary Pipher, *Reviving Ophelia: Saving the Selves of Adolescent Girls* (New York: Penguin, 1994), 22.

If adolescence, as Pipher wrote: Pipher, *Reviving Ophelia*, 22.

this age coincides: Riki Wilchins, "A Lesson in Feminine Norms: Why Philanthropy Matters to Educational Outcomes," NCRP, Spring 2014, www.ncrp.org/publication/responsive-philanthropy-spring-2014 /lesson-feminine-norms.

During the 2012 US presidential elections: Nona Willis Aronowitz, "Does Change.org Really Change Anything?" *Dame*, November 8, 2013, www .damemagazine.com/2013/11/18/does-changeorg-really-change-anything.

Peggy Orenstein writes: Peggy Orenstein, *Schoolgirls: Young Women, Self Esteem, and the Confidence Gap* (New York: Anchor, 1995).

spent a number of years studying grit: Angela Duckworth, *Grit: The Power of Passion and Perseverance* (New York: Scribner, 2016).

They can review studies: Jill Shelton et al., "The Distracting Effects of a Ringing Cell Phone," *Journal of Environmental Psychology* 29, no. 4 (December 2009): 513–21, www.ncbi.nlm.nih.gov/pmc/articles/PMC3018855.

If you look at a periodic table, you see: For more information, see www .compoundchem.com/2014/02/19/the-chemical-elements-of-a-smart phone and www.coolinfographics.com/blog/2013/2/4/the-periodic-table -of-iphones.html.

the tailings pond: Hongqiao Liu, "Can We Build a Clean and Smart Future on Toxic Rare Earths?" China Water Risk, July 20, 2016, http://chinawater risk.org/resources/analysis-reviews/can-we-build-a-clean-smart-future -on-toxic-rare-earths.

In our quest for the newest technology: EarthTalk, "How to Reduce the Toxic Impact of Your Smartphone," *Scientific American*, February 20, 2015, www.scientificamerican.com/article/how-to-reduce-the-toxic-impact -of-your-ex-smartphone.

disposable biosensors: Bill Gates, "Cell Phone Science," *Gates Notes* (blog), November 9, 2010, www.gatesnotes.com/Health/Cell-Phone-Science.

PLTW provides the curriculum: "Determining the Cost to Implement a PLTW Program," Project Lead the Way, accessed December 1, 2016, https://web .wpi.edu/Images/CMS/K12/Cost_discussion_document_2013.pdf.

Those with quadriplegia: Frank Jordans, "Mind-Controlled Robotic Hand Helps People with Quadriplegia," STAT, December 7, 2016, www.stat news.com/2016/12/07/robotic-hand-people-quadriplegia.

Magnetic microbots: Chris Schmidt, "Making Stuff Smaller," *NOVA*, PBS, January 26, 2011, www.pbs.org/wgbh/nova/tech/making-stuff.html#making -stuff-smaller.

Chapter 10: High School: Keeping the Door to STEM Open

Pam Laquidera is an expert in women's studies: Pam Laquidera, interview, September 2016.

a striking early example: "Jane Goodall's Story," *Nature*, March 3, 1996, www .pbs.org/wnet/nature/jane-goodalls-wild-chimpanzees-jane-goodalls -story/1911.

Could electrical engineering and jazz: Alice Parker, interview, September 9, 2016.

looking back to biology: Leah Burrows, "A Clean Way to Extract Rare Earth Metals," Harvard John A. Paulson School of Engineering and Applied Sciences, June 17, 2016, www.seas.harvard.edu/news/2016/06 /clean-way-to-extract-rare-earth-metals.

Pollack and a classmate: Eileen Pollack, "Why Are There Still So Few Women in Science?" *New York Times Magazine*, October 3, 2013, www.nytimes.com /2013/10/06/magazine/why-are-there-still-so-few-women-in-science .html.

20 percent of undergraduate courses might have: Jordan Friedman, "10 Universities Where TAs Teach the Most Classes," *U.S. News & World Report*, February 21, 2017, www.usnews.com/education/best-colleges/the-short -list-college/articles/2017-02-21/10-universities-where-tas-teach-the -most-classes.

Smith College made tests optional: Delece Smith-Barrow, "Test-Optional Schools Aim to Create Diverse Campuses," *U.S. News & World Report*, September 17, 2015, www.usnews.com/education/best-colleges/articles /2015/09/17/consider-test-optional-schools-as-a-minority-applicant.

Chapter 11: College: Getting Strategic

spent over two decades: Joan Lampert, interview, November 16, 2016.

it was Stanley Milgram: "Undergraduate Program in Applied Mathematics," Harvard John A. Paulson School of Engineering and Applied Science, www.seas.harvard.edu/programs/applied-mathematics

serves the needs of its liberal arts students: Carl Staumshein, "Computer Science as Liberal Arts Enabler," Inside Higher Ed., February 23, 2016, www .insidehighered.com/news/2016/02/23/liberal-arts-colleges-explore -interdisciplinary-pathways-computer-science.

Seventeen hundred biology students: D. Z. Grunspan et al., "Males Under-Estimate Academic Performance of Their Female Peers in Undergraduate Biology Classrooms," *PLoS ONE* 11, no. 2 (2016): e0148405, doi:10.1371/journal .pone.0148405.

professors tend to call: "Gender Issues in the College Classroom," Graduate School of Arts & Sciences Teaching Center, Columbia University. https:// edisciplinas.usp.br/pluginfile.php/3753817/mod_resource/content/1 /Columbia%20Gender%20Issues%20college.pdf.

When Ayat was offered an internship: Katianne Williams, "The Courage to Dream and Achieve: Advocating for Gender Equality," *IEEE Women in Engineering Magazine* 11, no. 1 (June 2017): 36–38.

Salma is a technologist, philanthropist, and social activist: Katianne Williams, "People Are Key in the ICT Partnership: e Worldwide Group Founder Salma Abbasi," *IEEE Women in Engineering Magazine* 6, no. 2 (December 2012): 43–46.

STEM Job Descriptions

Mars Curiosity rover deployed: Robert Perkins, "USC Aerospace Engineer Helps Curiosity Rover Land on Mars," USC News, August 16, 2012, https:// news.usc.edu/40315/usc-aerospace-engineer-safely-lands-rover-on-mars.

As an atmospheric scientist: "Choosing a Career in Atmospheric Science," NASA, www.nasa.gov/centers/langley/news/factsheets/AtmSciCareer.html.

Bioinformatics is a combination: Rochester Institute of Technology, "What Is Bioinformatics?" Thomas H. Gosnell School of Life Sciences, www.rit.edu /cos/bioinformatics.

studies biology at the molecular: Coriell Institute for Medical Research, "What Is Molecular Biology?" www.coriell.org/research-services /molecular-biology/what-is-molecular-biology.

In New Zealand, for example: Biotechnology Learning Hub, "Biocontrol," October 10, 2007, http://biotechlearn.org.nz/themes/biocontrol.

An elementary school in Washington: American Society of Civil Engineers, www.asce.org.

The all-women Trusst Lingerie company: Trusst Lingerie, "The Science of Support," www.trusstlingerie.com/pages/technology.

Silver nanoparticles kill: Nanobusiness, "The Nanotechnology Used in Clothes," www.nanobusiness.org/the-nanotechnology-used-in-clothes.html.

Environmental engineers are studying just this: Carnegie Mellon University Civil and Environmental Engineering, "Scanning for Silver: Investigating Nanoparticle Absorption in Plants," April 15, 2014, www.cmu.edu/cee /news/news-archive/2014/2014-nanosilver-research-lowry.html.

As soon as the Zika virus was first reported: UNC Gillings School of Public Health, "Gillings Epidemiologist Explains Zika Virus Basics," http://sph. unc.edu/sph-news/gillings-epidemiologist-offers-primer-on-zika-virus.

studies disease outbreaks: "Epidemiologist/Medical Scientist Overview," *U.S. News & World Report*, http://money.usnews.com/careers/best-jobs /epidemiologist.

Apps that allow people to diagnose: Marcel Salathé, "Digit Epidemiology: Tracking Disease in the Mobile Age," March 4, 2015, http://theconversation. com/digital-epidemiology-tracking-diseases-in-the-mobile-age-37741.

What materials should buildings be made out of: "Careers in Fire Protection Engineering," SFPE, www.sfpe.org/?page=CareersWhere.

such as at Dartmouth College: Kathryn Loconte Lapierre, "Humanitarian Engineering." *Dartmouth Engineer Magazine*, Summer 2011, http:// engineering.dartmouth.edu/magazine/humanitarian-engineering.

Materials engineers study the compositions: "Occupational Outlook Handbook: Materials Engineer," Bureau of Labor Statistics, www.bls.gov/ooh /architecture-and-engineering/materials-engineers.htm.

Promethean engineers developed: Michael Abrams, "Lightweight Power," March 2016, www.asme.org/engineering-topics/articles/energy/lightweight-power.

In Lake Erie in 2014 a toxic algae bloom: "Microbiologists Seek Answers to the Toxicity of Algae's in Lake Erie," *Daily Times Gazette*, April 12, 2015, http://web.archive.org/web/20151019230708/http://www.dailytimes gazette.com/microbiologists-seek-answers-to-the-toxicity-of-algaes-in -lake-erie/4393.

The boreal toad is endangered: "Toad Probiotic Fights Fungus," *Nature*, October 6, 2016, www.nature.com/nature/journal/v538/n7623/full/538009c .html.

a mining engineer will work in the office: "Summary Report for Mining and Geological Engineers," O*Net Online, www.onetonline.org/link /summary/17-2151.00.

Still, as journalist Steve Connor puts it: Steve Connor, "Nuclear Power Is the Greenest Option, Say Top Scientists," *Independent*. January 4, 2015, www .independent.co.uk/news/science/nuclear-power-is-the-greenest-option -say-top-scientists-9955997.html.

They work in the medical field: "Occupational Outlook Handbook: Nuclear
   Engineer," Bureau of Labor Statistics, www.bls.gov/ooh/architecture-and
   -engineering/nuclear-engineers.htm.
The need for statisticians: "Occupational Outlook Handbook: Statistician,"
   Bureau of Labor Statistics, www.bls.gov/ooh/math/statisticians.htm.
a rare marsupial in Australia: Dr. Jordan Schaul, "The Climate Change
   Conundrum: What the Future Is Beginning to Look Like for Wildlife,"
   National Geographic, January 10, 2013, http://voices.nationalgeographic
   .com/2013/01/10/the-climate-change-conundrum-what-the-future-is
   -beginning-to-look-like-for-wildlife.
If you want to be involved: "Green Jobs: Careers in Wind Energy," Bureau of
   Labor Statistics, www.bls.gov/green/wind_energy.

BIBLIOGRAPHY

Books

Bertram, Vince M. *One Nation Under Taught: Solving America's Science, Technology, Engineering, and Math Crisis.* Beaufort Books: New York, 2014.

boyd, danah. *It's Complicated: The Social Lives of Networked Teens.* Yale University Press: New Haven, 2014.

Cohen-Sandler, Roni. *Stressed-Out Girls: Helping Them Thrive in the Age of Pressure.* New York: Viking, 2005.

DeWinter, Jennifer. *Influential Video Game Designers: Shigeru Miyamoto.* New York: Bloomsbury Academic, 2015.

Duckworth. Angela. *Grit: The Power of Passion and Perseverance.* New York: Scribner, 2016.

Gold, Jodi. *Screen-Smart Parenting.* New York: Guilford Press, 2015.

Hacker, Andrew. *The Math Myth: And Other STEM Delusions.* New York: New Press, 2016.

Kaufman, Scott Barry, and Carolyn Gregoire. *Wired to Create: Unraveling the Mysteries of the Creative Mind.* New York: Perigee, 2015.

Lockhart, Paul. *A Mathematician's Lament.* New York: Bellevue Literary Press, 2009.

Orenstein, Peggy. *Schoolgirls: Young Women, Self Esteem, and the Confidence Gap.* New York: Anchor, 1995.

Phillips, Adam. *On Kissing, Tickling, and Being Bored.* Cambridge, MA: Harvard University Press, 1994.

Piaget, Jean. *The Construction of Reality in the Child*. New York: Ballantine, 1971.

Pipher, Mary. *Reviving Ophelia: Saving the Selves of Adolescent Girls*. New York: Penguin, 1994.

Russell, Bertrand. *Conquest of Happiness*. New York: Horace Liveright, 1930.

Sales, Nancy Jo. *American Girls: Social Media and the Secret Lives of Teenagers*. New York: Knopf, 2016.

Websites, Periodicals, Magazines, and Newspapers

Abrams, Michael. "Lightweight Power." ASME. March 2016. www.asme.org /engineering-topics/articles/energy/lightweight-power.

Achieve, Inc. "Topic Arrangements of the Next Generation Science Standards." November 2013. www.nextgenscience.org/sites/default/files /NGSS%20Combined%20Topics%2011.8.13.pdf.

Alexander, Bryan. "Merida's Hair in *Brave* is an Animation Sensation." *USA Today*. Last modified June 26, 2012. http://usatoday30.usatoday.com/life /movies/news/story/2012-06-26/brave-princess-merida-hair/55821498/1.

American Mathematical Society. "Two Views: How Much Math Do Scientists Need?" *Notices of the American Mathematical Society* 60, no. 7 (August 2013): 837–38 www.ams.org/notices/201307/rnoti-p837.pdf.

Anderson, Nicole Sallak. "Calling All Parents: Don't Let Calculus I Be the End!!!!!" *Code Like a Girl*. August 18, 2016. https://code.likeagirl.io /calling-all-parents-dont-let-calculus-i-be-the-end-6ece9cc5cc4e.

"Archive of NSF/RISD Bridging STEM to STEAM Workshop." STEM to STEAM. www.stemtosteam.org/archive/nsf-risd-workshop.

Aronowitz, Nona Willis. "Does Change.org Really Change Anything?" *Dame*. November 8, 2013. www.damemagazine.com/2013/11/18/does-changeorg -really-change-anything.

Beem, Heather. "Seal Whiskers Inspire Marine Technology." *Oceanus Magazine*. January 27, 2016. www.whoi.edu/oceanus/feature/seal -whiskers-inspire-marine-technology.

Beilock, Sian L., Elizabeth A. Gunderson, Gerardo Ramirez, and Susan C. Levine. "Female Teacher's Math Anxiety Impacts Girls' Math Achievement." *PNAS* 107, no. 5: 1860–63, doi:10.1073/pnas.0910967107.

Beliveau-Dunn, Jeanne. *Building the Human Capital for Sustainable Cities*. Meeting of the Minds. Video Webinar, 1:00:15. http://cityminded.org/cal /human-capital-sustainable-cities.

Bhatt, Meghanna, Johanna Blakely, Natasha Mohanty, and Rachel Payne. "How Media Shapes Perceptions of Science and Technology for Women and Girls." Fem Inc. October 2014. https://learcenter.org/wp-content /uploads/2014/10/femSTEM.pdf.

Biotechnology Learning Hub. "Biocontrol." October 10, 2007. www.science
learn.org.nz/resources/1743-biocontrol.

Bronson, Po, and Ashley Merryman. "The Creativity Crisis." *Newsweek.* July
10, 2010. www.newsweek.com/creativity-crisis-74665.

Burrows, Leah. "A Clean Way to Extract Rare Earth Metals." Harvard John A.
Paulsen School of Engineering and Applied Sciences. June 17, 2016. www
.seas.harvard.edu/news/2016/06/clean-way-to-extract-rare-earth-metals.

Carnegie Mellon University Civil and Environmental Engineering. "Scanning for Silver: Investigating Nanoparticle Absorption in Plants." April
15, 2014. www.cmu.edu/cee/news/news-archive/2014/2014-nanosilver-
research-lowry.html.

Cheng, Yi-Ling, and Kelly S. Mix. "Spatial Training Improves Children's
Mathematical Ability." *Journal of Cognition and Development* 15, no. 1
(2014): 2–11, doi.org/10.1080/15248372.2012.725186.

Chew, Jonathan. "How Lego Finally Found Success with Girls." *Fortune.*
December 30, 2015. http://fortune.com/2015/12/30/lego-friends-girls.

Cole, Diane. "Your Aging Brain Will Be in Better Shape If You Take Music
Lessons." *National Geographic.* January 3, 2014. http://news.national
geographic.com/news/2014/01/140103-music-lessons-brain-aging
-cognitive-neuroscience.

Connor, Steve. "Nuclear Power Is the Greenest Option, Say Top Scientists."
Independent. January 4, 2015. www.independent.co.uk/news/science
/nuclear-power-is-the-greenest-option-say-top-scientists-9955997.html.

Coriell Institute for Medical Research. "What Is Molecular Biology?"
www.coriell.org/research-services/molecular-biology/what-is-molecular
-biology (site now defunct).

"Dads Who Share the Load Bolster Daughter's Aspirations." Association
for Psychological Science. May 28, 2014. www.psychologicalscience.org
/index.php/news/releases/dads-who-share-the-load-bolster-daughters
-aspirations.html.

"Determining the Cost to Implement a PLTW Program." Project Lead the
Way. Accessed December 1, 2016. https://web.wpi.edu/Images/CMS/K12
/Cost_discussion_document_2013.pdf.

EarthTalk. "How to Reduce the Toxic Impact of Your Smartphone." *Scientific American.* February 20, 2015. www.scientificamerican.com/article
/how-to-reduce-the-toxic-impact-of-your-ex-smartphone.

"E-mails 'Hurt IQ More than Pot.'" CNN.com. April 22, 2005. http://edition
.cnn.com/2005/WORLD/europe/04/22/text.iq.

Environmental Science. "What Is a Petroleum Engineer?" www.environ
mentalscience.org/career/petroleum-engineer.

Fondas, Nanette. "Research: More than Half of Top Female Execs Were
College Athletes." *Harvard Business Review.* October 9, 2014. https://hbr

.org/2014/10/research-more-than-half-of-female-execs-were-college
-athletes.

Friedman, Jordan. "10 Universities Where TAs Teach the Most Classes." *U.S. News & World Report*. February 21, 2017. www.usnews .com/education/best-colleges/the-short-list-college/articles/2017-02-21 /10-universities-where-tas-teach-the-most-classes.

Furlong, Hannah. "Ford, P&G Looking to Gecko for Adhesive Innovations." Sustainable Brands. October 21, 2015. www.sustainable brands.com/news_and_views/chemistry_materials/hannah_furlong /ford_pg_looking_gecko_adhesive_innovations.

Garner, Richard. "Singapore-Style Teaching Helps Solve Problem of Maths Failure, Says New Research." *Independent*. June 17, 2015. www.independent .co.uk/news/education/education-news/singapore-style-teaching-helps -solve-problem-of-maths-failure-says-new-research-10327085.html.

Gates, Bill. "Cell Phone Science." *Gates Notes* (blog). November 9, 2010. www .gatesnotes.com/Health/Cell-Phone-Science.

"Gender Issues in the College Classroom." Graduate School of Arts & Sciences Teaching Center, Columbia University. https://edisciplinas.usp .br/pluginfile.php/3753817/mod_resource/content/1/Columbia%20 Gender%20Issues%20college.pdf.

Goodrick, Ryan. "Who Invented Velcro?" Live Science. May 21, 2013. www .livescience.com/34572-velcro.html.

Halverson, Heidi Grant. "The Trouble with Bright Girls." *Psychology Today*. January 27, 2011. www.psychologytoday.com/blog/the-science -success/201101/the-trouble-bright-girls.

Hanan, Ali. "Five Facts That Show How the Advertising Industry Fails Women." February 3, 2016. *Guardian*. www.theguardian.com/women -in-leadership/2016/feb/03/how-advertising-industry-fails-women.

Heimbuch, Jaymi. "Shark Week and Biomimicry: Four Futuristic Technologies Inspired by Sharks." Treehugger. August 2, 2011. www.treehugger .com/clean-technology/shark-week-and-biomimicry-four-futuristic -technologies-inspired-by-sharks.html.

Hemel, Daniel J. "Summers' Comments on Women and Science Draw Ire." *Harvard Crimson*. January 14, 2005. www.thecrimson.com /article/2005/1/14/summers-comments-on-women-and-science.

"Impact." MyBlock Education Program. Accessed September 23, 2016 www .myblockedu.org/impact.

"Jane Goodall's Story." *Nature*. March 3, 1996. www.pbs.org/wnet/nature /jane-goodalls-wild-chimpanzees-jane-goodalls-story/1911.

Jordans, Frank. "Mind-Controlled Robotic Hand Helps People with Quadriplegia." STAT. December 7, 2016. www.statnews.com/2016/12/07/robotic -hand-people-quadriplegia.

Kapp, Diana. "Can New Building Toys for Girls Improve Math and Science Skills?" *Wall Street Journal*. April 16, 2013. www.wsj.com/articles/SB10001 424127887324504704578411194039125724.

Kay, Katty, and Claire Shipman. "The Confidence Gap." *Atlantic*. May 2014. www.theatlantic.com/features/archive/2014/04/the-confidence-gap /359815.

Klein, Rebecca. "Working Class Kids Ask Fewer Questions in Class, and Here's Why." *Huffington Post*. September 10, 2014. www.huffingtonpost .com/2014/09/10/working-class-students_n_5799212.html.

Knapton, Sarah. "Men and Women Do Not Have Different Brains, Claims Neuroscientist." *Telegraph*. March 8, 2014. www.telegraph.co.uk/news /science/science-news/10684179/Men-and-women-do-not-have-different-brains-claims-neuroscientist.html.

Kristof, Nicholas. "The Man Who Stayed Behind." *New York Times*. October 22, 2011. www.nytimes.com/2011/10/23/opinion/sunday/kristof-the -man-who-stayed-behind.html.

Lapierre, Kathryn Loconte. "Humanitarian Engineering." *Dartmouth Engineer Magazine*. Summer 2011, http://engineering.dartmouth.edu /magazine/humanitarian-engineering.

Lenhart, Amanda. "Teens, Social Media & Technology Overview 2015." Pew Research Center. April 9, 2015. www.pewinternet.org/2015/04/09 /teens-social-media-technology-2015.

Liu, Hongqiao. "Can We Build a Clean and Smart Future on Toxic Rare Earths?" China Water Risk. July 20, 2016. http://chinawaterrisk .org/resources/analysis-reviews/can-we-build-a-clean-smart-future-on -toxic-rare-earths.

Lortie-Forgues, Hugues, Jing Tian, and Robert S. Siegler. "Why Is Learning Fraction and Decimal Arithmetic So Difficult?" *Developmental Review* 38 (2015): 201–21, www.psy.cmu.edu/~siegler/2015-LF-etal.pdf.

Maeda, John. "Artists and Scientists: More Alike than Different." *Guest Blog*. *Scientific American*. July 11, 2013. https://blogs.scientificamerican.com /guest-blog/artists-and-scientists-more-alike-than-different.

Makers. "Sheryl Sandberg Honors Single Moms in This Touching Mother's Day Facebook Post." www.makers.com/moments/gender-roles-home.

Marcel, Salathé. "Digit Epidemiology: Tracking Disease in the Mobile Age." The Conversation. March 4, 2015. http://theconversation.com /digital-epidemiology-tracking-diseases-in-the-mobile-age-37741.

McElroy, Molly. "To Get Girls More Interested in Computer Science, Make Classrooms Less 'Geeky.'" UW News. August 24, 2015. www.washington .edu/news/2015/08/24/to-get-girls-more-interested-in-computer-science -make-classrooms-less-geeky.

McGill University. "What Is Biochemistry?" Accessed January 2, 2017. www
.mcgill.ca/biochemistry/about-us/information/biochemistry.

McGregor, Jena. "This New Paid Leave Policy May Be the Smartest Perk for
Families Yet." *Chicago Tribune.* September 13, 2016. www.chicagotribune
.com/business/ct-deloitte-paid-leave-policy-20160913-story.html.

Menehan, Kelsey. "Singing and the Brain." Chorus America. December 4,
2015. www.chorusamerica.org/advocacy-research/singing-and-brain.

"Microbiologists Seek Answers to the Toxicity of Algae's in Lake Erie."
Daily Times Gazette. April 12, 2015. http://web.archive.org/web
/20151019230708/http://www.dailytimesgazette.com/microbiologists
-seek-answers-to-the-toxicity-of-algaes-in-lake-erie/4393.

Miller, Claire Cane. "How Elementary School Teachers' Biases Can Discourage Girls from Math and Science." *New York Times.* February 6, 2015.
www.nytimes.com/2015/02/07/upshot/how-elementary-school-teachers
-biases-can-discourage-girls-from-math-and-science.html.

Nanobusiness. "The Nanotechnology Used in Clothes." www.nanobusiness.
org/the-nanotechnology-used-in-clothes.html.

NASA. "Choosing a Career in Atmospheric Science." www.nasa.gov/centers
/langley/news/factsheets/AtmSciCareer.html.

"Nerd Girls Hit the Islands!" Nerd Girls. www.nerdgirls.org/thacher.

NPR Staff. "After Backlash, Computer Engineer Barbie Gets New Set of Skills."
All Things Considered. NPR. November 22, 2014. www.npr.org/2014/11/22
/365968465/after-backlash-computer-engineer-barbie-gets-new-set-of
-skills.

Perkins, Robert. "USC Aerospace Engineer Helps Curiosity Rover Land
on Mars." USC News. August 16, 2012. https://news.usc.edu/40315
/usc-aerospace-engineer-safely-lands-rover-on-mars.

Pollack, Eileen. "Why Are There Still So Few Women in Science?" *New
York Times Magazine.* October 3, 2013. www.nytimes.com/2013/10/06
/magazine/why-are-there-still-so-few-women-in-science.html.

Reese, Jennifer. "One Part Creativity: Zero Parts Recipe." *Slate.* June 2, 2009.
www.slate.com/articles/life/food/2009/06/one_part_creativity_zero
_parts_recipe.html.

Rochester Institute of Technology. "What Is Bioinformatics?" Thomas H.
Gosnell School of Life Sciences. www.rit.edu/cos/bioinformatics.

Rotherham, Andrew J., and Daniel Willingham. "21st Century Skills: The
Challenges Ahead." *Educational Leadership* 67, no. 1 (September 2009):
16–21, www.ascd.org/publications/educational-leadership/sept09/vol67
/num01/21st-Century-Skills@-The-Challenges-Ahead.aspx.

Rutkin, Aviva. "How Minecraft Is Helping Children with Autism Make New
Friends." *New Scientist.* April 27, 2016. www.newscientist.com/article
/mg23030713-100-how-is-helping-children-with-autism-make-new-friends.

San Francisco State University. "Getting in Rhythm Helps Children Grasp Fractions, Study Finds." *ScienceDaily*. March 22, 2012. www.sciencedaily.com/releases/2012/03/120322100209.htm.

Schaul, Jordan. "The Climate Change Conundrum: What the Future Is Beginning to Look Like for Wildlife." *National Geographic*. January 10, 2013. http://voices.nationalgeographic.com/2013/01/10/the-climate-change-conundrum-what-the-future-is-beginning-to-look-like-for-wildlife.

Shea, Christopher. "LED Lights Are a 'Transformative Technology' in the Developing World." NPR. October 13, 2014. www.npr.org/sections/goatsandsoda/2014/10/13/354845893/led-lights-are-a-transformative-technology-in-the-developing-world.

Schmidt, Chris. "Making Stuff Smaller." *NOVA*. PBS. January 26, 2011. www.pbs.org/wgbh/nova/tech/making-stuff.html#making-stuff-smaller.

Schrock, Karen. "Imaginary Worlds Are Early Signs of Highly Creative Kids." *Scientific American*. August 7, 2009. https://blogs.scientificamerican.com/news-blog/imaginary-worlds-are-early-sign-of-2009-08-07.

Sea Grant Michigan. "Marine Engineering: Designing a Ballast-Free Ship." www.miseagrant.umich.edu/research/research-themes/marine-engineering.

Smith, Megan. "Computer Science for All." *White House* (blog). January 30, 2016. www.whitehouse.gov/blog/2016/01/30/computer-science-all.

Smith-Barrow, Delece. "Test-Optional Schools Aim to Create Diverse Campuses." *U.S. News & World Report*. September 17, 2015. www.usnews.com/education/best-colleges/articles/2015/09/17/consider-test-optional-schools-as-a-minority-applicant.

Society for Research in Child Development. "Gender Gap in Spatial Ability Can Be Reduced Through Training." *ScienceDaily*. September 16, 2010. www.sciencedaily.com/releases/2010/09/100915080431.htm.

SFPE. "Careers in Fire Protection Engineering." www.sfpe.org/?page=Careers Where.

Staumshein, Carl. "Computer Science as Liberal Arts Enabler." Inside Higher Ed. February 23, 2016. www.insidehighered.com/news/2016/02/23/liberal-arts-colleges-explore-interdisciplinary-pathways-computer-science.

Steeh, Judy. "U-M Study Helps Define Why Fewer Women Choose Math." May 22, 2003. http://ns.umich.edu/Releases/2003/May03/r052203.html.

"Summary Report for Mining and Geological Engineers." O*Net Online. www.onetonline.org/link/summary/17-2151.00.

Thielman, Sam. "What Women Watch on TV." *Adweek*. Last modified March 13, 2014. www.adweek.com/news/televisionwhat-women-watch-tv-156621.

"Toad Probiotic Fights Fungus." *Nature*. October 6, 2016. www.nature.com/nature/journal/v538/n7623/full/538009c.html.

Trangbæk, Roar Rude. "Lego Friends Doubled Expectations for Sales in 2012." February 21, 2013. https://wwwsecure.lego.com/en-us/aboutus/news-room /2013/february/lego-friends-doubled-expectations-for-sales-in-2012.

Trusst Lingerie. "The Science of Support." www.trusstlingerie.com/pages /technology.

UNC Gillings School of Public Health. "Gillings Epidemiologist Explains Zika Virus Basics." http://sph.unc.edu/sph-news/gillings-epidemiologist -offers-primer-on-zika-virus.

Undergraduate Program in Applied Mathematics." Harvard John A. Paulson School of Engineering and Applied Science. www.seas.harvard.edu /programs/applied-mathematics.

University of Leeds. "Frog-Like Robot Will Help Surgeons." April 11, 2013. www.leeds.ac.uk/news/article/3388/frog-like_robot_will_help_surgeons.

University of Chicago Medicine. "History of Personalized Medicine Brings Future Hope to Lung Cancer Patients." Last modified December 2010. www.uchospitals.edu/specialties/cancer/patient-stories/victor-lung.html.

U.S. News & World Report. "Epidemiologist/Medical Scientist Overview." http://money.usnews.com/careers/best-jobs/epidemiologist.

Wilchins, Riki. "A Lesson in Feminine Norms: Why Philanthropy Matters to Educational Outcomes." NCRP. Spring 2014. www.ncrp.org/publication /responsive-philanthropy-spring-2014/lesson-feminine-norms.

Wilson, W. Stephen. "Elementary School Mathematics Priorities." www .math.jhu.edu/~wsw/papers2/education/14b-elem-math-priorities-pre- ferred-09.pdf.

Journals

Cheryan, Sapna, John Oliver Siy, Marissa Vichayapai, Benjamin J. Drury, and Saenam Kim. "Do Female and Male Role Models Who Embody STEM Stereotypes Hinder Women's Anticipated Success in STEM?" *Social Psychological and Personality Science* 2, no. 6 (2011): 656–64, http://spp.sagepub .com/content/2/6/656.

Courey, Susan Joan, Endre Balogh, Jody Rebecca Siker, and Jae Paik. "Academic Music: Music Instruction to Engage Third-Grade Students in Learning Basic Fraction Concepts." *Educational Studies in Mathematics* 81, no. 2 (2012): 251.

Grunspan, D. Z., S. L. Eddy, S. E. Brownell, B. L. Wiggins, A. J. Crowe, S. M. Goodreau. "Males Under-Estimate Academic Performance of Their Female Peers in Undergraduate Biology Classrooms." *PLoS ONE* 11, no. 2 (2016): e0148405, doi:10.1371/journal.pone.0148405.

Gurian, Michael, and Kathy Stevens. "With Boys and Girls in Mind." *Educational Leadership* 62, no. 3 (November 2004): www.ascd.org/publications

/educational-leadership/nov04/vol62/num03/With-Boys-and-Girls-in
-Mind.aspx.

Handley, Ian, et al. "Quality of Evidence Revealing Subtle Gender Biases in
Science Is in the Eye of the Beholder." *PNAS* 112, no. 43 (October 2015):
www.ncbi.nlm.nih.gov/pmc/articles/PMC4629390.

Hyde, Janet S., and Janet E. Mertz. "Gender, Culture, and Mathematics
Performance." *PNAS* 106, no. 22 (June 2009): www.pnas.org/content
/106/22/8801.full.

Kim, Kyung Hee. "The Creativity Crisis: The Decrease in Creative Thinking
Scores on the Torrance Tests of Creative Thinking." *Creativity Research
Journal* 23, no. 4 (2011): 285–95, http://kkim.wmwikis.net/file/view
/Kim_2011_Creativity_crisis.pdf.

O'Brien, L. T., and C. S. Crandall. "Stereotype Threat and Arousal: Effects on
Women's Math Performance." *Personality and Social Psychology Bulletin*
29, no. 6 (June 2003): 782–89, www.ncbi.nlm.nih.gov/pubmed/15189633.

Shaycroft, M. F., J. T. Dailey, D. B. Orr, C. A. Neyman, and S. E. Sherman.
"Project Talent: The Identification, Development, and Utilization of
Human Talents. Studies of a Complete Age Group—Age 15." Cooperative
Research Project No. 566, Project Talent Office, University of Pittsburgh,
Pittsburgh, PA, 1963. www.projecttalent.org/docs/Studies_of_Complete
_Age_Group_-_Age_15_(1963).pdf.

Shelton, Jill, et al. "The Distracting Effects of a Ringing Cell Phone." *Journal of Environmental Psychology* 29, no. 4 (December 2009): 513–21, www
.ncbi.nlm.nih.gov/pmc/articles/PMC3018855.

Wadley, Jared. "My Fair Physicist? Feminine Math, Science Role Models Do
Not Motivate Girls." Michigan News: University of Michigan. April 24,
2012. http://ns.umich.edu/new/releases/20355-my-fair-physicist-feminine
-math-science-role-models-do-not-motivate-girls.

Wai, Jonathan, Megan Cacchio, Martha Putallaz, and Matthew C. Makel.
"Sex Differences in the Right Tail of Cognitive Abilities: A 30 Year Examination." *Intelligence* 38 (2010): 412–23, https://www.psychologytoday
.com/files/attachments/56143/sex-differences-in-the-right-tail-cognitive
-abilities.pdf.

Williams, Katianne. "Bian Selected as the IEEE PES Wanda Reder Award
Winner." *IEEE Women in Engineering Magazine* 9, no. 2 (December 2015):
18–20.

———. "Building a Career that Works for You: Gras Writes Her Own Story."
IEEE Women in Engineering Magazine 11, no. 1 (June 2017): 27–29.

———. "The Courage to Dream and Achieve: Advocating for Gender Equality." *IEEE Women in Engineering Magazine* 11, no. 1 (June 2017): 36–38.

———. "Measuring the Effectiveness of Water Treatment Programs: Lantagne Focusing on Developing Countries." *IEEE Women in Engineering Magazine* 8, no. 2 (November 2014): 21–23.

———. "Orbiting Next-Gen Technology: The Women Behind Boeing's Mex-Sat Satellite." *IEEE Women in Engineering Magazine* 8, no. 2 (December 2014): 6–10.

———. "People Are Key in the ICT Partnership: e Worldwide Group Founder Salma Abbasi." *IEEE Women in Engineering Magazine* 6, no. 2 (December 2012): 43–46.

———. "The Scientists Driving Cancer Care." *IEEE Women in Engineering Magazine* 2, no. 1 (June 2011): 6–8.

———. "Shall We Dance?: Entering the World of Robot Choreography." *IEEE Women in Engineering Magazine* 11, no. 1 (June 2017): 24–25.

———. "A Smarter Way to Play: Einstein's Workshop Is a Techie Community Center." *IEEE Women in Engineering Magazine* 9, 1 (June 2015): 23–25.

———. "Stranger Visions: Creating Realistic 3-D Portraits." *IEEE Women in Engineering Magazine* 10, no. 1 (June 2016): 11–14.

Government Sources

Bureau of Labor Statistics. "Green Jobs: Careers in Wind Energy." www.bls.gov/green/wind_energy.

———. "Occupational Outlook Handbook: Materials Engineer." www.bls.gov/ooh/architecture-and-engineering/materials-engineers.htm.

———. "Occupational Outlook Handbook: Nuclear Engineer." www.bls.gov/ooh/architecture-and-engineering/nuclear-engineers.htm.

———. "Occupational Outlook Handbook: Statistician." www.bls.gov/ooh/math/statisticians.htm.

National Education Association. "An Educator's Guide to the 'Four Cs.'" Accessed April 18, 2016. www.nea.org/assets/docs/A-Guide-to-Four-Cs.pdf.

US Department of Commerce, Economics and Statistics Administration. "STEM: Good Jobs Now and for the Future." ESA Issue Brief #03-11. July 2011. www.esa.doc.gov/sites/default/files/stemfinaljuly14_1.pdf.

US Department of Education. Prepared Remarks of US Secretary of Education Arne Duncan on the Report, "Arts Education in Public Elementary and Secondary Schools: 2009–2010." April 2, 2012. www.ed.gov/news/speeches/prepared-remarks-us-secretary-education-arne-duncan-report-arts-education-public-eleme.

Vilorio, Dennis. Bureau of Labor Statistics. *Occupational Outlook Quarterly* (Spring 2014): www.bls.gov/careeroutlook/2014/spring/art01.pdf.

Interviews

Debbie Berebichez, email interview, June 28, 2017.
Alex Caram, in-person interview, September 12, 2016.
Min Chen, telephone interview, November 10, 2016.
Skip Fennell, telephone interview, October 24, 2016.
Sarah Gretter, telephone interview, September 19, 2016.
Joan Lampert, telephone interview, November 16, 2016.
Pam Laquidera, in-person interview, September 2016.
Alice Parker, telephone interview, September 9, 2016.
Erin Winick, telephone interview, September 13, 2016.

INDEX